Geoffrey Best was a Scholar of Trinity College and a Fellow of Trinity Hall, Cambridge. In 1954–5 he was Choate Fellow at Harvard, from 1966–74 was Sir Richard Lodge Professor of History at Edinburgh University and in 1969–70 he was Visiting Fellow of All Souls College, Oxford. In 1974 he became Professor of History in the School of European Studies at the University of Sussex and in 1978–9 was Fellow of the Woodrow Wilson International Center, Washington DC. His published works include *Temporal Pillars* (1964), a study of the Church of England since 1700, *Shaftesbury* (1964), *Bishop Westcott and the Miners* (1968) and (as co-editor with Andrew Wheatcroft) *War, Economy, and the Military Mind*. Since 1974 he has been editor of *War and Society Newsletter*. He is currently editor of the *Fontana History of European War and Society* series which includes his forthcoming book, *War and Society in Revolutionary Europe, 1770–1870*.

GEOFFREY BEST

Mid-Victorian
Britain
1851–75

FONTANA/COLLINS

First published in Great Britain, as part of the
series *The History of British Society* edited by
E. J. Hobsbawm, by Weidenfeld and Nicholson
1971

First issued in Fontana 1979
Second Impression 1982
Copyright © Geoffrey Best 1971

Made and printed in Great Britain by
William Collins Sons & Co. Ltd, Glasgow

Set in Linotype Plantin

For Paul Longland
who first showed me the road

Contents

Maps

General Editor's Preface

Social history is a comparatively new *genre*, though the name itself has long been familiar. It has been widely used as part of the combination 'social and economic history', as a label for the history of labour and popular movements and other topics of interest to scholars of the left, for miscellaneous studies of customs, social behaviour and everyday life, or even, as with the late G. M. Trevelyan, as a residual category of traditional history: 'history with the politics left out'. Its aim today is the ambitious one of writing the history of society. Ideally, it ought therefore to embrace and coordinate the numerous historical specialisms, since all are relevant to its task. In practice, social historians are, at least for the present, likely to concentrate on a number of topics which have tended to be neglected, or to be treated only peripherally, by the general and specialist historians, with some honourable exceptions.

Class and social structure is the most obvious of these, but the historical demographers have also opened up the study of the pattern of birth, marriage, death, household and kinship, 'urban studies' has explored the cities, while the pattern of culture (in the anthropologists' sense of the word) and ideas has attracted what the French call the historians of 'mentalities'. More generally, all aspects of the life and activities of the common people, that is to say those who have left little documentation behind as individuals, have been studied with increasing intensity. A great deal of work in social history has concentrated in these areas since 1950, when the subject began to be systematically developed. However, these studies have been unsystematic, both because the topics themselves have been treated patchily, and because other and equally relevant ones have been neglected. Though of course a good deal of important material has been accumulated by historians of one kind or another in other contexts.

The present series attempts to bring together, for the period from the industrial revolution on, what we know (and don't yet know) about the structure and changes in British society. Since social history is itself in the process of development, the individual authors have been left to define their field, though they have all agreed to treat certain common questions and subjects. Though they are all experts, they have not written for a specialist public, but for students—of history, of sociology or indeed of any subject which requires some understanding of British society since 1780—and for the general reader, who, contrary to a widespread opinion, is not a myth. Not everyone who wants to know about the past and the present also wants to pass an examination. However, it may be hoped that the attempt to draw together the threads of our present knowledge, and at least some of those of historical discussion, may help to advance the work of the numerous and active force of social historians, if only by stimulating them to do better than the authors of this series.

E. J. Hobsbawm

Preface

To three friendly masters in the profession of nineteenth-century British history I have been particularly indebted. When, about five years ago, I told the first that I was going to write this book, he said it couldn't be done, and he for one wouldn't wish to read it. The second said it was an interesting project and he wished me luck. The third said he thought it would be very difficult to do properly. To my intense regret the book appears too late for me to have the pleasure of discovering whether Edward Welbourne would in the event resist the temptation to see what I had made of it, or the joy of drawing from W. L. Burn some characteristic wry dictum. Of that senior trinity, only George Kitson Clark remains; and I hope he will not disapprove to such an extent as to incline him to disavow the, so to speak, grandparental responsibility which I cannot help attributing to him, since it was he who first made me wish to study nineteenth-century history.

Part of my problem in writing this book has been my knowledge that, however different may be the case in respect of most other periods represented in this series, this mid-Victorian period has been—and with the happiest results—already much exposed to authors. The seeker after mid-Victorian knowledge finds the way already well signposted in Kitson Clark's *Making of Victorian England*, Burn's *Age of Equipoise*, or Asa Briggs's *Victorian People*; not to mention the inexhaustible quarries of Sir John Clapham's *Economic History of Modern Britain* and the not yet exhausted diamond mines of G. M. Young's essays and *Portrait of an Age*; let alone more recent books by Eric Hobsbawm himself, by Sidney Checkland, by R. K. Webb and others. My justification, such as it is, for adding another book to that shelf, rests on these grounds. Whatever ideal, 'agreed' definition and explanation of mid-Victorian British society may one day be attained, we are not yet anywhere near attaining it; and since History knows no way of approaching that ideal goal but by the trial-and-error method of repeated range-finding salvos from historians with firm enough attitudes and large enough vision to enable them (perhaps) to measure range and enforce pattern and proportion, there is no harm in another historian chancing his arm. Firm attitudes and bold vision are not lacking in most of those unusually good books already occupying the field; though in some cases the attitudes are a good deal more explicit than in others! My own chief interest is quickly declared. I simply wanted to know what it might have felt like to be alive about 1850 and how different it would have felt about a generation later. From that simple seed the work grew, and at the end of it I find that all I have done to satisfy my original curiosity is to locate and to follow through the years some of the principal conditions and circumstances which must have helped determine the quality of life, and to relate them to contemporary expressions about it.

I have welcomed the help of mid-Victorian novelists, where their representations of aspects of contemporary life, their distillations of certain of its essential qualities, seem sharper than those of writers of non-fiction. If to use 'literary evidence' in social history is to be 'unscientific' and 'impressionistic', then I must be called so. Some fellow historians whom I highly respect make no use of imaginative literature even where it could save them space (because literary genius may be able to put volumes into nutshells) and the reader tedium (because not many of us can write as well as, for instance, Dickens, Hale White or Hardy). 'Impressionism' or not, the intelligent use of all relevant evidence can produce plausible generalisations and judgments about matters that must otherwise, without such alchemy, stay unspecific and unfocused. I have felt the more inclined to use literary sources where appropriate, because a group of readers I have had much in mind are students of Victorian literature, some of them anxious to find out (provided the finding won't take them too long) what the society behind the novels was like, and how society and novel related to each other. Those readers at any rate will not mind my use of the clergyman Crawley, the schoolmaster Headstone, *et al.* It will have to be judged on its merits by another group of potential readers, historically curious students in various of the social sciences and studies. To them, and to professional colleagues of the more sociological kind, I address the last part of this preface. What I have written will probably be considered social history of rather an old-fashioned sort; more traditional, indeed, than I expected when I began it. There is (partly, I must say, because so much statistical research remains to be done) less quantification than I hoped to provide, and less application of sociological theory than, zealous for modernity, I thought it might be useful to achieve. For failure to learn more sociology, I am clearly to blame. But even had I learnt more, I am not sure how much of it would have been fruitfully applicable.

It is probably in respect of *class* that I shall be found, by the sociological, most wanting. I have used the language of class more as it was used by mid-Victorians than as it is used by any ancient or modern school of social theorists; i.e. I have used it continually and confusedly. Mid-Victorian society, it is hardly too much to say, was obsessed by class, and riddled with class-consciousness, and perhaps not quite clear what it all meant. David Owen (another revered master gone!) cited in his big and useful book *Philanthropy in England* this opaque but confident utterance by the Director of HM Convict Prisons in 1852: 'With us,' he told a Commons' Select Committee, 'the distinction of classes is a national characteristic. There may be considerable kindness between classes, but there is no cordiality.' At the end of the day I am not sure what Captain O'Brien meant. I was willing, when I started, to draw from the evidence as simple a class structure as the evidence would stand: the simpler, the better, since I like clear analysis as much as anyone, and am prepared to accept a Marxist structure of indelible class antagonisms if I have to. The evidence about mid-Victorian class however has not seemed to me to make possible a simple analysis in those or any other terms, for the following reasons. (1) Although men used the conventional terms upper, middle and working or lower class, and their usual variants, they were acutely aware that men actually thought and acted in terms of a more considerably stratified and confused class structure than that nominally tripartite one; as if their social structure was more like that we commonly ascribe to the eighteenth century, of multiple gradations or ranks in a pyramidal order, with as many opportunities for 'class consciousness' both upwards and downwards. (2) The feelings of class antagonism which were obviously there—feelings largely economic in source, and representing so to speak 'horizontal' social divisions, though more than two of them—were not often or for many people stronger feelings than those attaching to their so to speak 'vertical' connections with classes below and above them. (3) Often stronger than any other social division, so far as I can see, was that 'vertical' one between the Respectable of any 'horizontal' class and the Non-Respectable of the same—a distinction I discuss at length in Chapter Four. (4) Such feelings of 'horizontal' class hostility as there were seem not to have prevented plenty of men 'rising in the social scale' and slipping at once into the attitudes of the class attained; and class attitudes which could be slipped on and off like that don't indicate the deep-dyed attitudes predicated of class by the Marxist analyst. All these matters are treated of more largely in Chapters Three and Four; but I take this early opportunity to spotlight them because I don't want anyone to get that far and then feel defrauded.

The book is not elaborately foot-noted. It does not need to be. It is not much of a work of 'research', as conventionally understood. Some of it is derivative, much of it is synthetic, and there is no concealment of how much I owe to others, both those who have gone into print and those who have not. I have tried to give references for all actual quotations, and for the sources of the more complicated figures. For the rest, my good faith and professional self-respect may, I hope, be thought sufficient guarantee that I have sought to be accurate in my summaries of situations and developments. For whatever errors of *fact* may nevertheless have slipped in, I am profoundly regretful.

It remains only to express my gratitude to a great number of people for taking trouble to help me, and my hope that they will not think I have put their help to bad uses. For that help, in all its shapes and sizes I thank (and this list cannot be as complete as ideally it should be): Eric Hobsbawm, H. J. Dyos, John Harrison, Harry Hanham, Owen Chadwick, Charles Chilton, John Kent, James Cornford, Henry Parris, W. H. Chaloner, Antony Jay, Philip Collins, R. K. Webb, Michael Flinn, Christopher Smout, Hector Macdonald, Iain MacIver, Daniel Paton, Christopher Harvie, Peter Mathias, Kenneth Fielden, Kenneth Fielding, Sydney Checkland, T. D. Jones, J. T. Coppock, Brian Harrison, Raphael Samuel, John Roach, John Vincent, John Myerscough, R. J. Morris, Clyde Binfield, E. P. Hennock, Robert Storch, Michael Wolff, Rhodes Boyson, J. A. Banks, Jack Simmons, M. J. Cullen, Calvin Woodward, Nicholas and Hazel Taylor, Margaret Walgate, Sir Nikolaus Pevsner, Henry Pelling, Kitty Michaelson, Owen Dudley Edwards, Wray Vaplew, my mother, my children and my wife.

1 : The Mid-Victorian Environment

Introduction: the Economic Background

The least disputable ground for regarding the period of years covered in this book as in some sense a unity is an economic one. These were years of unchallenged British ascendancy over the family of nations in commerce and manufactures: a sort of ascendancy upon which peace-loving British optimists were inclined to congratulate the world. If this ascendancy in fact involved a kind of sterling imperialism and an economically enforced Pax Britannica—and most historians believe that it did—it was arguably a beneficent one; everyone got richer, while some got richer quicker than others. If Britain got richest quickest of all, who should complain of that? The world's eagerness for British goods, skills and services, was matched only by British eagerness to sell them. There were no inducements or pressures but those of the market. For twenty rare years, something like free trade nearly prevailed; and idealistic free-traders' dreams of international prosperity and concord seemed sometimes to be coming true.

Through the fifties and the sixties this illusion could just be sustained by rational men. It wore out early in the seventies. The big boom begun about 1850 petered out as the Franco-Prussian War restored national rivalries to bad old intensities of truculence, and as the economic euphoria of the boom decades gave way to the relative (it was never more than relative) gloom of the so-called Great Depression; the beginning of which is precisely datable from 1873. Quite quickly, the conditions of international trade became less attractive for Britain. Prices, which had risen steadily since 1851, faltered and actually began again to fall. What had, for thirty years and more, seemed regular stable markets for staple British manufactures, showed signs of saturation. Worse still, British manufacturers were now encountering what, in the fifties and early sixties, almost all of them (except silk and worsted men, who never beat the French at their own fine textiles game; and Black Country clocks never went as well as American or Swiss ones) had been comfortably able to forget about: competition. From the United States, from Belgium, France and Germany it came. The most that Britain could hope for now, in the markets of the world, was to be *primus inter pares*: a noble and profitable position indeed, if one considered it dispassionately—but galling to businessmen who had known what it was like to have virtually no peers or rivals at all.

This is not an economic history book, but I cannot fail to sense the prime importance of economic history to my story. The character of British society in the mid-Victorian period was more or less conditioned by its remarkable economic development. 'More or less', because such interesting characteristics as the extraordinary interest shown by landowners in the welfare of pheasants and foxes, or the preference shown by the prosperous and, presumably, more educated parts of the community for a remarkably non-utilitarian and expensive style of education for their sons, seem not to derive more directly from economic causes than from sociological ones; if even, in any more effective style, from these. The economic substructure must always be there, but it often lies so deep that one may do better to concentrate on the demonstrably proximate causes of phenomena one is curious about. Yet, whether the ultimate economic explanation lies close or distant, the limiting terms of mid-Victorian British society were prescribed by economic forces. Its 'economic miracle', such as it was, alone made possible that unprecedented degree and diffusion of wealth which allowed its citizens, as consumers, to reveal their characters in the choices they actually made out of such an unparalleled variety of goods; while the large degree of citizens' dependence on overseas trade made the ups and downs of at any rate that sector of the economy of very immediate and vital interest to them. The truth about British mid-Victorian society in its domestic aspects cannot be told without some preliminary understanding of how Britain stood in relation to the rest of the world, and what consequently were the economic contours of British social history through our period.

Britain was, in the eighteen-fifties, by far the richest country in the world. By just how huge a margin, is uncertain; accurate measurements of national income at even such recent epochs still rest partly upon intelligent guesswork; but an eminent authority, writing within the last decade, thinks it likely that the *per capita* incomes of the UK, France and Germany about 1860 were respectively £32·6, £21·1 and £13·3.[1] With comparative figures of something of this order, economic historians do not quarrel. Such figures are only what one would expect, for they evidently reflect, in not too distorted a glass, the position then freely accorded to Britain by the rest of the family of nations. The wealth of Britain was regarded as fabulous; and the prosperity of the wealthier of its citizens was all the more conspicuous for the sharpness of their juxtaposition with the many (about how many, will be considered in Chapter Two) who appeared to remain in something like immemorial poverty.

The wealth of Britain was going up fast all through our period: faster, so far as we can judge with the imperfect tools at our disposal, than it had gone up during the earlier years of the century. The latest attempt at a definitive estimate of the gross national income makes it £523·3m. in 1851, £668m. in 1861 and £916·6m. in 1871.[2] The outlines of the industrial distribution of these totals are sketched below (pp. 99–100). Merely to state the huge quantity of Britain's wealth in our period—huge, compared both with all past and all contemporary experience—and simply to discern the sides of the economy from which it chiefly derived does not, of course, say anything about either the means of production or the distribution of that wealth. The ways of life made possible or obligatory for those who produced it by the manner of its distribution remain all to be explained, and will fill three-quarters of this book. But such economic facts are, as one of the greatest and carefullest of our economic historians said, the foundations on which social history rests. He went on to point out that 'foundations exist to carry better things';[3] the best foundations are those which, once installed, need never more be thought about. I am nearly finished with them now. But one more reinforcement of basic economic history demands to be noted: the general course of prices and prosperity.

What were the long- and what the short-term conditions of economic activity? So far as the long-term conditions are concerned, the years we are dealing with have a neat peculiarity about them; they constituted a phase of generally rising prices which was exceptional in a century of generally falling prices. This exceptional upsurge lasted about twenty years. From a trough in 1851 this long-term price-pattern went up via plateaux and bumps to a peak in 1873; whereafter the pattern of general fall reasserted itself, and lasted till the century's price-nadir in 1895. The principal cause of our price rise was the new gold from California and Australia. With reserves of bullion abundant as they had never been before, the Bank of England (like the other central banks of Europe) felt able to follow a more relaxed credit policy; and where the central bank led, the other credit institutions did not hesitate to follow. 'The great pyramid of debt could be built higher, fostering speculation in commodities and securities, facilitating the formation of new companies and the operation of old.'[4] Hence came the great credit booms of 1852–7, 1861–6 and 1869–73; hence came the buoyant optimism and bold confident enterprise that made our period 'unique in history for rapidity and magnitude of economic expansion'.[5]

From year to year, and month to month, of course, this price-rise looked and felt different. To point out that its long-term consequence was industrial and commercial boom and, for those whose bargaining power was strong or whose social position was such that they had no need to bargain, a generous share of its benefits, is not to say anything about its short-term pattern. This was not so smooth. The contour lines, on closer inspection, are seen to be less even. The changes which in the long run brought a fortune to this Liverpool merchant and that Wolverhampton manufacturer, gave them a few nasty shocks en route, and sent some of their workers to the workhouse. The general happiness, such as it was, was marred by two sudden crises and collapses, in 1857 and 1866. Each brought in its train the usual harsh purge of under- and unemployment. Our imperfect statistics, drawn solely from the better-organised skilled men's trade unions (see below, p. 148) show 11·9 per cent unemployed in 1858; 8·4 per cent in 1862; over 7 per cent in 1867 and 1868.[6] For unskilled men, things were worse all the time. It is certainly a fact that some workers managed to push up their wages fast enough during these years to more than match the rise in prices, but such 'facts', we must remember, are the bloodless facts of social science fiction: all averages and long-term reckonings. (As Clapham remarked, 'The "average wage-earner" ... is not a man of flesh and blood. He is a most important figure, but not human.'') Later on we shall consider in what ways and just how often unemployment befell mid-Victorian working-men (below, p. 149); here it is necessary only to note that each statistical year within each statistical quinquennium had its own distinct character, and that most statistical months and weeks, if only we could know enough about them, would be found to have had the same. What can be affirmed as true of 'the working-man' in the roaring early seventies, may not be so true of Thomas Entwistle, joiner, in Keighley in the last week of March 1872. Year-by-year indices are only a qualified improvement on quinquennial ones; but it looks as if they are the nearest we shall ever get. It is better to be probably than possibly correct.

The Urban Environment

Britain was, in these years, regarded by other nations in very much the same way as America was popularly regarded in the nineteen-twenties. Britain had the most and the biggest of everything; except, for sure, population (and, arguably, culture). At the 1851 census the population of Great Britain was about 20,817,000 (plus 6,552,000 in Ireland): in 1861 the round figure was 23,128,000 (plus 5,799,000). France (just swollen by the annexation of Savoie) then had about 37,500,000; the United States about 32,000,000; Austria, something under 34,000,000; Russia-in-Europe, something over 56,000,000 (but no one really knew). It was not on account of the absolute size of population that Britain was, economically, 'top nation'; what that population did, and where it lived, were what excited wonder and, sometimes, alarm. The census of 1851 appeared to show that, for the first time, more people were living in 'urban' than in 'rural' situations; and the best recent work on this aspect of the census figures confirms that judgment.[8] For the first time in modern history a body politic had got into a mainly urban condition. No other country in the world approached such a condition until after 1900. The official mid-Victorian definitions of 'urban' and 'rural' were indeed calculated to make the 'urban' sound, at any rate to a modern ear, more intensely so than it often was. But we need not quarrel with the basic fact that, in the still-continuing process of siting population in cities and towns rather than in towns, villages and hamlets, the fifties were the decisive turning-point. Here are the relevant figures for our period, extracted from a very valuable article by C. M. Law.

Figures Illustrating Urban Growth in England and Wales, 1841–1881

	1841	1851	1861	1871	1881
Urban Population as % of total population	48·3	54·0	58·7	65·2	70·2
Urban Population growth as % of last census	25·0	25·9	21·6	25·6	22·8
[Total England and Wales Population growth as ditto]	14·3	12·6	11·9	13·2	14·7
Urban Areas:					
No. over 100,000+	7	10	13	17	20
No. between 20,000 and 100,000	112	141	160	196	235
Population in Urban Areas as % of total population:					
areas over 100,000	20·7	24·8	28·8	32·6	36·2
areas between 50,000–100,000	5·5	5·8	6·1	5·5	7·3
areas between 20,000–50,000	6·8	7·0	7·5	9·6	9·4
areas between 10,000–20,000	5·3	6·4	6·6	6·6	6·6
areas between 2,500–10,000	10·0	9·9	9·8	10·5	10·5

By far the largest of these built-up areas was of course London—Greater London—which could already well have been called a conurbation if men had yet known that barbarous but useful word. From J. T. Coppock I take most of the following figures.[9] Only those in the last column are my own.*

Growth of the Metropolitan Conurbation

	Inner London '000s	% increase per decade	Outer London '000s	% increase per decade	Total Conurbation '000s	% increase per decade	Conurbation as % population of E. & W.
1841	1,949		290		2,239		14·1
		21		11		20	
1851	2,363		322		2,685		15·0
		19		30		20	
1861	2,808		419		3,227		16·6
		16		50		21	
1871	3,261		628		3,889		17·1
		17		50		23	
1881	3,830		940		4,770		18·4

This London was in fact the largest city in the Western world. The nearest approaches to it in the eighteen seventies were made by Paris (reaching two million about 1877–8) and New York (in 1871, about one and a half million). Berlin and Vienna, the next in line, lagged a long way behind, with about a million each in the middle seventies. The scale of London by itself could make it seem frightening to the newcomer and the unattached, but it was not size alone that drew from so many observers, British and foreign alike, one or both of two standard reactions: astonishment at the scale and starkness of the contrasts it presented, and a half-fascinated, half-terrified, loving-hating recognition that, while remorseless, it was irresistible. The contrasts presented themselves in as many

*His 'Inner London' is the old London County Council area: roughly that of the Metropolitan Police District from 1829 onwards. His 'Outer London' includes the remainder of the Registrar-General's Greater London Conurbation area: i.e. starting in the south-west, Esher, Staines, Uxbridge, Harrow, Potter's Bar, Chigwell, Barking, Bexley, Orpington, Croydon.

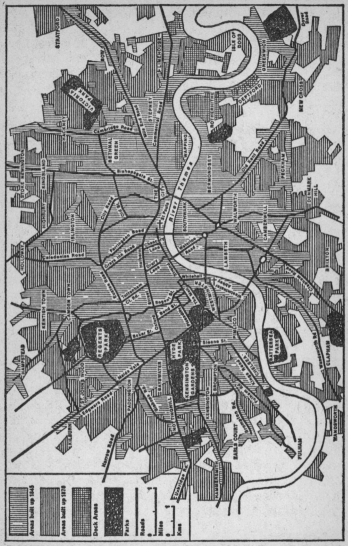

LONDON growth between 1845 (Wyld's New Plan of London) and 1870 (Reynold's New Map of London and Suburbs). N.B. What this map does not show! It omits railways and canal lines, including them and their premises within the 'built-up' areas; it is far from comprehensive even in main roads and bridges; and some parks (e.g. Battersea's and Primrose Hill, just N. of Regent's) were not enclosed at the earlier date.

forms as there were sensibilities to observe them: to the sociological moralist, London was 'at once the emporium of crime and the palladium of Christianity';[10] to the French or American visitor, the city where the worst poverty and the wealthiest magnificence of the world could be seen almost side by side; to the aesthetic observer, the city where atmosphere was all, where no light from whatever source came unfiltered or unenriched by steam, mist, haze, smoke or fog; to the psychological contemplative, a city where you could be unutterably lonely in the midst of millions. This latter sense was well expressed by Henry James, recollecting his first arrival in London in 1868:

'...a wet, black Sunday, about the first of March ... that drive from Euston, after dark, to Morley's Hotel in Trafalgar Square ... dusky, tortuous miles, in the greasy four-wheeler to which my luggage had compelled me to commit myself ... [London's] immensity was the great fact, and that was a charm; the miles of house-tops and viaducts, the complication of junctions and signals through which the train made its way to the station had already given me the scale. The weather had turned wet.... The low black houses were as inanimate as so many rows of coal-scuttles, save where at frequent corners, from a gin-shop, there was a flare of light more brutal still than the darkness.'

He took lodgings and a few days later, alone in them, experienced what came so often to so many: 'A sudden horror of the whole place came over me, like a tiger-pounce of homesickness which had been watching its moment. London was hideous, vicious, cruel, and above all overwhelming; whether or no she was "careful of the type", she was as indifferent as Nature herself to the single life ... a dreadful, delightful city.'[11]

Yet by the standards of our own day this immense London was not yet all that extensive. Reynolds's *New Map of London and its Suburbs* in 1870 shows a quasi-country belt of farms, market-gardens, small parks and estates, brickfields and cemeteries running from Willesden south to Barnes, broken only by the streets beginning to spread on either side of the Uxbridge and Hammersmith roads. Hampstead and Acton were not quite yet tied to London by bonds of brick. Wandsworth and Battersea on the south west were only patchily built over, while the Lea valley on the north east marked the limit of intense development, with little of Greater London beyond it but the railway town of Stratford, the industrial rampancy of West Ham, and that notorious fever-patch, Canning Town. *Mutatis mutandis*, the same is true of the other great towns of the mid-Victorian United Kingdom. Whatever it was that made them inescapable for some of their inhabitants, it was not size pure and simple.

Opposite is a table of the towns which had, by 1881, topped the 100,000 mark, together with an indication of the order of size in which they stood after the national capital.[12] (It is remarkable how many of them still retain the same position.)

Some of these were monsters by the standards of the day, but they were still physically much smaller than they are today: partly because their populations were smaller, partly because those populations tended to be more tightly packed. Contemporaries who commented on the great size of their cities did so because they were making comparisons with the past and because the recent growth had produced problems they were only beginning to learn how to solve. Our appreciation of their plight should not allow us to overlook the fact that their cities put no physical obstacle in way of the pedestrian who was free to get out of them.

Towns kept growing at this rate mainly because they offered a variety of more or less irresistible attractions to a superabundant population. These attractions were not entirely economic. J. A. Banks has reminded[13] us that these nineteenth-century towns, in many respects so grim and unwholesome, must yet have exercised some attractions better called social than economic: for girls and young women, a wider choice of marriage partners and a better chance of marriage; for young persons of both sexes, the prospect of a more independent and autonomous way of life; for the adventurous and restless of all ages, the legendary lure of city lights; for the troublesome and criminal, the city's immemorial anonymity

Towns of 100,000+ by the 1881 Census

	1851		1861		1871		1881	
	'000s	Order	'000s	Order	'000s	Order	'000s	Order
Aberdeen	72	16=	74	21	88	23	106	24
Belfast	103	11	122	10	174	10	208	9
Birmingham	265	5	351	5	433	4	437	4
Blackburn	47	22	63	25	85	24	104	26
Bolton	61	19=	70	23	83	25=	105	25
Bradford	104	10	106	13	147	11	194	11
Brighton	66	17=	78	19=	93	22	108	23
Bristol	137	8	154	9	183	9	207	10
Dublin	405	1	410	3	405	5	419	5
Dundee	79	15	91	17	119	16	140	16
Edinburgh	202	6	203	7	244	7	295	7
Glasgow	375	3	443	2	568	1	673	1
Hull	85	14=	98	15	122	15	166	14
Leeds	172	7	207	6	259	6	309	6
Leicester	61	19=	68	24	95	21	137	17
Liverpool	395	2	472	1	540	2	627	2
Manchester	338	4	399	4	444	3	462	3
Newcastle	88	13	109	12	128	13	145	15
Nottingham	57	20	75	20	139	12	187	12
Oldham	52	21	73	22	83	25=	111	22
Plymouth	90	12	113	11	188	17	123	20
Portsmouth	72	16=	95	16	114	18	128	18
Salford	85	14=	102	14	125	14	176	13
Sheffield	135	9	185	8	240	8	285	8
Stoke-upon Trent	66	17=	78	19=	101	19	125	19
Sunderland	64	18	80	18	98	20	117	21

(N.B. These figures are not absolutely fair because some will conceal occasional boundary changes; but I believe them to be good enough for this purpose of general comparison.)

and sanctuary. Such motivations must have influenced some country minds; how much, and how mixed with economic ones, it is impossible to say. The economic ones were, I suppose, the more important. The demand for labour in the countryside was at best stable, while the birth-rate exceeded the death-rate there as almost everywhere else:

'The first absolute declines in county totals were enumerated at the 1851 Census ... [says John Saville]. Then, during the decade of the eighteen-fifties, absolute declines in county populations became more widespread. The decrease in total

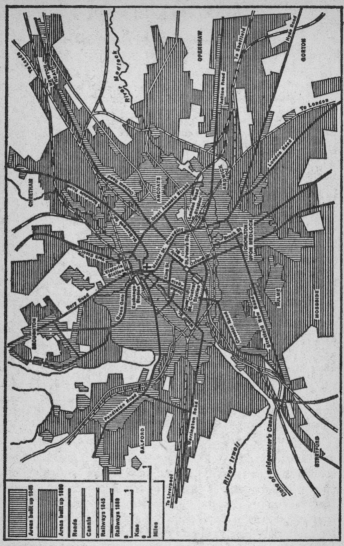

MANCHESTER growth between 1845 and 1889 (from the Ordinance Survey 6" Maps). I have marked as 'built-up' all ground occupied by canal wharfs and (what were very extensive) railwayyards, as well as industrial and domestic premises. I have not shown the great late-Victorian Ship Canal along the line of the Irwell.

numbers at the 1861 census was found to have continued in Wiltshire and Montgomery and to have begun in Cambridge, Huntingdon, Norfolk, Rutland, Somerset and Suffolk in England, and in Anglesey, Brecknock and Cardigan in Wales.'[14]

The sixties showed a check to this depopulation; 'many rural areas which had been showing an absolute loss of population now showed slight gains'; but this was only a temporary halting of the tendency which reasserted itself in the seventies and persists, with whatever local variations, into our own day. There simply was not work enough for all the hands brought up to do it; or else the work that was (perhaps irregularly) available was not well enough paid to make the more enterprising sort of country folk prefer it to what they (usually correctly) believed they could get elsewhere. So they responded to the pull of the urban and industrial magnets; not necessarily the same thing, as a moment's thought about the coal-fields will show. Their response was not usually more direct than the pull was immediate.

Long-distance migration—as it might be, from Dorset direct to London—seems to have been uncommon, except among the Irish and Highlanders, for whom it had perforce become an accepted fact of life with the result that there were, by 1871, 567,000 Irish-*born* in England and Wales (over a third of them living in Lancashire) and 105,000 in Scotland (making nearly 14 per cent of the total population). For most other British citizens the usual pattern of migration was of short-distance shifts, producing ' "currents of migration" setting in the direction of the great centres of commerce and industry'. This absorptive process was thus summarised by its first serious investigator: 'The inhabitants of the country immediately surrounding a town of rapid growth flock into it; the gaps thus left in the rural population are filled up by migrants from more remote districts, until the attractive force of one of our rapidly growing cities makes its influence felt, step by step, to the most remote corners of the kingdom.'[15]

Add to this seemingly incessant immigration the increase of local population by 'natural' means—sheer excess of births over deaths—and you have the basic general explanation of

the growth of the towns. In itself it does not say much about
them. What was happening in our period was in general no
different from what happened before or after, and there are
limits to what the census can tell one anyway. As Dyos neatly
puts it, 'What came into the Registrar-General's view-finder at
each ten-year interval was ... merely the frozen climax to a
decade of movement'.[16] He might as well have said, 'decade or
lifetime of movement'. The only fact about an individual's
movements recorded in the census was the place of birth. Thus
the parents of a Bermondsey family recorded as having been
born in 'Galway' might have lived twenty years in Liverpool
before moving South, and the statement concerning their surviving children that they had been born in 'London' would
conceal the fact that before reaching Bermondsey the family
had lived in St Giles's and Stepney. Unless they were rather
unusual, their life in Bermondsey would have been one of
frequent flits from place to place. Of these varieties of movement, which made up much of most individuals' experience of
urban life, the censuses say little or nothing. But they do make
possible such overall measurements of migration as Shannon
made of Victorian London.[17] His figures may be simplified
thus:

Estimated Decennial Immigration to London [N.B. not 'Greater'
London]

Immigrants, Where Born	1851–61		1861–71		1871–81	
	'000	%	'000	%	'000	%
England and Wales	232	81·1	276	83·6	421	84·5
Scotland	11	3·8	12	3·6	19	3·8
Ireland	14	4·9	7	2·1	19	3·8
Abroad	29	10·2	36	10·8	39	7·9

Shannon's summary is that 'London would appear to have
increased its population through immigration by a little over
12 per cent in the sixties, by some 15 per cent in the seventies,
and, slackening off, by some 10 per cent in the eighties.' Of
these increases, 'between a third and a fifth' came from extra-

metropolitan Middlesex, Surrey, Kent, Hertford and Essex: i.e. the immediate hinterland; and 'about a quarter' came from no further than the line Norfolk–Cambridgeshire–Huntingdonshire–Northamptonshire–Oxfordshire–Hampshire. Irishmen and Scotsmen and foreigners made themselves, or were held to be socially, more conspicuous than their absolute numbers warranted; and any modern Londoner who supposes that his city's cosmopolitanism is a new thing may be surprised to see, already by the eighteen-seventies, how substantial was the intake from overseas. Dyos's analysis of migration into South London leads him to the conclusion that its 'cumulative effect ... was to create urban communities in which not more than half their members had been born within South London at all'.[18] In the even faster growing industrial towns of the midlands and the north, the proportion of new arrivals was greater still. To the ordinary pressure of numbers must have been added, in all such situations, the social problems that always accompany the melting-pot cramming-together of groups from different countries and regions. The Irish kept very much together wherever they went—and they were liable to turn up whenever there was a brisk demand for coarse hard labour—and the Highlanders who came South to Glasgow and Edinburgh tried to do the same. It seems possible that regional groups (North Walians, Cornishmen, East Anglians and so on) did the same too.

The character of the population movements of the fifties and sixties may not be clearly distinguishable from those of the preceding and subsequent periods, but the case is otherwise in respect of the cities' central parts as they stretched and strained to cope with the pressures of prosperity, rising standards and relentless numbers. It was in our period that the Victorians began decisively to tackle the sanitary, administrative and cultural problems of their cities; and one consequence of this belated activity was a change in the shape and character of city centres as municipal pride and commercial opulence combined to 'improve them' and give them greater distinction and amenity. Partly because of these 'improvements', etc. (of which more anon), partly because the central residential parts were in any case already disagreeably packed with poor people and small shopkeepers, the residential developments of our period were almost all in suburbs. Most of these suburbs were however for the most part unlike the suburbs of our own day. They still had a strong flavour of the city about them, since only towards the end of our period did the growth of suburban railways and the invention of trams begin to create that substantial separation between city life and suburban home. Train and bus travel to work was not uncommon among the middle classes; by 1855 about 20,000 persons are reckoned to have been commuting by bus into London daily; about 15,000 by steamboat; about 6,000 by rail.[19] The working class suburb, such as it was, still had to be close enough to its denizens' places of employment for them to walk to work in the morning and, ideally, to get home for the midday meal. Higher class suburbs—except in Scotland, where the practice of living in 'flats' was familiar to all classes, and looked down on by none —invariably meant gardens, and the higher the class, the greater the quantity of timber left standing, to heighten the illusion of *rus in urbe*. Flats seem to have been very uncommon among respectable and prosperous English families before the seventies. I have traced none before those around Ashley Place, Westminster, *c.* 1852–4, and I am not sure that any more such big blocks were built—though housing reformers like George Godwin certainly kept the idea going—before the seventies, when at last they began to catch on.

It marked no novelty in the social situation that these great acreages of new bricks and mortar had from the start had a strong flavour of social differentiation. Those who built them expected—indeed, usually intended—them to do so. This was in natural conformity with established practice, and with the character of British society. Since early in the century social commentators had been deploring what they said was a new tendency towards the segregation of the classes into separate residential areas. It is not easy to judge whether they were accurately observing a new tendency, or beholding an established tendency with newly anxious eyes. At any rate it was there; and by our period every new-built street and neighbourhood was endowed from the hour of its conception with the social character which the promoter wished it to maintain. Often he was speedily disappointed—but that is another matter (see below p. 51).

Rich people bought or rented villas or the more splendid kind of terrace houses; and there is no doubt that the detached villa was, outside London, the most characteristic residence for the prosperous mid-Victorian Englishman. The terrace style was, socially speaking, in a state of decline. It was still compatible with unquestioned respectability, but it had ceased to be fashionable or smart except in London, where there was no room for anything else in or near the West End, and in towns like Leamington, Cheltenham, Bristol and Brighton, where the style had a powerful momentum of fashion to sustain it, and also in Scottish cities, where rather a different style of urban living prevailed. In Glasgow, indeed, one of the greatest architects of the century, Alexander Thomson, was throughout these years housing his upper middle class clients in villas and terrace houses indiscriminately. The social difference between his Great Western Terrace (1867–9) and, say, Lancaster Gate (1865–6) or Queen's Gate (1853 onwards) in London, is simply that the Scottish tradition allowed him to conceal the separateness of the included dwellings within a single monumental design, while the London designers frankly expressed that separateness, as if to suggest that the houses would have been villas if they could.

A villa, detached for preference, in a private estate, became the rich mid-Victorian town dweller's ideal: a spacious garden or even 'grounds' round the house, walls round the grounds, and gates and gatekeeper to control access to the road (in the suburbs very likely a private, 'unadopted' one) and thus to keep the neighbourhood free of such undesirables as itinerant musicians, carts, omnibuses, loafers, street-vendors and beggars. These gates or barriers were a regular feature of the wealthiest areas. Surviving only in rather rare instances, they are not easy for modern man to envisage. But wherever the proprietorship could maintain them, they were maintained, and not in suburbs only; the drive to single-class exclusiveness and privacy was such that the number of them in the metropolis only grew with time, until there were, by 1875, about 150 in the central and western districts. Many, tucked away in side-streets or blocking off cul-de-sacs, were of little public significance, but two dozen or so barred thoroughfares of such importance that they provoked a running fire of outraged criticism throughout our period, and several attempts at legislation: all blocked and beaten by the proprietors' parliamentary influence, despite such scandalous aspects of the situation as delays to fire-engines, the maintenance of the enclosed streets at public expense, and endless brawls between gatekeepers and enraged citizens, at least two of them ending in fatality. Belgravia, Marylebone, Mayfair and St Pancras were the most afflicted areas. Not until 1890 did these barricades of privilege crumble in the metropolis. They survived in suburban areas till later, and Kensington Palace Gardens still gives a good idea of what they were like.

Semi-detached villas were the next best thing to wholly detached ones, and the nearer the suburb was to the centre, the more there were of them; they cost less than detached houses, were nearly as private, and gave the casual passer-by an impression of being grander than they actually were. Sir John Summerson ascribes their invention to the men who soon after 1800 built the Eyre Estate at St John's Wood: 'the first part of London, and indeed of any other town, to abandon the terrace house for the semi-detached villa—a revolution of striking significance and far-reaching effect'.[20] By our period the effects were felt all over England. In every suburb, wherever the price of land was not so high as absolutely to prescribe some sort of terraced development, the semi-detached abounded.

Between the less pretentious sort of semi-detached houses and the unabashed terrace, there was no significant difference in either social or economic terms. Once below the carriage-owning or carriage-suggesting level (few men with incomes below £600 a year could keep up even the most modest two-wheeler) it became largely a matter of geographical chance and personal choice whether a semi-detached or a terraced house was taken. The dearer the land, the likelier a terraced house was to provide the quantity and kind of rooms required by the more stylish kind of respectability. Terraced houses were, as I have already insisted, rarely *fashionable* outside mid-Victorian London; but they could undoubtedly look *respectable*, and that was what was wanted by virtually every mid-Victorian who could afford to consider a house of his own. By the later Victorian nineties, suburbia was spreading into hinterlands where land was relatively cheap enough for the semi-detached and detached house to be within the reach of the less affluent, and that was the end of the terrace idea until its revival after the Second World War. In the eighteen-fifties and -sixties, however, the terrace was fairly standard for all but the more affluent town-dwellers: a normal form in which estate-developers and speculative builders put up houses for the great majority of their customers, the middle and lower middle class people whose incomes did not exceed about £300 a year and all the working class people who could afford a small house. Sameness and straightness characterised these streets. The 'garden suburb' idea—mild suggestions of woodland and wildness by means of winding roads and natural timber—could only work at the detached and semi-detached level; departures from the straight and narrow could only be economically justified where the contours of the land required them. The rule was, that the lower the class, the plainer and more frankly terraced the house. Bay-windows above all marked the better-off terrace houses; together with variously elaborated porches, door surrounds, string courses, balustrades, cornices and attics, more often in classical and Italianate modes than Gothic until about 1870, they gratified their generation's equation of decoration with beauty, and their occupiers' preference for the illusion of variety. The lowest-class terraces of course were innocent of all such embellishments: straight rows of brick boxes cut into by rectangular door and window spaces, relieved perhaps by a semi-circular fanlight.

These brick terraces or rows at their worst were of the two or three storey 'back-to-back' kind. The description speaks for itself. Back-to-backs (according to Flinn, a late eighteenth-century innovation[21]) had only one open face; they shared a common back wall, and stood one on each side of it. Untold thousands had been built during the first half of the century. Mid-Victorian Nottingham had at least 8,000 of them (i.e. about two-thirds of its whole stock of houses). Thousands were still being lived in, and some were still being built. Manchester prohibited their construction in 1844 but Bury did not forbid them till 1866; Liverpool, not (I believe) till 1864; from conflicting evidence about Nottingham I gather that a nominal ban in 1845 did not become absolute till after 1874. Their nastiness lay not merely in the flimsiness of their construction, the lack of a back-yard, the impossibility of ventilation, and their geographical position which was inevitably in the middle and/or earliest industrial parts of the older cities; it was made especially apparent to eye and nose by the accompanying sanitary arrangements, the privies and ash-pits, which (added perhaps subsequently to the houses themselves) had to be either inserted into the fronts of the houses or put into the street or courts.

The courts which, especially in the bigger towns, would often be found behind the rows (as also behind bigger dwellings fallen on evil days) were every bit as mean and nasty as back-to-backs: even nastier, if they were back-to-backs themselves. Birmingham was particularly strong in such; it had at least 2,000 courts. Liverpool in 1842 was found to have 1,982, containing 10,692 houses in which lived over 55,000 people, and most of them were still there in 1850. The closed court might or might not offer a pleasanter prospect and a better life than the open street. It was unlikely to be better ventilated. It was certain to be even less adequately cleansed; courts had usually been expressly excluded from the jurisdiction of improvement commissioners (for whom, see below, p. 58) and where they were nominally the responsibility of a public authority, they came at the bottom of its list of scavenging priorities. Privies, where present, would certainly be shared ones in a common place; water, where supplied at all, would be obtained at a common tap.

Houses lining streets, if they were not back-to-backs, could hardly help being better than the worst; they would have *some* sort of yard or garden at the back, and probably privies of their own. Two-up-and-two-down was the commonest arrangement of rooms, with an attic or a cellar often making a fifth. Whether they were ill-built or well-built depended entirely on circumstances. Those erected, for example, by self-respecting industrialists as homes for good workers, or by estate developers as homes for out-servants, would be good of their kind; those flung up by speculators or small capitalists for instant profit would be bad. We read of such being built in Birmingham in the late forties for as little as £60 a-piece: 'The capital cost was kept down by making the supporting walls only 4½ inches thick, putting in joists measuring 5½ by 1½ inches, and fixing them 17 inches apart'.[22] Building regulations, prescribing minimum sizes of rooms and windows, widths of streets, thicknesses of walls, provisions for drains, etc., were rare before the later forties, and (as for example in London, where building regulations were theoretically comprehensive) unevenly enforced. During the forties, local authorities began increasingly to make such building by-laws as their sense of local practicality suggested, and thus to prevent the continued building of the very worst sort of housing in the very worst situations.

Local boards of health had power to insist on something better, and it seems that all self-respecting towns were, by the sixties, using that power. But beyond their boundaries—in most mining areas, for instance, and almost everywhere that was still nominally rural—anything might still go; we are reminded how fragile and incomplete was the rule of sanitary law even within bounds when we hear MOHs complaining in the seventies that they still could not stop the building of houses on abandoned refuse-tips. Dr Dyke told the Adderley Commission sitting about 1870 what was happening just outside the limits of his jurisdiction, near Merthyr Tydfil:

'If a new colliery is opened in an upland valley 200, 300 or 400 houses are built very rapidly, and they are inhabited long before they are dry. The foundations, as a rule, are simply upon the sod, which is merely turned over, and a flag is put upon that sod. There is a population sprung up in a neighbouring valley to ours which has now ... 40,000 people, the whole of whom are living in houses that had never been looked after by any surveyor before they were inhabited.'

Within his boundaries, standards were higher. Foundations had to be drained; 'the walls of the foundation up to a certain height' had to be built 'of lime that is waterproof'; rooms not less than eight feet high; windows of a certain size; and so on.[23] These requirements, where they could be imposed, were the more important for the labouring family because so often, to cite Macclesfield's MOH in 1857: 'The working man has no choice whatever in the selection of his cottage.'[24]

Housing and Homes

The topic of building regulations, for the most part sanitary in object, leads the mind naturally to larger questions of house design and furnishing. I wish I felt better able to handle them. Shifts in the proportions of floor-space allotted to rooms for particular purposes; the disappearance of rooms for this function, the appearance of rooms for that; changes in quality or quantity of structure or fittings following price changes or technical innovations: these and cognate matters are obviously of immense potential interest to the social historian, but they have hardly yet begun to attract serious historical enquiry. The prescribed limits of this volume would in any case have prevented me from dwelling long upon them, but absolute lack of professional guidance keeps me from straying far beyond the kitchen and the privy, two important rooms about which some fragmentary information is available. Every aspect of the bedroom remains, alas, mysterious. By what social groups, if any, were separate beds or separate bedrooms sought? What social types had dressing rooms, why and how did couples manage their dressing who could not afford a dressing room? To move to other parts of the house: when did central heating by hot-water radiators begin to take the chill off corridors and corners far from the fire? How cheap had upright pianos become by the seventies, and what proportion of them was imported? How cheaply could a six-room house be furnished by 1870? How grand had a house to be for a bathroom to be built into it? A new house did not have to be very grand to get a privy, even in the fifties; but whether that privy would contain a water closet, or some other form, would depend for many years yet on local law and custom.

Water-closets were officially discouraged for all classes of users in some mid-Victorian cities (e.g. Manchester) because of the strain their outpourings imposed on the drainage and sewerage system, and I believe it is true to say that outside privies, whether serving one house or many, were almost always, until after our period, of an older-fashioned non-mechanical kind. That meant they were either earth or 'dry' closets, where the excrement fell into deposits of earth or ashes supposed to be regularly renewed, or they were some species of 'wet' closet: perhaps directly over a drain or cess-pit, perhaps over a pail, perhaps over that 'greatest of all forms of sanitary barbarism', a wet midden. Sir Arthur Newsholme, chief MOH to the Local Government Board, recorded that Manchester in 1871 had over 38,000 privy middens; pail-closets replaced most of them by the mid-eighties; water-closets later still.[25] Glasgow did not enforce a general replacement of middens by WCs until after 1890; Nottingham as late as 1908 had ten thousand more pail-closets than water-closets. One must not antedate the impact of the water-closet on the working classes. Water companies did not like supplying water-closets in poor districts, complaining that the delicate machinery got bashed up, the china smashed, the metal fittings stolen, the water thus left running; and although MOHs were not all of one mind about the water-closet question, many of them (including Edinburgh's) were convinced that the sanitary advantages of an efficient water-closet system were outweighed by the nuisances that, among the lower classes, so often followed their breaking or blockage. Only in 'model' lower class dwellings were water-closets, of whatever design (the unsavoury pan and valve lever-operated types remained unaccountably popular long after sanitary experts proclaimed the superiority of syphon types), to be commonly found. In better-class town houses, where the proprieties of respectable life were supposed to be observed (and where moreover a cistern-full of water could be relied on to keep the flush working during the dry hours which continued to characterise some water companies) water-closets were, I gather, common.

If water technology was one major source of domestic change in the nineteenth century, gas was another. By the fifties gas light was normal in middle- and upper-class houses in most towns and in all cities. It was not the brilliant white gas light made possible by the invention of the incandescent mantle from the nineties onwards; it was yellower, smellier, smokier and hotter; but it was so much handier and, for any quantity, cheaper than the alternatives, that few town-dwellers who needed a lot of light and who could afford the cost of installation went without. Gas was also, from the later forties onwards, being commercially applied to cooking, but the excellent researches of Alison Ravetz make it clear that despite their efficiency and controllability, gas cookers were not widely used before the eighties and nineties, though gas rings may have been on account of their suitability for economic and delicate stewing.[26] Gas seems to have been little used by the lower classes in their own homes before the invention of the slot meter about 1890, and it can be left entirely out of any account of how the conditions of their lives changed through the mid-Victorian period. Their light came, rather expensively, from wax, oil, tallow and (from the later fifties) paraffin; their heat, when and where they could afford it, from wood and coal; their cooked meals from the same fuels in open fires or little kitchen ranges, which facilitated boiling and frying but less usually baking or roasting—operations still often performed by the baker down the street.

I return now to the types of dwelling in which the poorer mid-Victorians lived. For many, home was a plain new cottage or house, as already described: cheaply built, perhaps following the prescription of local authority by-laws, perhaps not. But such simple houses were not the only places in which the lower classes lived. They might also be found in three other kinds of building: in what we should nowadays call flats; in what were then called lodging-houses; and in houses that had declined from some former better state. (Not so often in cellars, however, the occupation as well as the building of which was generally prohibited from the forties onwards. Illegal occupation might of course continue.)

Flats were, from an English point of view, virtually invented during the forties, and in the course of our period they became quite a conspicuous feature of the central working-class districts of the larger industrial cities. Contemporaries most commonly called these blocks 'model dwellings'. The name exactly described their purpose. They were (often philanthropically) meant to show how, by building what were, in effect, tall blocks of small flats, the rather poor could be housed relatively well. In practice they did not work out quite like that. The standard of accommodation they provided was indeed, compared with what could be got for the same rent locally, quite good: solid and sanitary, even if tending to the utilitarian and barrack-like. Their tone is well caught by a sympathetic respectable observer in 1866:

'Though there is nothing picturesque in these buildings [he wrote of the Shoreditch Peabody Buildings in Commercial Street, opposite the Cambridge Music Hall (which he considered wicked)] the architect has done wonders for the health and comfort of the residents ... The closets are numerous, private and convenient, light and spacious; the lavatories [I think he meant wash-places] are ample and accessible—closets and lavatories for men and women are separate and far apart ... The ventilation of every house and room is beyond praise; around the upper portion of each house [i.e. flat], fresh air has constant admission, and sweeps the ceiling ... The uppermost storeys ... are lofty, pleasant-looking, breezy drying rooms.... On this lofty flat [i.e. floor] are bathrooms for men and for women, separate and remote from each other. The fire-grates maybe too large for some families; the ovens too small; the heat of the fire ... may go too much up the chimney; the walls, being merely whitewashed brick, may wear a poorhouse or gaol-like look. There being no supply of hot water for the baths, is almost tantamount to there being no baths at all. But tenants should not complain too much . . .'[27]

Indeed they should not; unless they sought more liberty of action in respect of animals, hours, noise, window-boxes, etc., than the usually rather stringent rules permitted. In model dwellings of this and allied kinds (the Peabody Trust ones subsidised their tenants, while Sir Sydney Waterlow's very successful Improved Industrial Dwellings Company set out to show that five per cent profit could be returned) the tenant was certainly getting more room space and more amenities per penny of rental (e.g. cooking range with water heater at the back; sink with draining-board; ventilated larder) than he could have done in an ordinary house. By the mid-eighties, when the housing of the working classes had become so pressing a public concern that a royal commission looked into it, about 150,000 people were inhabiting model dwellings in London, and some smaller number elsewhere. The achievement though absolutely impressive is relatively insignificant; it made only a tiny dent in the problem, which could not under British circumstances be solved without vast injections of subsidy from somewhere; and the classes of people thus housed were in general not the classes for whom decent housing was otherwise out of the question. Even the most philanthropically-minded managers of model dwellings had to have a care what sort of tenants they took in. Waterlow's organisation, which provided probably the best quality flats, was said to take in none below artisan level. The Peabody Trust and the other giant of the metropolitan business, the Artisans' Labourers' and General Dwellings Company, late-born in 1867, were reputed to take a higher proportion of sub-artisans but of course—and who could blame them?—they only wanted men with steady jobs, whose prospects of being able to pay rent regularly were encouraging. The big organisations of familiar names were copied by many smaller ones and by private individuals like Shaftesbury's friend Lord Kinnaird who founded the model lodging house mentioned below (p. 47). The model dwellings movement was a noble ornament to mid-Victorian philanthropy, but the market was too tough for it. By the end of our period everyone concerned had come to a clear realisation that the difficulties were simply economic ones: commercial men were not much attracted by Waterlow's example, because they could get bigger returns on their capital elsewhere (it seems to have been a rule, that the bigger the city, the less commercially attractive was the provision of *good* working-class housing), while the men who could afford them—relatively prosperous artisans, low-grade clerks, etc.—often disliked the stigma of dependence and tameness that hung over them, not to mention the low character of neighbourhoods in which they so often stood. They made the mistake of demanding respectability from those who could not afford it.

Model dwellings were not the only original idea produced by the men of our period in hopes of improving the standards of working-class housing. 'Model cottages' became fashionable among benevolent country landlords (see below, p. 86) and 'model lodging houses' an active concern among social and sanitary reformers in the bigger towns. The importance of the 'common lodging house' can easily be missed by the modern reader to whom the word 'lodging' must usually suggest a more or less respectable residence for students or single working men and women. Mid-Victorian lodging houses were more often than not disreputable, were rarely if ever inhabited by students, and were as likely to be used by the (supposedly) married, the infant, the decrepit, the out-of-work, the vagabond and the criminal as by the single and industrious. They were in fact catch-alls on the penultimate rung of the social ladder: temporary shelters and even makeshift 'homes' for all who, while able to afford nothing better, were not quite yet reduced to the workhouse, the river-bank and the railway arch. For a modest payment (exacted on entry!), modest provision was made of bed and board; the bed perhaps no more than a heap of (dirty) straw, the board usually consisting of some common cooking facilities. For migrants on the move and for new arrivals in a town, a lodging house was the obvious, perhaps the only place to go; where houses and room were scarce and dear, it was often an obvious place to stay, and it was a positively attractive one to all who operated on the shady side of the law. Henry Mayhew collected much information on them about the beginning of our period, when he learnt from habitués in what parts of London they were most thickly and easily to be found, and came to the conclusion that about 10,000 people must be 'domiciled, more or less permanently, in the low lodging houses of London'—i.e. in the cheaper, nastier ones: for with the more expensive ones, which were scarcely distinguishable from boarding or rooming houses for single or married artisans, clerks, and commercial travellers and other relatively monied people, no one had any quarrel. An official estimate a few years later was that London's lodging houses had room for over 80,000 persons per night. 'Some of the lodging houses present no appearance differing from that of ordinary houses; except, perhaps, that their exterior is dirtier.... Some ... are the worst class of low brothels, and some may even be described as brothels for children.' An experienced patron of these places told Mayhew that the country ones were on the whole less physically abominable—less bug-ridden, less liable to be promiscuous—than the London ones, but that the keepers of the country ones were usually receivers of stolen goods while the London keepers, though perfectly well aware of what so many of their customers were up to, usually kept clear of their criminal transactions except in those which were in fact 'thieves' kitchens', sub-stations of crime. 'Nothing can be worse to the health than these places', he said in a striking sentence, 'without ventilation, cleanliness, or decency, and with forty people's breaths perhaps mingling together in one foul choking steam of stench.'[28]

It was not surprising that these ubiquitous, indispensable and almost uniformly deplorable places should have attracted the attention of authority. The corporation of Glasgow took power to control their worst abuses in 1840; that of Liverpool, in 1842. The city of London did the same some time before 1851, the year when Lord Shaftesbury piloted through both Houses (he was only Lord Ashley when he introduced it to the Commons) the general act which enabled any police authority to establish the same system of inspection and control. This was especially valuable in London, where the metropolitan police at once took charge of the matter and within a few years had closed down the worst and imposed some minimal standards of superficial hygiene and decency on the cheapest. A variety of contemporary reports, official and unofficial alike, leave no doubt that substantial improvement was effected. It was difficult by 1860 to find lodging houses as noisome as was common in 1850. But the cheaper ones remained, by the rising moral and sanitary standards of the reign, very nasty; the demand for their facilities remained so great, and could in no other way be met, that local authority officials often deliberately neglected to enforce the law; and (it is important to remember) this general power to regulate common lodging houses (except in Glasgow and Liverpool) to houses or rooms in houses let as lodgings, the frequent nastiness of which had to be tackled in other and more roundabout ways, where they were tackled at all.

While the operations of the police were tending throughout our period to improve the character of the common lodging houses (tending also, of course, to make them less accessible to the *very* poor and dirty), philanthropy was moving in the same direction by means of 'model' ones. Like the 'model dwellings', these had their origins in the great philanthropic awakening of the forties; like them again, their success was only partial so far as the really poor were concerned. Mayhew reported in 1850 that the best of the London ones, in George Street, St Giles's, was of a character and cost to be well above the means of the people who needed it most. The one established in Westminster by Shaftesbury's friend Lord Kinnaird worked well: civilised amenities, optional attendance at religious worship, an honest capable master and beds for only 3d a night. But he concluded that many of them were either unsympathetically, even cruelly, strict in their regulations ('adding insult to wretchedness') or simply bogus:

'Many private adventurers have thus dignified their domiciles, and ... it is only a cloak for greater uncleanliness and grosser immorality.... The sham model-houses to which I more particularly allude ... are in Short's-gardens, Drury Lane; Mill-yard, Cable-street, Thrawl-street, Spitalfields; Plough-court, Whitechapel; and Union-court, Holborn. All of these are, *without exception*, twopenny brothels, head-quarters of low-lived procuresses, and resorts of young thieves and prostitutes.'[29]

Corruptio optimi pessima. Such places came under police control in 1851 and, whether claiming to be 'model' or not, were willy-nilly made to conform to the new minimum standards; while genuinely 'model' ones, like that in Eagle Court, opposite Somerset House (see plate 6) continued to be opened. While housing remained in such short supply, there could hardly be too many of them.

The 'model dwellings' and the common lodging house justify so much space because they were eminently characteristic of our period, not because of the numbers they housed. The majority of the lower classes lived either in more or less recently built little cottages or houses of the kind that have been described, or in sub-divisions of bigger houses fallen from a better, former state. 'Made-down', was the expressive Scottish word for the process familiar (then as now) throughout the UK. Hardly a big city in the western world has not its lower class (often immigrant) area where overcrowding and every sort of social and sanitary inconvenience half-hide behind façades of once 'respectable', even grand, houses. It is probably an enduring feature of urban society in circumstances of growing wealth and population:

'As towns increase [wrote Robert Rawlinson, a prominent sanitarian, in 1858] there is an engulphing or lowering of whole streets and of entire districts of houses, built orginally for the merchant and superior tradesman. Examine some of our great sea-ports and inland manufacturing towns, and it will be found that streets of houses originally erected for the 'merchant princes' are now in ruins ... now the abodes of the improvident, the vagrant, the vicious, and the unfortunate....'[30]

The sites where this perhaps protracted process of decay

and descent was often most concentrated were known as 'rookeries', an expressive term applied to big old houses (maybe even palaces!) gone utterly to seed, and the congeries of tenements, cottages, courts and alleys grown behind them. The rookeries' reporter Thomas Beames, an admirer of Dr Arnold devoting himself to work in the Westminster slums where, as he colourfully put it, 'Europe's grandest hall is flanked by England's foulest graveyard!', assured his readers in 1850 that such were not limited to the well-known ones off the Strand, and in St Giles's, along Saffron Hill, in the Minories, Westminster ('the Devil's Acre') and Bermondsey (Jacob's Island); you could find them, if you looked hard enough, almost everywhere: Mile-End Road, Lambeth, Maiden Lane, Paddington. . . .[31]

But such extreme collapse could be very recent too. Some new-built areas were never anything but ghastly slums (Agar's Town, for instance, which crawled out of the mud between the Euston Road (as it now is) and the Regent's Park Canal about 1810, and was obliterated by St Pancras station fifty years later) and some damp low-lying areas like 'the Potteries, Notting-Hill' attracted thousands of 'squatters' and accommodated them for years. In older-built areas, that process of decay, which sometimes took (as it may still take) many years to reduce a neighbourhood through many strata of shabby gentility to real slum status, could be brought about with a lightning rapidity uncommon in our own times. It has become uncommon because public authorities nowadays exercise a variety of controls which were then almost wholly lacking: powers enabling them to control the use of land and buildings, to 'zone' development, to prescribe transportation provisions, to preserve historic or otherwise meritorious buildings, to compel owners to do this or that with what they may still fondly regard as their own. One of the effects of the growth of all these powers—a growth which had hardly begun by 1875—has been that residents in any given districts usually have plenty of warning of an impending drastic change in the local amenities; a change which in any case nowadays takes place in a society somewhat softer, in its class-consciousness and observance of conventional forms, than it then was.

The Railway and the City

For wealthy and respectable mid-Victorians the shape of things to come would be as starkly clear as it was in Boston, Mass., to George Apley's father when he looked out of his South End bow window one morning and saw standing on the doorstep of a house over the way *a man in shirtsleeves*. 'Thunderation!' he said; and sold the house within twenty-four hours.[32] The tocsin of social collapse, however, would more often be sounded by the picks and shovels announcing the start of work on a new railway line or goods yard, a factory, workshop or warehouse. Railways and industrial or commercial building were the most potent instruments of character change in neighbourhoods. Occasionally, in the inner parts of cities, they might enforce or mark a change for the better, in some respects: the extensive demolition of usually low-grade property that made way for the new railway termini of our period. The first termini, sited before the drawing power of the railways was realised, generally lay on the perimeters of cities. Paddington, Nine Elms, London Bridge, Euston and Shoreditch were not 'central'. By the end of the fifties it was clear that more central stations would be profitable, and so the rails marched through or over the existing bricks and mortar to Victoria, Charing Cross, Holborn Viaduct and Cannon Street, to St Pancras and to Liverpool Street. London was of course exceptional, but similar things happened when the big provincial stations were built. Then there was the replacement of older smaller property by grand new palaces of business and finance and civic magnificence in the city centres: a less spectacular but perhaps not in the aggregate less momentous operation, progressing all over industrial and commercial Britain in rhythm with the surge of confidence and prosperity. These rebuildings, often called 'improvement schemes', abolished many slums, however little good they did the wretched slum-dwellers (see below, p. 81).

But throughout the whole inner suburban area, the effect of new railways and industrial premises was almost always to lower the tone of the adjacent districts. At its most dramatic, it could do what Michael Sadleir described in one of his two wonderfully accurate historical novels about the darker side of Victorian London:

'Until the early forties the residential status of the northern stretch of Waterloo Road remained good. . . . But lower down the hill building was going on too rapidly, and by 1845 an infiltration of rough characters from the Borough ... had already begun to flutter the comfortable bourgeois who occupied the respectable terraces. Nothing was said or admitted; but here and there a family moved out and no other took its place. . . . Then something occurred which turned a northward trickle into a mass-migration . . .'

Suddenly, late in 1845, the South Western Railway's plans for a line from their Nine Elms terminus through Waterloo to London Bridge became known. By the time the first Waterloo station was opened, in 1848, the terraces were already half deserted and the houses stood empty and forlorn. . . . Then a second blow fell. The railway mania dissolved and the LSWR's scheme for the London Bridge link-up was abandoned. 'The immediate result was that the station near York Road, instead of being a mere temporary terminus, became an official and established one. The ruin of Waterloo Road as a street of residential decency was now complete.' Its neighbourhood became mid-Victorian London's most lurid and beastly red-light quarter, best known by the name of its main mart, Granby Street.[33]

With less instant but equally lethal effect a railway or industrial development would, so to speak, seal off a neighbourhood and doom it to proletarian use: lowering the character of housing already there, determining that the houses that were bound sooner or later to fill the gaps would be low class ones. Our period was a significant one in this respect, because these mid-Victorian years saw the near-completion of the surface railway systems of the inner urban areas, and thus fixed upon the British city the social geography that has so largely

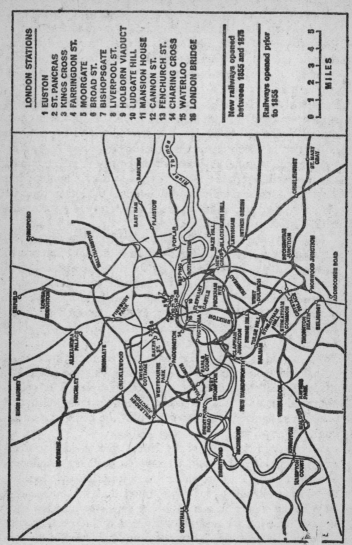

LONDON STATIONS

1 EUSTON
2 ST. PANCRAS
3 KINGS CROSS
4 FARRINGDON ST.
5 MOORGATE
6 BROAD ST.
7 BISHOPSGATE
8 LIVERPOOL ST.
9 HOLBORN VIADUCT
10 LUDGATE HILL
11 MANSION HOUSE
12 CANNON ST.
13 FENCHURCH ST.
14 CHARING CROSS
15 WATERLOO
16 LONDON BRIDGE

New railways opened between 1855 and 1875

Railways opened prior to 1855

0 1 2 3 4 5
MILES

The development of London railways, 1855–75

survived into our own day. My own Edinburgh is a notable case in point. Whatever chances it had after the thirties of pursuing the tidy and rational principles of development that had governed it hitherto, were substantially spoiled by the arrival, before the recommencement of large-scale building in the sixties, of a mess of railways and yards, breaking up several logical lines of residential and road development and casting a lasting blight over several large areas which, 'outer-suburban' though they were then, lie now within the inner suburban ring. Edinburgh suffers from this still.

Not in every respect was the local government of the mid-Victorian city inactive. Its power to control land-use was indeed as non-existent as its will to control it; therein it reflected a national state of mind, which, on the slow reluctant march towards collectivism, had not yet got further than to accept in the name of the public, the necessity of certain interferences with the use men made of their own premises, and the style in which they built them. These interferences were indeed startling enough to most mid-Victorian men of property, and they justify a closer inspection; which it will be convenient to give them as part of the whole important business of local government.

Local Self-government

Local *self*-government was what the mid-Victorians usually called it, the better to convince themselves and others that the increasing activity of their local authorities was voluntary and spontaneous, and that they were not being pushed around by Whitehall. In the passion of their hostility towards the idea of 'centralisation', they exaggerated the extent of their local independence, but their point was nonetheless worth making. It can certainly be plausibly argued that, from the forties until the seventies, the urban local authorities of Britain were, *vis-à-vis* Whitehall, more independently active than ever before (since the sixteenth century, anyway.) or since. The eighties saw, not indeed a diminution in the scale of their activity, but the marked beginnings of that progressive decline in their independence which has gone on ever since. The forties had seen the beginning of that serious (and overdue) endeavour to grapple with the problems of industrial urbanisation with which we are still preoccupied. The fifties and sixties saw the towns and cities of Great Britain engaged in a not unpraiseworthy campaign to come to terms with this new society. These were the years when the industrial city at last got a grip of itself, and when the social requirements of the industrial age began, however slightly, to make themselves felt in local government all over the country.

Thus to place the mid-Victorian phase in the general history of local administration is one thing; to define its character, and to depict its operation, is another, and much more difficult. The fact is, that local government during our period became extraordinarily complicated. It presented a scene of mounting confusion, attaining its climax between 1871 and 1875, and it assumed such a variety of forms that no short account can confidently anticipate every enquiry that may be made about it. But some account of it I must attempt, because it affected so much the daily lives of the people of our period. It affected them more directly and closely than local government affects us now: directly, because it was virtually the *only* active force of government that bore upon them, 'Whitehall' being then relatively so insignificant and closely, because its operations (which sometimes were surprisingly numerous and costly) could literally make the difference between life and death. The local government of mid-Victorian Britain is thus much more than part of its administrative history; it is, to a greater degree than the analogy of modern local government would lead you to think, a big part of its social history too. But it is not easy to describe. Growing fast through our period and the period before it, the way it grew after 1830 was such as to perpetuate in it just the same confusion and disorder that the Utilitarian reformers denounced before 1830. The early Victorians manfully set about bringing it into line with modern needs, and partly succeeded, but the means they adopted were not such as to make it economical and orderly. For reasons which are more the administrative and political historian's business than ours they spread responsibility instead of concentrating it, multiplied local authorities instead of consolidating them, and allowed these authorities a large measure of liberty to develop at what pace and in what manner they would. The result of forty years of this sloppy practice was that a town-dweller in 1872 in an ill-organised place might find himself 'governed' by five or six local authorities; he would vote on as many separate occasions under a different franchise each time, and pay as many different rates, collected by as many different officials.

This piling-up of additional authorities had begun in the early thirties. (Even much earlier, if you include all the bodies of local improvement and police commissioners that were by then established alongside the ancient authorities of county, borough and parish.) The Poor Law Unions established by the Poor Law Amendment Act of 1834 began the new era in local government with a bang; Parishes, governed by the Vestries, were left intact for all other purposes and as Poor Law rating authorities, but everything else to do with pauperism was taken over by the new authority, the Union, and controlled by its new body of elected local representatives, the Board of Guardians. Boroughs were reformed after a fashion in 1835, and became the seats of municipal corporations that might or might not extend their activity beyond the narrow sphere statutorily required of them. The year 1836 added Registration Districts; usually coterminous with Poor Law Unions but with separate officers and responsibilities, and, unlike the others in my list, levying no rate. Baths and Washhouse Boards became generally possible after 1846. (Liverpool had independently shown the way.) The Public Health Act of 1848 introduced what was, alongside the Union, to be the most important local authority of our period, the Local Board of Health; like most of the other local boards, it might or might not be the municipal corporation under another name, where there *was* such a corporation. The invention of Burial Boards, Highway Boards, and Sewerage and Drainage Boards assisted the process of proliferation which attained its climax in the establishment of School Boards in 1871.

So far as any principle can be detected beneath this multi-plication of local authorities, it was 'for each function, its own authority'. This was at any rate a rational principle, and from its consistent application a perfectly workable and efficient system of local government could have resulted, however much less efficient it might have been than one based on the opposite principle of consolidation. Being however neither clearly realised nor consistently applied, it allowed the func-tions supposed to be separate to become in practice shared and diffused; as they did especially in the case of public health, to such an extent that when the Medical Officer for Merthyr Tydfil was asked in 1869 by a Royal Commission to say who was locally responsible for public health, he told them: 'The local Board of Health, two Burial Boards, the Board of Guard-ians, the Superintendent and district Registrars, and the In-spector of Factories and his subordinates'.[34] Confusion and fragmentation were probably at their worst in the English countryside where, as the greatest public health expert of the day said, there was 'one authority [the Vestry] for every privy, and another [the Guardians] for every pigsty'.[35] But it was not much better in towns where, after 1866, as the Commission learnt from another distinguished sanitarian, hospitals and ambulances were to be provided by different authorities, the local authority empowered to provide hospitals had no medical staff, while the local authority with medical staff was not empowered to provide hospitals.[36]

Responsibilities for roads, drains, refuse-collecting and housing standards could become not less diffused. But this tendency to diffuse or fragment responsibility was only one of the disorderly elements inherent in the style of development of local administration in our period. There were several others. Municipal corporations were in two respects less straight-forward than the unsuspecting modern reader might suppose. In the first place, not every 'town' that looked big enough to be governed by a municipal corporation was actually so gov-erned. Many insignificant and stagnant little towns had mayors and councils; some large and bustling towns did not. It mainly depended on whether the place had been a municipal corporation before 1835. Every town of any size that had possessed a charter before 1835, retained it thereafter. 'Towns' or even, as in the cases of Manchester and Birmingham, 'cities' that had not previously been chartered, could thereafter become so. Twenty-nine had done so by 1861. But many that might have done so had not; and among them were places as large (I give the 1861 population figures) as Bury, 87,563; Merthyr Tydfil, 83,875; Birkenhead, 41,649; Cheltenham, 39,693; Chatham, 36,177; Hudderfields, 34,877; Croydon, 20,325; Glossop, 19,126; Whitehaven, 18,824; and St Helens, 18,396. The second 'catch' about municipal corporations was that their performances were so variable. I do not mean simply that what they did, some did well and some did badly. I mean rather that, beyond a certain point, they were all doing different things, and doing them more or less as and how they pleased. The 1835 Act actually *required* them to do surprisingly little; indeed its only positive requirement was that a reformed borough should set up a watch committee to run its own police force; the rest of its constructive provisions were permissive: boroughs could make by-laws for suppressing new nuisances, they could make arrangements for assuming the powers of existing improvement commissioners, they could assume similar powers for themselves if no such commissioners already existed, etc. It left everything to the initiative of the borough; it required hardly anything; and its consequences were exactly what you would expect. The vigorous boroughs with go-ahead men in them got things done, and the sluggish ones stagnated. 1848 gave them another chance. The Public Health Act of that year *enabled* them to facilitate sanitary improvement by becoming local boards of health; most did, but some did not: unsanitated Stafford, Tiverton, Basingstoke, Chichester and Seaford, for example, were municipal corporations.

They were laws unto themselves in a still more substantial and literal way. Most boroughs to some extent, and some boroughs to a very large extent, helped themselves to the powers they needed by getting their own private and local acts of parliament. In so doing they were carrying on an ancient

tradition, the tradition of legislative self-help which had engendered, by similar means and for similar mixed local government purposes, all those improvement or police commissioners
of the late eighteenth and early nineteenth centuries: many
of which were in operation at the start of our period. Not until
the later forties was any kind of common form or content
given to the local acts, and what was offered by the Clauses
Acts of 1846 and 1847 did not have to be accepted. Those
Acts (compendia of 'model clauses' for legislation concerning
baths and washhouses; nuisances removal—nuisances was the
polite portmanteau word for *every* variety of refuse and waste;
markets and fairs; gasworks; waterworks; harbours, docks and
piers; towns improvement—i.e. slum clearance, street widening etc.; cemeteries; and police) were designed to cheapen the
getting and to improve the calibre of local acts, and did nothing
to diminish their proportionate importance in local government. The richer and prouder corporations continued to use
them throughout our period and thus acquired their own individual constitutional histories, which only at certain unpredictable points intersected the yearly lengthening series of
public and general acts to which the lesser towns more largely
conformed. But not only because it leaves local acts out of
sight is that series an unreliable guide to the actual development of local administration, either in its general state or as it
stood in any particular place. A reader who assumed the
greater force of a statute of general rather than local application would almost certainly be misled. Local acts cost money,
and could not be prudently promoted without some assurance
of local approval. Readiness to pay for a local act in fact usually
went with a readiness to pay for much besides. Local acts
almost necessarily meant local action. General acts did not.
It was easier for a sluggish or malignant locality to accept,
even with some show of virtue to adopt, the minimum requirements of a general act and then to do nothing about the
optional parts. Whitehall could do little to force them, even
when it wished to, which was not all the time. Whitehall's
sanitary department, which had as the General Board of
Health begun in 1848 with a brave display of coercive fire-

works, was by 1858 reduced, under the title of the Local Government Act Office, to the stature of a branch of the Home Office, and seems actually to have been embarrassed and bothered by the demands of the more go-ahead local boards to be allowed to do things. Go-slow local authorities were fairly sure to be left alone, in not doing what was not absolutely compulsory for them to do, while they could often get away with not doing much that was, in theory, compulsory!

The last general point that needs to be made about the qualities of local administration during our period is that a great deal of its legislation was not mandatory but permissive, and that much of what was mandatory was difficult, even impossible, to enforce. As with its characteristic diffusion or fragmentation of responsibilities, one asks what principle underlay this making of so much permissive that should have been mandatory, and one finds it summarily defined in the *Report of the Royal Sanitary Commission* (alias the Adderley Commission), 1871:

'LOCAL SELF-GOVERNMENT ESSENTIAL TO ENGLAND. The principle of local self-government has been generally recognized as of the essence of our national vigour. Local administration under central superintendence, is the distinguishing feature of our governments. The theory is, that all, that can, should be done by local authority, and that public expenditure should be chiefly controlled by those who contribute to it . . .'[37]

Until the seventies, this theory was so ardently embraced by so many citizens and politicians, that it more or less governed the practice. After the seventies, it mattered less and less, and the history of public administration entered the so-called 'collectivist' phase, in which the collection of public money and the control of its expenditure was increasingly undertaken or positively ordered by 'Whitehall' and Parliament. The seventies marked the water-shed between this 'collectivism' and what has not unsuitably been known for long as the age of 'individualism'.

The description has much point, provided it is recognised as meaning not that men could or should enjoy freedom to do just as they liked but that, whatever controls they placed or suffered to be placed upon their freedoms, those controls ought ideally to be accepted from any quarter but Parliament or 'Whitehall'. Westminster was welcome to propose but not to impose.

'If the country had taken the thirty or forty times repeated hints offered them by Parliament, [wrote Dr Stewart, an eminent sanitarian, in 1867] how very different would our sanitary condition have been at this good hour! But when I have said this, I have said all that is due to the Parliaments and Governments of the last thirty-five years. . . . Throughout our sanitary laws—which we cannot yet properly call a system or code—three things are tacitly assumed, viz. 1. That to the local authority . . . belongs the duty of caring for the health of its constituents. 2. That the local authority will neglect that duty, and 3. That the local authority must not be expressly enjoined to do its duty.'[38]

After nearly twenty years of 'intervention' in public health, the staple means of enforcement of the major provisions of the 1866 Sanitary Act was the conferring upon householders the right to call 'recusant' authorities to account for their failure to the Home Secretary: a means of enforcement more like the usual eighteenth-century one of offering rewards to informers than the usual twentieth-century one of placing the local authority under central compulsion.

'In this way [concluded Dr Stewart] and also by empowering the [Medical Officer of the] Privy Council to institute sanitary enquiries and report the results thereof annually to Parliament, the legislature, with a becoming jealousy of anything like undue interference with local self-government, has long been endeavouring to create a public opinion in favour of sanitary reform, and so to direct it as to overcome the sluggishness and prejudice of niggardly and self-complacent 'bumbledom' both in town and country. Some places, as, for instance, Liverpool and Leicester, have for many years enjoyed the services of able, energetic and judicious medical officers of health; and other towns—such as Birkenhead, Bristol, Doncaster, Dundee, Edinburgh, Glasgow and Leeds—have more recently recognized the necessity of appointing such officers ... and have shown themselves ready to lend a hearty support to their officials in the discharge of their disagreeable and arduous duties. But if they be otherwise minded ... the law, beyond the limits of the Metropolis, while suggesting the propriety of appointing, acquiesces in the non-appointment of medical officers of health; and since 1860, the injunction of the Nuisances' Removal Act, 1855, to appoint inspectors of nuisances, has actually been withdrawn!'[39]

So far my concern has been to sketch the dominant characteristics of mid-Victorian local administration, partly to suggest what in general was the legislative atmosphere in which this administration functioned, partly to warn the persistent enquirer against expecting uniformities and consistencies which were in fact hardly ever there. From the general let us now turn to the particular, and sketch some features of a few specimen local authorities and the places under their charge.

Liverpool

Liverpool, by the period we are considering London's only rival as a port, was governed by a corporation under its own local acts. Its urban administration had for long been exemplary. The enterprising vigour with which, throughout Victoria's reign, it combated the most appalling social and sanitary problems was only the survival, after the Municipal Reform Act, of a tradition established long before it. Local acts of 1842 and 1846 gained for the corporation, working through committees, a fuller set of powers to control housing and sanitation than were yet owned by any other city government; and, more remarkably still, those powers were forcefully employed. Britain's first Medical Officer of Health was Liverpool's: Dr William Henry Duncan, who took office on 1 January 1847. About the same time the corporation set seriously about the improvement of the city's basic public utilities: gas and water. The two gas companies were driven by the threat of a municipal take-over to amalgamate and to improve the quality of service; the buying out of the water companies was begun under a Local Act of 1847, and an extensive new municipal system of supply, from reservoirs thirty-six miles away, was working by 1857. The corporation adopted useful clauses of the 1858 Local Government Act but continued to rely on local acts for its most striking powers. Only Glasgow (which also worked by local acts) interfered with private property rights to the same extent as Liverpool did under its Act of 1864. Nine local acts, between 1858 and 1883, enabled the corporation to 'improve' the central parts of the city by the standard means of driving spacious new streets through old congestion. Thus did Liverpool present an example of municipal self-government at its most independent and admirable: an old corporation meeting the challenges of the mid-Victorian period in its own determined way and, by the standards of the time, creditably.

Manchester

Manchester will serve as an example of a new corporation behaving in much the same way. It did not have a municipal corporation till 1838, and that corporation did not break through the financial and legal meshes cast over it by hostile local interests until 1842. Late starter though it was, the new corporation of Manchester showed from the beginning a determination to be as independent of Whitehall as it could be. The place had been locally self-governed, before incorporation, by a variety of improvement commissioners under local acts. The new corporation absorbed these many unrelated authorities (they, for the most part, vehemently protesting) and improved and extended their services under a series of local acts beginning in 1843. Manchester men were very proud of these, and it became an article of faith with them that the Public Health Act of 1848 was modelled on Manchester's Local Act of two years earlier. They used (successfully) their influence to prevent its forcible application to all urban places, maintaining that it would 'destroy, in a great degree, the principles of self-government ... and virtually transfer the power of managing their own affairs ... from the inhabitants to an irresponsible [*sic*!] Central Board'.[40] Whitehall was no more permitted to interfere in Manchester than Manchester chose. Whether or not Manchester was, under this régime of touchy provincial independence, as well-governed as it might have been had it conformed more closely to Whitehall's standards, was and is an open question. One shrewd observer thought not. Observing that Manchester still had not appointed an MOH, he said that 'the only ground of hope for future sanitary reform would seem to be the existence of its justly celebrated sanitary association', the members of which had 'applied themselves to the ... herculean task of stirring up the local authorities to the discharge of some of the more obvious responsibilities devolving upon them, as the guardians of the health of the great and prosperous community which, by a pleasant fiction, they are presumed to govern for its good'.[41] It is indeed difficult not to conclude that Manchester's not appointing an MOH till 1867 had something to do with the fact that Whitehall had been urging the appointment of MOHs since 1848. But that was the way of it in the mid-Victorian town. A town that insisted on doing things in its own way and in its own time could not before the seventies be much moved by Whitehall. Only public opinion could hustle it.

Bury and Barrow-in-Furness

These towns can stand as examples at the administrative antipodes from Liverpool and Manchester. The way they were run was absolutely different. Each was thoroughly industrial: Bury almost exclusively based on cotton, Barrow on iron. Neither was an old municipal corporation and each was therefore necessarily governed by the local vestry until, in the case of Bury, 1846, and, in the case of Barrow, 1867. A Local Act in 1846 established a body of improvement commissioners, who governed the town, so far as it was governed at all, until it was at last incorporated in 1875. The Bury Improvement Commissioners were not a prestigious body, and one must presume that their generally sluggish record was largely due to their inability to make way against the opposition of local property interests. Incorporation finally came as a combined result of pressure from Whitehall (about 1870, beginning at last to feel strong enough really to put the squeeze on) and of local public opinion, roused at last to a sense of the indignity of Bury's position. Barrow was able to remain so long without formal local government other than it got from its own vestry and from the Ulverston Board of Guardians because it was, to an unusual degree, a 'works town', owned and run by the Furness Railway Co. together with the booming iron companies which formed a sort of syndicate to run things as suited them best. It was not in their interest that their workmen should absolutely lack roofs over their heads or drains beneath their privies, and they therefore built tight-packed blocks of quite solid houses conveniently close to the works, of sufficiently symmetrical appearance and supported by enough amenities of water and gas, schools, places of worship, etc., to enable enthusiasts to acclaim it as some sort of an achievement in town planning. Such enthusiasm cannot, unqualified, survive reference to the statistics of its overcrowding, intemperance and disease. But everything that was done for the town of Barrow up to 1867, the year of its incorporation, was done by industrial self-help. Until that year no public and general acts of parliament in the sphere of public health and local government had any applicability to Barrow at all. They could not become applicable until Barrow acquired a local authority capable of applying them.

Merthyr Tydfil

This town illustrates another quite different urban administrative growth pattern. Like Barrow, it was very much a 'works town', relying for its fluctuating prosperity on four huge ironworks and associated coal-mines. Unlike Barrow, its local industrialists, beyond providing a relatively small number of houses for their work force, let it grow as it would. Merthyr grew fast and nastily. It became indeed something of a by-word for its neglect of natural opportunities; the surrounding hills were full of water but the poor townsfolk could hardly ever get it undefiled and in hot weather had to queue up for it at public spouts; the force of gravity was everywhere ready to operate an efficient sewerage system and yet Merthyr was, until the later sixties, exceptionally ill-drained. Until mid-century (by when its population was already 50,000) it was governed by the parish vestry, the board of guardians, and a turnpike trust which occasionally cleaned the main street. The public health movement of the later forties produced in Merthyr two schools of thought about the means of improvement. Some advocated the establishment of improvement commissioners by way of a local act (the Bury way); others preferred to form a local board of health under the 1848 Public Health Act. The latter won the day and a local board was set up in 1850. So reluctant were local interests to sink their fears and jealousies of each other and of anybody that might claim to represent 'the public interest', that the local board (which was anyway packed with representatives of the big firms) got on but slowly. Water was not freely flowing in until 1863; sewage was not flowing out till five years later. By the late sixties Merthyr Tydfil was cleansed under the ultimate authority of several general acts: the 1858 Local Government Act, the 1866 Sanitary Act, and Torrens's Act of 1868. Its condition however was still awful. Even all the resources of every general act between 1848 and 1870 proved inadequate to put Merthyr right, without the fructifying response of local zeal and self-respect. The history of Merthyr Tydfil during our period admirably illustrates the actual gulf that could separate what a standard local authority was authorised to do by general statutes, and what it in fact did.[42]

Surbiton

Surbiton, subject of an exceptionally good local history, invites brief notice as an example of yet another type of unincorporated mid-Victorian town.[43] Until in 1838 the London and Southampton Railway came pressing through the fields between Wimbledon and Woking, Surbiton was nothing but the name of the hamlet that straggled along the southern bank of the river between Kingston and Thames Ditton. Its development began the moment the first train stopped there. Only twelve miles out; near the river; excitingly close to such socially distinguished places as Esher, Hampton, Ham and Richmond Park; and from an early stage backed by Coutts's, who had the acumen to get Philip Hardwicke to design the biggest houses on their central part of it, and Cubitt's to build them; it could hardly fail. Land prices soared as the villas went up, and before they knew where they were, the self-reliant men of Surbiton had a serious local government problem on their hands: unmade, undrained and unlit roads, and ditches, watercourses and wells fouled; and, perhaps worst of all, the neighbouring borough of Kingston seeking to annex them by a boundary extension in their direction. Having fought that off, in 1855 they secured their future interests by means of a local act (Coutts's guaranteed the costs) establishing a body of improvement commissioners, to govern exactly the area of the ecclesiastical district marked out in 1841 for the new church which Coutts's prudently provided as both a community centre and a guarantee of gentility. The Surbiton Improvement Commissioners needed no other powers than were taken from various of the 1847 Clauses Acts to make up their own founding statute. Showing such a regard for property that, time and again, their schemes had to be reshaped to accommodate the preferences and prejudices of local citizens, they slowly got a system of sewers and drains going and brought the greater number of local roads under their care. Shopkeepers they were able to ignore: their one great amenity improvement, the planting of lime trees along the main roads, was carried out in the teeth of shopkeeper opposition. (Surbiton, governed by its oligarchy of proprietors, must have been unusual in this respect; the shopkeeping interest was usually much more powerful.) Dust removal and street lighting, they put out to contract. Until after the end of our period, the Surbitonians remained in this idyllic state of minimal local self-government of an increasingly archaic

form; congratulating themselves on the relative lowness of
their rates and the stability, even reduction, of the price of
season tickets; and keeping the burghers of Kingston ever at
arm's length.

Dublin

Throughout our period the biggest city in Ireland, Dublin
was nevertheless of all the major cities of the UK the most
nearly, in economic and demographic terms, stagnant. Its
wharves and jetties indeed hummed with activity: exports of
people, farm produce from the interior, and locally produced
liquors both malt and spirituous, the textiles known as poplin
and tabinet, and (perhaps surprisingly) footwear; imports of
almost everything that a slowly prospering and hardly in-
dustrialised country needed to bring in from economically advanced neighbours. There was a little iron-founding and ship-
building, and a good deal of furniture making; but apart from
that and the local products already mentioned, Dublin was
not at all industrial and no one seriously thought of it as
such. Belfast was already the obvious focus of Irish industrial
growth. Dublin was the administrative, military and cultural
capital, boasting a compact assemblage of handsome public
buildings unmatched anywhere else in the kingdom. It boasted
also more than its fair proportion of the nastiest private buildings, on which its lord mayor and corporation was making, so
far as I can judge from scanty evidence, no great impression.
Faced by sanitary and social problems hardly less acute or
weighty than those of Liverpool, Manchester and Glasgow,
the municipality of Dublin moved slowly in the wake of
those more bustling and prosperous places. Perhaps it could
not afford to do better; perhaps the pressure was taken off
them by the multitude of charitable and philanthropic institutions (over 200 such schools alone in 1850!) inherited
from a glorious capital past, but apparently most people entertained lower expectations of the material quality of life
than in the confident centres of material progress. Whatever
the reason, the way the poor lived in Dublin was awful. The

Social Science Congress was told by Nugent Robinson in 1861 that over a third of Dublin's houses were let in rooms, and that about half its people were living in single-room dwellings. Overcrowding was worst in 'the Liberties', where classic rookeries abounded in former abodes of pre-mechanical textile manufacture. In 134 of the worst streets and alleys he counted 40,319 persons in 11,214 rooms. The prime essentials of mid-Victorian sanitary improvement had been attended to: a main sewerage system was installed (emptying into the Liffey); cellar dwellings (never numerous by Lancashire standards) and the worst common lodging houses had gone. Regular early morning circuits by the scavenging squads kept low class courts and streets passable. So Dublin's meaner parts survived; but not, one gathers, with much to spare.

Edinburgh

Edinburgh's meaner parts, which so conspicuously jostled its public buildings and smart thoroughfares, were by the sixties under better control. Contemporaries often bracketed Edinburgh with Dublin as being similar in so many respects: each a former political capital, still administratively powerful; each remarkably handsome to look at and rewarding to walk round; each with a good university and a fine equipment of literary and scientific institutions; each with peculiar problems of poverty and pauperism; and neither conspicuous for modern industry. Yet Edinburgh, I judge, had more of it than Dublin, and Edinburgh's professional men were successfully engrossing all the top legal and much of the top financial business of a country which, unlike Ireland, was already achieving industrial and commercial eminence and was looking forward to still more of it. Behind the grandiose terraces of the new town and, less concealed behind the picturesque beetling street fronts of the old town, there indeed lay formidable concentrations of destitution and squalor. But the scavenging service was celebrated as perhaps the best in Britain, and the police had been only less vigorous than Glasgow's in regulating common lodging houses. Hospital and dispensary services were predictably excellent; I have not discovered anywhere else as universally available a medical service as that given by the Royal Infirmary and its doctors. The big sanitary talking-point of the fifties was, as in so many cities, the problem of sewerage, and it was solved before it became insufferable. The Water of Leith was in effect becoming the common sewer for the whole of the western side of the city, and in the sixties a main sewer was constructed along its course to intercept the filth. Edinburgh's appointment of Henry Littlejohn as MOH in 1862 was probably not because of any dramatic climax of insanitation (as for example the second cholera epidemic, which had brought Duncan to the salvation of Liverpool and Simon to the City of London; or 'the great stink' of the Thames in 1858, which drove parliament at last to make up its mind about metropolitan sewerage) but because, in the existing state of legislation and Edinburgh's quite active local administration, there seemed to be little room for such an officer to manoeuvre in. And the historian of Victorian Edinburgh's public health, Hector Macdonald, tells me that the chain of circumstance that led in the end to his appointment was set off by the spectacular collapse, in late 1861, of a huge old tenement house in the High Street, with loss of thirty-five lives, and consequent revelations of the sordid swarm of people living there.

London

The capital's local government, which had hitherto been fragmented between an extraordinarily confused mosaic of unions (since 1834, the only standard unit of local government), parishes, improvement commissioners for every sort of purpose, turnpike trusts and quarter sessions, was between 1847 and 1855 put into a shape which lasted with little change till after the end of our period. That shape was neither firm nor attractive; only in comparison with what it superseded did it seem to be much of a shape at all. It was certainly unworthy of its subject. London presented the anomalous spectacle of a great capital city without a unitary government;

a natural whole, allowed to remain in a condition of separate parts. The cause of this absurd and lamentable anomaly was The City proper: the square mile (approximately) of territory within boundaries running roughly parallel to the ancient city walls on the north bank of the river, between the Tower and the Temple. There reigned the Lord Mayor and Corporation of the City of London, wealthy, proud and privileged. Once the City had in itself been London, for all practical purposes. Westminster remained quite a separate and different place until the later seventeenth century, when the line of The Strand at last became sufficiently built up to make it seem more natural to talk of the Cities of London and Westminster together as 'London'. So the modern London—the natural London, 'Greater London', the metropolis as it was then generally known—grew all round the ancient City and became locally governed or not governed in the variety of ways which survived until the early fifties. The City kept itself to itself, and in particular kept its wealth to itself. Its separation from the surrounding parts had already by the later eighteenth century become theoretically indefensible, and during the early nineteenth was proved by radical reformers to be practically so. Their foamings at the mouth, more political than administrative in motivation, were fruitless. The City's power and prestige were enormous, and the early Victorian radicals were almost contemptuously brushed off. It looked after its little territory on its own, contributing not a penny to the revenues of the circumambient authorities upon whose efficient maintenance of the roads etc. it so much relied, continuing to spend much of its great wealth on conspicuous ceremony and feasting and 'jobs for the boys' and their children. It managed its own little territory quite efficiently (its record in sanitary matters and street improvements was actually a good deal better than its socio-political critics liked to admit) but conceded hardly an inch outside. By 1850, its administrative autonomy had been sapped only in the fundamental matter of sewerage; a compromise between the City's characteristically 'go-it-alone' sewerage scheme and the sanitary reformers' equally characteristic pan-metropolitan scheme had given the new Metropolitan Sewers Commission jurisdiction over *main* sewers while leaving the City in sole charge of the subsidiary ones; the reformers secured their point, and the City saved its pride. Apart from that, the City remained a kind of administrative citadel in the heart of the metropolis, foraying from time to time to establish outposts (a meatmarket in Holloway, a pauper children's boarding school in Norwood, a foreign cattle market in Deptford) in the territories within its sphere of influence, and perhaps making up by its ceremonial splendour for its diminishing administrative importance. The City —and this was mainly why it stood so secure upon its eternal rock—could put on a splendid show when it chose. Either in the lord mayor's mansion house or in one of the livery companies' halls, England's most lavish entertainments were unstintingly staged for the astonishment and gratification of foreign visitors. Only the Inns of Court and the wealthiest peers and financiers could, less frequently, match them; Buckingham Palace was not in the same league. Thus the City stood without much competition from England, and with no competition at all from the metropolis. Yet, with most of the metropolis, it had no official relationship. The City was as ostentatiously self-conscious as the local authorities of the other parts of that great swelling urban mass were, in their corporate characters, insignificant and anonymous. In none of those authorities could you before 1855 have found any more magnificent public occasion than a board of guardians' dinner; after 1855, they offered no more impressive civic spectacle than a plenary session of the representative body then created, the Metropolitan Board of Works. From its headquarters in Spring Gardens, Charing Cross (just by the Admiralty Arch), the board attempted to give the Metropolis as a whole (except for the City!) the first beneficial experience of unified government it had ever had. Two great sewerage systems, one north and one south of the Thames, were operating by 1865—an undertaking, as the board truthfully noted, 'of greater magnitude than anything of a similar kind that had previously been accomplished'; the north bank of the Thames itself, thitherto a turbid and feculent waterway between mudbanks, was stylishly embanked all the way from Chelsea to Blackfriars; new thoroughfares were sliced through slums—Charing Cross Road, Shaftesbury Avenue, Victoria Street, Northumberland Avenue, Clerkenwell Road—and if the results were architecturally less impressive than Haussmann's in Paris, that was mainly because the board had not his freedom to lavish public money. At the time of its birth, London was ill-served with parks: Battersea and Victoria Parks were on the drawing board but still several years from completion; Hyde Park, Green Park and Regent's Park were peculiar mixtures of elegance and vice; Kennington Common was about to be made into a recreation ground; Hampstead Heath was a sort of no man's land of woods, turf, artists and gravel pits, focus for many years of a celebrated battle between private right and public benefit. To the board and some pioneer amenities societies (the first being the Metropolitan Playground and General Recreation Society, 1857) was due the securing for the public of Hampstead Heath (at last, in 1870), Wormwood Scrubs, Clapham Common, Finsbury Park, Southwark Park, etc., and a lot of smaller places. The Thames bridges were freed from tolls and turned into public thoroughfares maintained out of the rates. Only Westminster, Blackfriars and London Bridges were free at our period's opening. Southwark Bridge was liberated in 1864; the rest not until 1878. Another of the board's achievements was the establishment of an efficient fire brigade; Captain Shaw's, which the City too relied on. Thus did the Metropolitan Board of Works do something to give mid-Victorian London both the sense and the reality of being a city at unity with itself. Its wholesale dealings in local government were unambitiously effective, so far as they went. They could not go far, because all the, so to speak, retail business of local administration was left by the 1855 Act in the hands of independent and irresponsible inferior (one cannot truthfully say, 'subordinate') authorities: either vestries—governing pre-1855 parishes considered big enough to survive unchanged—or district boards, governing groups of smaller parishes. These vestries and district boards were the principal providers of local government in the mid-

Victorian metropolis, and very uncertain providers they were. The only lingering trace of their historic origin lay in the religious respect they paid towards property owners. Some were certainly corrupt; few were more than spasmodically efficient; and they were responsible to no higher authority (except the courts of law, where they could be, and on rare occasions were, prosecuted by private citizens for not doing their statutory duty). The Metropolitan Board of Works had no control of them, nor had any other higher body. Local boards of health all over the rest of England—authorities whose functions their own were very like—owed some responsibility to the Local Government Act Office; but not the metropolitan vestries and district boards. 'In fact they are not under anybody?', as an incredulous MP put it to an expert witness in 1870. 'No', he replied; 'nothing in London is under anybody.'[44] *Eppur si muove*. Mid-Victorian London must have been the most vigorous city in the mid-nineteenth-century world.

Public Health and Civic Amenities

Governed or misgoverned in this great variety of ways, and for the most part growing without intermission, the towns and cities of Britain remained, throughout our period, hazardous places to live in. They became in some ways pleasanter and more interesting to live in (see below, pp. 81–4); they did not until just after our period begin to become markedly more healthy to live in. Yet throughout our period the sanitarians were busily laying the foundations of modern public health: resolutely counter-attacking the armies of disease and death, engineering channels for the city's compound excrement to get out and away to somewhere else where it might be less harmful (or even be agriculturally useful), trying to teach citizens the elements of sanitary sense. Their achievement was the great one, considering all the circumstances, of preventing the cities from becoming even more lethal than they already were.

The nature of that achievement is indicated by the dimin-

ishing role as killers of the 'filth diseases' depending on the
fouling of water or food by infected excrement. Cholera virtually disappeared after its last epidemic visitation in 1866–7.
The lethal propensities of diarrhoea markedly diminished.
Cleaner water and milk, cleaner privies, the removal and prevention of 'nuisances'—all the main concerns of the sanitary
movement—did the trick. 'The history of the water-supply
of Glasgow', remarked its third MOH, 'is punctuated in its
successive stages [1848 and 1859 being the main ones] by a
progressive reduction of the diarrhoeal rate'.[46] Typhoid alias

Annual Death Rates per 1,000 Persons in London and elsewhere[45]

	E. & W.	London	Liverpool	Birmingham	Glasgow
1850	20·8	21·0	28·0	24·96†	—
1855	22·6	24·3	31·0*	—	—
1860	21·2	22·4	26·0	24·98†	29·9*
1865	23·2	24·5	36·5	—	30·6*
1870	22·9	24·1	31·1	24·94†	30·2*
1875	22·7	23·6	27·5	25·2*	30·4*
1880	20·5	21·7	27·2	—	26·6*
1885	19·2	20·4	25·6	20·7*	—

*average for preceding five years
†average for preceding ten years

enteric fever, which also came mainly from filthy environment,
became much less common a killer in the better-run cities, and
the national statistics (which of course increasingly represented
urban conditions) showed an unbroken decline through the
seventies. But the diseases which, whatever the state of the
environment, could still thrive on undernourished, ill-cleansed
and overcrowded bodies—especially little ones—showed (with
the solitary and unaccountable exception of tuberculosis,
which steadily diminished from the early fifties onwards) no
serious sign of diminution before, at earliest, the later seventies.
Typhus, smallpox (never deadlier than during the pandemic
of 1871–2) and scarlet fever (then of a much deadlier character than in our present century) became less troublesome to
the late-Victorians than they ever were to our mid-Victorians.
But diphtheria (apparently new to some places during our

period) remained a grim menace till the twentieth century, and was one cause of the persistence of infant mortality at a terribly high rate until it in turn began to follow the general death rate's downward course just after 1900. (The only recorded years more lethal than 1899 to infants under one year old were 1846 and 1847.)

Public health statistics provide reasonably hard evidence about one side of urban life. During our period they became collected with enough self-conscious expertise for us to be sure about what they say, to be able to judge how much or how little they mean. They enabled the making of such judgements as, e.g.:—that, save only in 1854, London with all its hazards was at any rate safer to live in than Berlin; that in any year of our period a newborn child had a better chance of reaching its first birthday if it came into the world in Manchester rather than Liverpool, a much better chance if it arrived in Glasgow; but that in each of these cities (and presumably anywhere else) its chances of survival were better if it was born during the fifteen years after 1875 than during the twenty-five years before 1875; that although the national general death rate of children under one improved hardly at all between 1850 and 1900 (after slight average decline between 1876 and 1892, it then became as high again as ever it had been until 1900), the same death rates of children under five, under ten and under fifteen all declined steadily (and even, in the two last-named cases, dramatically) through the second half of the century. Such facts have their interest and value. They do not however say much about the quality of urban life. We know fairly accurately how many died, and what they suffered from; we are not at all so sure about those who did not immediately die, however much they suffered. Registration of deaths itself was far from perfect; notification of infectious diseases was even less so; the businesslike collection of statistics concerning other diseases and ailments was still in its infancy. As for all the elements of the quality of life that lay outside the sanitary circle, it seems impossible to get any closer to the truth about them than by using intelligent estimation. Some mid-Victorians thought they could do better than that. They collected what they liked to call 'moral statistics' —criminal or moral statistics (number of arrests and convictions), educational statistics (school attendances and evidences of illiteracy mainly), religious statistics (denominational membership) and mixed cultural statistics (figures relating to book and periodical sales, museum attendances, etc.). The bold deductions they often drew from figures of these kinds have little value for the modern enquirer. Their 'moral statistics' in particular were worthless. But the questions which they were trying to answer with the aid of this sort of evidence, are the very questions we still most dearly want to get answered. Was the general quality of urban life—or was the quality of life of this or that particular group of town dwellers—improving at all during our period?—And what was it like anyway?

In all industrial towns and in most big towns whether industrial or not, it was, for a start, grimy. Coal was plentiful, though not particularly cheap. Coal fires and furnaces were then much less efficient; each industrial establishment had its own belching chimney, and there were many more separate establishments per industry than there are today. Prospects of mill-towns could *literally* be described as forests of chimneys. Coal was moreover the only source of heat for cooking as well as house-warming. London's 'pea-soup' fogs were not at all new; but they were credibly said to be worse than they ever had been. Coal smuts in the fog or drizzle would sometimes be described as a sort of sooty snow. And not only was there this pervasive coal-dirt. Except where the roads were of the hardest metal (cobbles or stone flags before the sixties; asphalt, granite sets or wood blocks slowly thereafter) they sent up quantities of dust, clouding the air in dry weather and making mud in wet, and requiring the services of the watercart and the crossing-sweeper. City streets could be just as crowded then as now. Traffic jams and rush-hours were normal in London in the sixties; over 20,000 vehicles were crossing London Bridge daily in 1860; the Metropolitan Board of Works' new streets had less aesthetic, police and sanitary purposes than economic. The centres of cities were normally full of mixed and teeming life. They were indeed becoming the citadels of big business we have known them as ever since, but few had by 1860 gone far towards losing their old-fashioned furnishings of small retail shops, multitude of churches, run-down inns (giving way fast to hotels now), labyrinths of courts and alleys—and residences. Residences no longer for the natural leaders of the urban community. Their shift to more select neighbourhoods had begun at least a century earlier and was by now complete. But lots of small employers in the shop, catering and entertainments businesses still lived in among them, and 'the poor' were still plentiful in the city's inward parts.

Two characteristics of the way of life of the poor majority of town-dwellers were so constant and so directly related to the urban environment as to merit separate mention here. I mean, overcrowding and proximity to work. Whatever other common conditions of life and work may have got better during Victoria's reign, overcrowding did not. In many places it got worse. Cheap housing almost always lagged behind the demand for it; and that demand itself was less buoyant than it might have been, inasmuch as many people whose good wages, when they were in work, were demonstrably adequate to pay the rent for something better than the cheapest, nevertheless stuck to the cheapest they could bear to live in because experience taught them that a good deal could be borne, and because of prudent suspicion that those good wages were too good to last. So better-class blocks of flats and houses sometimes stood half-empty, while lower-class ones nearby stood over-full; lice, lodgers and all. An ingrained habit of domestic overcrowding that had become part of a familiar and intermittently satisfying way of life was proof against many reformers' representations. But quite often people had no choice but to accept overcrowding whether they liked it or not. They had to stay near enough their place(s) of work to be able to get to them on foot or ferry, for there was no other means of travel for working men before at earliest the later sixties (and then only in selected slices of London). Unskilled men about whose jobs there was any element of the casual dared not live far from the places of opportunity. But skilled workmen too could, for no matter what different reasons, be in the same fix. They were so most notoriously in London, where rents were universally high, and skilled men with their families had to live in homes much inferior to what they could have got in the midlands and the north. The five shillings a week that would provide six rooms in Lancashire could not be sure to get more than two in London. But it was not only in London that even the would-be respectable had to live hugger-mugger. Wherever mines or manufactures boomed and the housing supplies were for whatever reason cramped, overcrowding could quickly become horrific. One might not have expected it in, for instance, Barrow-in-Furness, that bustling boosted company town squeezed between the sea and the Lakes. Four hundred houses were built each year (on average) between 1861 and 1868, but rents rarely sank below 5s a week and four-room houses were often found to contain two or three families. The woollen towns of the West Riding were in 1891 (when figures were first collected) found to have so many more overcrowded homes than the cotton towns across the Pennines that one supposes they had long been that way. Some of them—Huddersfield, Bradford and Halifax, for instance—were half as bad again as Liverpool, and over twice as bad as Manchester, where only 8·2 per cent of the people were reported as living more than two to a room. Newcastle and Gateshead, with 35 per cent and 40 per cent respectively, were far above the English urban norm and getting on towards the Scottish one. One- and two-room dwellings were commoner in the north, too. In Scotland they remained until much later (indeed, remain today) *relatively* common. Thirty per cent of Glasgow's population in 1871 was living in one-room dwellings; 41·5 per cent in two-room ones. By 1881 those proportions had changed to 24·7 per cent and 44·7 per cent respectively. These rooms were indeed usually larger and better equipped than those inhabited by one-room families south of the Tees, and Glasgow's creditable mortality rates compel one to believe that the Scottish one- and two-room way of living was—especially after the urban authorities got to grips with things in the sixties—neither as deadly as one would have expected, nor as bad as in some other cities. But the moving lecture on 'Life in One Room' given by Glasgow's second and greatest MOH, J. B. Russell, prevents one from thinking that it can ever have been *pleasant*.[47]

This overcrowding, broadly understood as comprising number of persons per room (the most sensitive indicator), number of people per house, and number of houses per acre, was peculiarly worrying to the mid-Victorians, wherever they found it. Overcrowded houses could of course be found as easily in the countryside as in the town, and with sanitary and moral consequences (actual or presumed) of like kind, if not like quality. It was the quantity and concentration of over-crowding in the towns that gave its urban form unusually sombre tints and overtones. 'This pestilential heaping of human beings', Dr John Simon called it in December 1850 in his *Second Sanitary Report to the City of London*. His preoccupation was its consequences in terms of disease and death. 'Only because of the physical sufferings,' he said, 'am I entitled to speak; only because pestilence is forever within the circle; only because Death so largely comforts these poor orphans of civilisation.' But he felt unable to leave it at that. In a peroration of unusual power, he told his employers: 'You cannot but see that side by side with pestilence there stalks a deadlier presence, blighting the moral existence of a rising population; rendering their hearts hopeless, their acts ruffianly and incestuous; and scattering, while society averts her eyes, the retributive seeds of increase for crime, turbulence and pauperism.'[48] Simon was only saying 'what oft was thought but ne'er so well expressed'. The slums of the cities terrified respectable mid-Victorians. Unless strongly motivated by phil-anthropy, public service or the spirit of adventure, they never went into them if they could help it. Ofter they had little idea what the city slums were like inside. It was one thing, a per-fectly manageable thing, to visit the homes of the rural poor. The gentry knew—at least their wives and daughters knew —what a rural slum was like; and they were not afraid to visit it. Town slums were, reputedly, unsafe to visit without

police escort. The better-class people who shopped and strolled
in the main streets sometimes did not know how close they
stood to the slum courts and yards that huddled behind the
street fronts, their existence perhaps suggested merely by the
low arches and narrow passages that gave access to them.
These permanently overcrowded central city districts remained
substantially intact throughout our period, and even got worse.
Some were demolished in course of street improvements,
commercial redevelopments, railway works, etc. (Our supreme
authority in this field approves the estimate of 56,000 persons
displaced by London's new railway lines and stations between
1853 and 1885;[49] 3,084 were reckoned to have been dislodged
by the building of the Strand Law Courts; between 2 to
3,000 people 'driven out of Dale Street', Liverpool, in 1867;
etc.) People thus unhoused would not usually dare to go far
from where they had acquired some precious experience as
to the means of living and partly living. While better-off persons took advantage of the rapidly (in the sixties) improving
facilities for getting in and out of the centre by train, the
poor for the moment stayed there; they crowded into already
crowded quarters close by, and made their overcrowding
worse.

One major aspect of the mid-Victorian city remains to be
described. While the suburbs extended, taking with them a
growing proportion of the better-off; while dominantly lower-
class districts solidified or spread around the central and the
industrial parts; the central parts themselves were changing
and acquiring characteristics that seem essentially modern:
relative lack of resident population, increasing devotion to
business, administrative, cultural and inter-city transport func-
tions. The resident population of the City of London, which
had hardly varied since 1801, fell from its 1851 peak of
129,000 to 113,000, 76,000 and 51,000 in 1861, 1871 and
1881 respectively. From no other city central areas were residents likely to be drained at the same brisk rate; but there
seems to be no good reason for not supposing that all big
cities were experiencing the same process through our period.
In most of them, indeed, its small beginnings lay in the forties:

i.e. in Birmingham, Leeds, Liverpool, Manchester and Glasgow; and everywhere the causes were the same: demolitions for wider streets, railway lines and stations, big new buildings sacred to 'business' and government, and, starting in the sixties in Glasgow, Edinburgh and Liverpool, 'slum clearance'. The net result (as also, in part, the intended purpose) of these structural changes was the palpable modernisation of the city, a more or less conscious and deliberate adaptation of its forms to the requirements of 'modern' mid-Victorian city life.

Conspicuous among those requirements was a proper presentation of the public buildings, civic ornaments and palaces of commerce which should embody and represent the city's proud sense of its own identity. This desire to make a good civic showing was rather a new thing about the middle of the century. Fine public buildings in the central parts were not in themselves new. Birmingham's great town hall was begun in 1832; Manchester's Athenaeum was its contemporary; the noblest civic edifice of the century, Liverpool's St George's Hall, was designed in 1839 even though it wasn't finished till the fifties. These and many more such grand pieces were early Victorian, and all were of course responses to distinct civic needs: cultural and educational needs, in the cases of Athenaeums, Literary and Philosophical or Mechanics' Institutes, and halls big enough for music festivals; governmental needs, where the object was to clothe justice in marble or to dignify a local legislature; needs variously economic, as most obviously in the case of corn and coal exchanges. Such buildings were far from new in our period; they only continued to be erected; the only functional novelty—very significant in its way!—was the modern style 'office block', the spread of which through the City has been traced to a principal source in I' Anson's Royal Exchange Buildings, 1842–4.[50] New from about 1850 was the reverent yet enthusiastic interest in the central urban *ensemble*, the public buildings and the more commercial buildings that thronged around them in a potential unity that could to some extent be deliberately shaped. Mid-Victorian cities began to take new pride in themselves:

not as 'county' capitals, local second-bests to London for an old-fashioned social round, not just as places where a lot of money was made, but as growing points of a new world order, where the expansive power of trade could be allied to traditional cultural standards of amenity and style. Their rate-paying citizens were often, to use the expressive American word, 'boosters'; but 'boosters' with the Guildhall, Chatsworth, St Paul's and perhaps also St Peter's at the back of their minds! Safely emerging from the acute anxieties of the radical thirties and the hungry forties, and (however reluctantly) aware of the necessities of local government, they began to cultivate a civic identity more respectable and representative than it had generally been in the 'corrupt' old days, and were not ashamed to enjoy the prestige and the social connections which conventionally accompanied participation in the more pretentious kinds of municipal government and civic display. So mayors and corporations—representative men *now*, and truly embodying the wealth and virtue of the town —came into the open; ceremony and ritual, frowned on by the stern reforming radicals of the thirties, revived; the legislators and officials of the corporation were moved from their usually mean offices (economical reminders to the administrators not to lord it over their paymasters) to town halls that unmistakably stood for something. Asa Briggs has told how the rivalry of Leeds and Bradford translated itself about 1850 into architectural terms. The latter's St George's Hall, completed in 1852–3, stood for Bradford's bold pretensions to the commercial primacy of the West Riding and to a place in the top city set; its promoter, Mayor Samuel Smith, compared it with Birmingham's Town Hall and London's Exeter Hall to the latter's disadvantage. (London indeed could never compete in this line with the proud provincial cities of the midlands and the north.) To Leeds men these pretensions of their booming neighbours were intolerable. They countered with the project for a grand new town hall and a splendid one was in fact ready by 1858, their economical instincts having, for the time being, been worsted by their desire to make a gorgeous splash. The more economical citizens were particu-

larly worried by the idea of its tower: 'a tower would cost
money and would be only good at look at, not to use.' The
protagonists of splendour urged them to think not of pennies
but 'dignity and beauty', 'nobility', 'elevating influences' and
'pretensions'; 'like the noble halls of France, of Belgium and
of Italy', their town hall would 'attract ... the visits of strangers,
dilettanti tourists, and the lovers of art from distant places'.[51]

While the offices and officers of local governments became
thus magnified in our period, civic pride and self-respect were
improving the aspects and amenities of cities in other ways too.
Public parks became for the first time objects of deliberate
desire, and ratepayers recklessly advanced to the point of
readiness to pay for the upkeep of parks presented by wealthy
citizens. After Paxton's pioneer park at Birkenhead, Manchester led the way, with three parks opened during the later
forties; Bradford was given Peel Park, towards which its first
mayor Milligan and the worsted king Salt contributed a thousand each, in 1850; Dundee got The People's, alias Baxter,
Park in 1863; Bolton, Heywood Park in 1866; and so on. The
Metropolitan Board of Works was meanwhile, as we have
seen, doing the same for London. Museums and public libraries like wise became not uncommon; see p. 234, below.

The central parts of Britain's cities thus through the fifties
and sixties became gradually more tidy, business-like, and
consciously impressive. The quantity of people living in them
usually diminished, although the overcrowding of those living
in them usually got worse. New buildings burgeoned and they
were (except for the big hotels which were a significant phenomenon of the times) not for living in. Old streets were widened,
old graveyards closed; insanitary and/or dangerous commercial
activities like cattle markets and slaughterhouses were brought
under control and/or bodily moved to less annoying sites,
away from the business man, the shopper and the tourist.
Hospitals, endowed schools, almshouses, and all other such
kinds of institutions began also to shift to where land was
cheaper and air cleaner: to the suburbs or to the country,
now becoming easy to reach by rail. Not only by losing the
last of the domestic residences of its major money makers

did our mid-Victorian city experience that separation of function which was to turn its middle parts, by the end of the century, into a dead-on-Sundays concentration of commerce and 'culture'.

The Countryside

Of the smaller town environment, and of the circumambient green sea of village and countryside that still surrounded at no great distance the urban-dwelling population, it is not necessary to say much. Except in one important respect (see below, p. 89) it changed so little compared with the towns and cities during our period, and such changes as did occur were usually slow and piecemeal. The main topographical elements of the British countryside were all laid down well before the eighteen-fifties, and except in Ireland neither economic nor social change enforced substantial alteration until the so-called 'great depression' period later on. The social order of the Engglish, Welsh and at any rate lowland Scottish countryside and its market towns remained unaltered in essentials: a governing hierarchy of landowners, clergy and professional men; an intermediate fringe order of farmers, hardly before the later sixties dreaming of pursuing any political or social goals distasteful to their landlords; a largely landless labouring class, upon which the (not apparently numerous) appeals of country town radicals and 'open village' malcontents were wasted before the same years which witnessed the beginnings of farmer disaffection, the end of the sixties.

Ireland's differences from this general order were that landowners were less commonly resident, clergy of the established church less influential, professional men far fewer on the ground, the intermediate farmer element only beginning to form (as during the post-famine reconstruction, the land system jolted and crashed into some semblance of modern equivalence to the British, in whose market if anywhere it had to compete); and the labouring class much more open to rebellious suggestions. Except, again, in Ireland, where the face of the countryside was changing quite fast in some areas through this economic reconstruction (small fields being banged together to make big viable ones, drainage schemes turning bog into meadow, new roads everywhere, deserted cottages and cabins mouldering ...), the aspect of the still agricultural countryside was much the same in 1870 as it had been twenty years before, and it looked more like the countryside of the nineteen-sixties than like that of the seventeen-sixties. (I say 'the still agricultural', because the countryside was of course being steadily eroded all around growing towns and by developing non-urban industries like coal in South Yorkshire, South Wales and Fife, and iron quarrying in the Cleveland Hills.) The 'agricultural revolution' had by the middle of the nineteenth century wrought the English and Scottish countryside into a physical shape suitable for its purposes; what further draining and ditching remained to be done, what improved equipment of barns and sheds and yards could still be installed, only tinkered with the detail of an appearance to which the rural ruling class was, not least for sentimental and recreational reasons, passionately attached; agricultural revolution there may have been, but social revolution, no! The woods, commons (such as remained), coverts, spinnies and fields therefore stayed secure and were even made to seem almost unnaturally so, as each element of these attractive landscapes was carefully trained and preserved, so far as its controllers could contrive it, for its destined purpose in their scheme of things: sense of community, profit and livelihood, sport, sheer pleasure of heart and eye. It was a work of art as well as (in effect) a great industrial plant: a beautiful and profitable contrivance, fashioned and kept in smooth working order by that happily undoubting class to whom the way of life it made possible seemed the best the world could offer. Wherever this rule predominated—and I have the impression that it did predominate through most of the cultivated counties—the built environment only changed to the extent that 'the big house' was added to or rebuilt, and the walls or fences of its park or grounds strengthened; farm buildings were modernised; villas and towny-looking houses intruded into village and small town streets and environs for the clergy, doctors, lawyers, etc., tradesmen who made their money out of rural society, and that increasing army of persons with pensions or other 'private means' who liked living in it; and new dwellings of humbler class appeared too, some of them the rural equivalents of those 'model' blocks of flats or rows of cottages which philanthropy or the profit motive had prompted in cities and close to factories.

Virtuous landowners throughout our period were much given—with what quantitative effect, it is impossible to say —to building better cottages for the families which worked on their estates or for the farmers on their land. They were made aware, or more uncomfortably aware, that the cottages in which the bulk of the rural labouring class lived (cottages perhaps so picturesque!) were from a sanitary point of view dangerous and from a moral point of view (because of their lack of rooms and usual squalor) deplorable. Landowners who were prepared to spend money on a good cause had no lack of architects' designs to choose from; and many of the (unless they were olde-Englishe gabled or thatched ones for landscape purposes) brick-box or stone consequences of their concern are still to be seen. Official reporters (of whom the most important was Dr H. J. Hunter, in the middle sixties) and morally agitated observers reported that rural labouring-class housing conditions remained generally dismal until at least the seventies. The 1873 Social Science Congress heard without astonishment Lord Napier and Ettrick's reckoning that 'one-third of the agricultural houses of Britain required to be rebuilt': i.e. about 700,000.[52] The difficulties in the way of improving them were mainly economic, but partly social; the motive for improving was wholly social. The economic difficulty for the philanthropically minded country gentleman was simple and huge; the labourer could not afford decent housing. It was barely possible for decent-standard housing (I do not mean overcrowded housing!) to pay its way, let alone make a modest profit (let further alone make the 8 to 10 per cent profit which the mid-Victorian considered normal for real estate), in prosperous industrial towns; it was usually impossible throughout most of the British agricultural world.

Labourers' rents were often in fact quite high but only because they had to live somewhere and there was nowhere else to live. No more than in most towns was housing superabundant in the countryside. The aggregate rural population was, as we have seen, in process of decline; fewer workers were needed and, as emigration to towns or other lands continued, fewer people were seeking work; the effective demand for working-class houses was therefore, even allowing for the period's drift towards higher standards in these matters, not going up. Meanwhile, economic and social motives combined actually to reduce wherever possible the quantity available. The economic motive was that immemorial one, of reducing the poor rate; until the passage of the Union Chargeability Act in 1865 it was virtually automatic that, the fewer houses within the parish, the lower would the poor rate be. The social motives for reducing the quantity of housing were, first, the landowner's normal desire to have only just as many cottages nearby as would house the essential labour for the estate and the farmers who paid the rent; and second, the concern, normally shared by landowner and farmer, to make sure that no more cottages were beyond their own control than could possibly be avoided. Ownership of cottages was a cardinal point in the grand schemes of subordination. We read therefore of a positive shortage of cottages in many southern and eastern agricultural areas, of labourers having to take what they were offered, and of many of them having to walk miles daily to and from their places of employment, which might well be in other parishes. Contemporaries divided the rural world into 'open' and 'closed' parishes: 'open' parishes being those where there was no concentration of landownership, where there might be freehold land, and therefore likely to be some variety of accommodation and occupation for workers; 'closed' where concentration of ownership made possible—what was assumed would normally follow—the disciplining of a village by means including the elimination of uncontrolled dwellings.

The Railway and the Country

Such were the essentials of the rural environment, in all but
one important respect, and at last I deal with it: the railway.
Here again we find the railway making a giant and novel impact on society. Elsewhere in this book I notice its revolution-
ising of leisure patterns and its enriching of family life. Here
all I wish to notice is the extent to which the railway changed
the face and pace of the countryside. Other forms of transport changed hardly at all. There were no shiny-surfaced hard
roads; such were indeed still uncommon in the towns. Country
roads were variously surfaced with grass, earth and stones.
The very best of them, tended by an unusually go-ahead
Parish or (from 1862) a Highway District (of parishes) or a
self-respecting Turnpike Trust (there were still over 800 in
Britain at the turn of the seventies) might be macadamised in
the proper, expensive way, with a fine firm crust of granite
chips, resting on the inferior beds of broken flints and gravels
which, whether for top or lower use, still made the stone-
breaker a familiar figure of the roadside and the work-yard.
But good roads of this calibre were rare. The mass of them
were adequate only for a comfortably slow-moving traffic of
country coaches, farm carts, droves of cattle, family vehicles
of every kind—and horses. Traction engines were the heaviest
and noisiest objects to be met. All fast traffic and most heavy
traffic now went by rail. Canals still, in some areas, retained
a declining share of the heavy stuff.

But railways brought momentous big change with them.
Their impact and effects of course began earlier, in the thirties,
but they had not gone far before the later forties. Map 4
shows just how much further it had gone by the seventies.
Nothing like this had happened to the countryside before.
The cuttings and embankments, the bridges and viaducts, the
straight swathes cut through field and forest, the attendant
semi-domestic paraphernalia of stations, signal boxes, plate-
layers' huts and coal-dealers' cabins—here was a giant new
phenomenon which not only transfigured the appearance of
the countryside wherever it went (and by no means always

for the worse; the stations were—as those still standing allow
one to see—often architecturally delightful, while the viaducts
and bridges echoed noble Roman themes) but also brought
guarantees of a revolution in most of the terms of economic
and social relationships. Yet the working of that revolution in
rural Britain was, through our period, subterranean. The little
country town of Barleyboll, wrote Surtees, was perfectly
representative of its kind at the turn of the fifties.

'It had a pound at one end, an inn in the middle, a church
at one side, a fashionable milliner from London, a merchant
tailor from the same place, and a hardware shop or two, where
they also sold treacle, Dartford gunpowder, pocket-handker-
chiefs, sheep-nets, patent medicines, cheese, blackings,
marbles, mole-traps, men's hats, and other miscellaneous
articles.'[53]

What would have changed by the seventies? No longer gunpowder in the shop, some modern middle class houses, a
branch of a bank, a couple of agents for agricultural equipment and supplies—and, perhaps a mile and a half outside the
town, a neat little gothic Barleyboll Station on the Wessex
and Loamshire line, opening the door through which the first
trickles of the twentieth century were beginning to seep.

The main railway lines of England were by 1852, remarks
their best historian, either completed or authorised to be so;
and 'the most important English towns not yet served by a
railway were Hereford, Yeovil, and Weymouth'.[54] Their isolation, and that of most of Wales and Scotland, soon ended. By
the turn of the seventies the railways served everywhere that
mattered, and served it more efficiently. It marks a big difference from the experience of our own day that roads were,
by comparison, of negligible importance; not such a difference,
that the canals were scarcely less so. The coastal shipping
business too was (relatively speaking) past its peak, and
beginning to undergo strange changes. Wherever the railway
stretched its iron finger, there once busy little ports went into
sometimes quite sudden declines—except where, as at Cardiff
and Barry, Southampton and Fleetwood, the railways actually
made or refashioned ports in their own industrial image; or

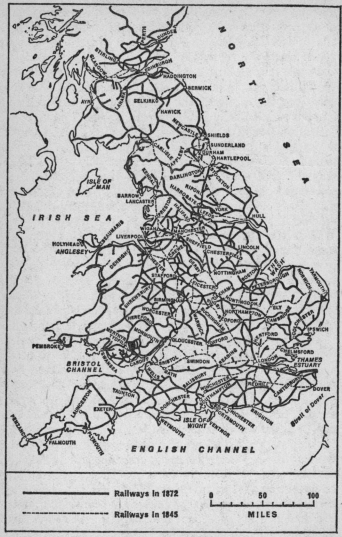

The railway system in Britain in 1872

where, as in the case of the Durham and Northumberland coal trade with London, strength of demand and convenience of transport combined to keep the coasters busy. It was in the railways' power, in this the beginning of their greatest age, as it once had been in that of 'overmighty subjects', to make or break communities. They could supply them more cheaply with most of the bulky goods that used to have to come by sea; they could bring in, and take over most of the local distribution of the lighter goods that always used to come, by no matter what means they did come, slowly and expensively; they were of prime importance in making possible such improvements in the standard of working class living as (for those outside the coalfields who could afford it) coal for keeping warm in winter, and the fresher, cheaper supplies of milk and meat and vegetables which just began to raise the quality of the common diet during the sixties; they could introduce and sustain the novel phenomenon of passenger traffic.

Passenger trains were, by the sixties, becoming plentiful, though the uninstructed or uninspired could not be expected to make much sense of Bradshaw. But on every line where passengers could go, at least one train each day could (because parliament had so willed it in 1844) be travelled on by third class passengers at the standard rate of a penny a mile. This amenity seems to have quickly become appreciated and used by the third class public; cheap fares were introduced as a further facility for them in the sixties; by 1872 it was worth the Midland Railway's while to put third class carriages on every train. We may presume that families were thus helped to keep together, that work-seeking migration over longer distances become more easy and usual than it had been in the early industrial revolution, and that the 'tramping artisan' in particular was benefited.

In such ways did the institution of the railway much increase its hold over the nation during these years. The lengthening mileage of track is by itself a far from adequate measure. Tracks themselves thickened, as swelling traffic demands turned some single tracks into double, some doubles into quadruple, and all along them more elaborate provisions of yards and sidings. The railway had no rival. Individual railway companies were often in rivalry among themselves; waged price-wars, bade for take-overs, threatened or effected amalgamations, got up parliamentary oppositions to rivals' bills. It is debatable whether the public suffered more than it benefited from these alarums and excursions. It is certain that the public used the railway more and more. In 1850 British railways carried 67·4 million passengers; in 1875, 490·1 million. Their freight loads more than trebled during the same years. One may well doubt whether railways ever mattered more in the life of the nation than they did between the seventies and the First World War. By the mid-eighties, says Clapham, 'most people in Britain were within ear-shot of the crash or mutter of a town by day. Many of those who were not, unless they lived North of the Highland Line, could yet catch the clank of trains in a still night.' Some new lines had recently been laid (about 14 per cent increase between 1875 and 1885) 'but in most places the railway had sunk into the landscape, like the road and canal before it. All that it brought in sight and sound had become established, and familiar as the uninterrupted spreading of the mutter of the towns.'[55] Not only the mutter of the towns asserted itself over the circumambient countryside. Their mounting demands for food controlled the countrymen's economy; and by the seventies, the railway was the principal way they got it. The urbanising Britain we are looking at was Britain entering the intensest phase of its Railway Age.

2: The Making of Livings

This chapter will deal with how the people of Great Britain and Ireland made their livings or otherwise kept alive, and in what major respects the conditions and rewards of those operations changed during our period.

A historian who were, for comparative purposes, to jump from the eighteen-sixties to the nineteen-seventies would presumably concern himself much less with how people in the later decade earn their livings and under what conditions they earn them, for the good and sufficient reason that most people now spend more weekday waking hours away from income-providing premises than on them, and most work-places are tolerably healthy to work in. If the problem of the nineteen-seventies is, for many people, finding ways of filling leisure, the problem of the eighteen-sixties was, for most people, finding some leisure to fill. Not that the sixties or the fifties were in this respect any tougher a time to inhabit than the forties or the thirties had been. Indeed for workers in the better organised trades, for shop and office employees and for many children they brought a hopeful promise of easier times to come. The extent to which the conditions of earning a living improved during the fifties and sixties—as they more or less did, for quite a large range of occupations—must not be left out of the reckoning, when it comes to assessing the quality of life in mid-Victorian Britain.

The Cult of Work

But it seems to remain true that work dominated people's lives to an extent that nowadays, in an 'advanced' industrial economy, is scarcely conceivable. Visitors to London from the Continent commented on the haste and push of its pedestrians, their ruthless pursuit of their own or their master's business, in much the same way as European visitors to New York fifty years later were to comment on the pace and intensity of business life in that city. The Swiss industrialist, J. C. Fischer, was so struck by the solemn business ritual in a City bank that he made a special record of it:

'When I returned to the bank a little before nine o'clock I was shown to a seat facing a counter where five cashiers conducted their business. At five minutes to nine the official to whom I had to give my cheque took his place behind the counter. I had it in my hand and showed it to him. He did not say a word but emptied several little bags of gold coins into a drawer. Then he produced the well-known little cash shovel that is used for coins in banks. And then he just waited. At the stroke of nine he asked me if I wanted gold or banknotes. I said I wanted gold. He did not count any of the sovereigns and half sovereigns but simply weighed them on his scales and then put them on the counter without taking any further notice of me. . . .'[1]

A few years later *Bradshaw's Handbook to the Manufacturing Districts* awestruck, reported 'the utmost order and regularity' in great cotton mills like Birley's at Chorlton and Houldsworth's in Ancoats. But, it warned the tourists,

'. . . unless the applicant has a letter of introduction from some person known to the proprietors, there is considerable difficulty in the way of obtaining admission. As it has been justly observed by a local authority, "the objection generally entertained is not founded so much upon a fear of admitting person who might take away information that the owners wish to monopolise, as it proceeds from the fact, that visitors occupy the time of an attendant, and disturb the attention of the operatives throughout the mill. The loss accruing from this cause is frequently more than can be readily estimated." '[2]
Visitors were thought to upset the routines of workhouses and prisons on like grounds. A French observer of the seventies alleged that 'On entering an office, the first thing you see written up is: "You are requested to speak of business only." '[3] Work, it is not too much to say, was a cult for the respectable classes. Carlyle never wasted breath less fruitfully than in recommending them to give themselves to work. They had it in their bones and they made sure that their employees

got it in theirs: women and children as well as lads and grown men. Not until the seventies were young children (i.e. till 1874, under nine; thereafter, under ten) statutorily barred from all forms of regular wage-earning labour. The industrial employment of women was very slowly diminishing—its diminution was indeed one of the larger changes in work-patterns of our period (see below, pp. 118 ff.)—but the 1871 census found 26·8 per cent of English and Welsh females (not counting girls under fifteen) still 'at work' for as many hours a day as they could get. The hours of men's work were tending to diminish but the severity of industrial work itself, if it changed at all, generally increased (see below, pp. 138–9) and the terrors of losing your job remained as great as they had always been. Herein lay one of the distinguishing marks of the whole Victorian period, compared with post-1945 Britain: the loss of your job *at almost any level of society* was a much more fearful thing than it now need be; and security of employment was therefore worth a huge sacrifice of income. There was, for virtually the whole of the period we are considering, a surplus of applicants for almost every employment going. Only 1872, a boom year if ever there was one, was a year of 'full employment' and that was only in respect of the men who by the standards of their day had reasonable hopes of employment; as was rarely the case with the lowest stratum of society (see below p. 150). Masters were still so well situated for wage bargaining that it remained the practice for men even in relatively unskilled occupations to provide or rent their own tools and other necessities; not only skilled men like cabinet-makers and saw-grinders had thus to subsidise their employers but also navvies, dustmen, sewer cleaners and clerical employees. 'A stove is provided for the benefit of the clerical staff'—at a Burnley mill in 1852, but—'It is recommended that each member of the clerical staff bring four pounds of coal each day during cold weather'! The owners provided 'Brushes, brooms, scrubbers and soap' for the clerks to clean their offices 'Forty minutes before prayers'; but nothing more in the writing lines than a 'sharpener'.' The girls who made 5s to 6s a week sorting and sifting on the coal, coke and slag heaps at iron works got no protective clothing; a puddler at Pen-y-Daran told Mayhew's collaborator that his regular pay stoppages included 6d a month 'for clay to repair the furnaces'.[5] These burdens had to be patiently borne. For most men, in most trades, jobs were scarce. Workmen who got bad names as trouble makers (e.g., and especially, as union organisers) were usually blacklisted and compelled to leave the district, unless they ventured to set up as independent tradesmen or, as was common in the north-eastern coalfields, as managers of co-operative stores. We read of dock labourers fighting to get to the front of the crowd outside the dock gates, of skilled workmen, clerks and shop-assistants dying their hair black so as to look younger and brisker than they actually felt. After sixty, wrote the coolest statistician of the period, 'a man becomes unfit for hard work; and if he loses his old master, cannot find a new one. In some trades, a man is disabled at fifty-five or fifty. A coal-backer is considered past work at forty.'[6] (No wonder. His normal daily lift was sixty tons.) No unemployed or unemployable person needed to die of starvation—the much maligned, on some accounts justly maligned, Poor Law looked after that—but the terms on which public relief was offered were usually humiliating, and so were those of private charity except when they were so indiscriminate as to be morally valueless. The official Poor Law outdoor relief given in the manufacturing districts as a sort of unemployment dole was never in itself adequate and was expected to be supplemented by whatever the members of the family taken as a whole could scrape together by begging, sponging, casual work, etc.; few but the utterly degraded or helpless looked forward to an old age inside the workhouse, yet few working people could hope to have enough savings left at the end of their working lives to keep them independent.

Skilled workmen were in fact rather better placed than most other Britons, inasmuch as their skills were less replaceable than most. A member of a craft union which had successfully resisted employers' attempts to break down its self-protective restrictions on recruitment and training (and maybe machinery too) was most unlikely to make more than between 30s and £2 a week (see below, p. 115) but he was much better placed for industrial bargaining than the Bob Cratchit whose skill went not beyond letters and ledgers, and he cannot be considered badly placed in comparison with the perhaps very expensively educated professional men who overcrowded the 'gentlemanly' professions—clergymen, lawyers, doctors, civil servants.... Clergymen who could not get a footing on the ecclesiastical escalator made livings by teaching (a business for which a clerical character was a conventional selling-point); fully trained solicitors were all too often glad to take posts as solicitors' clerks; medics who could not get on to the fashionable circuits wore themselves out in the service of Poor Law Unions, friendly societies and sick clubs. Even with connections and capital, professional success was not guaranteed; without either, it seems to have been exceedingly difficult for men honestly to make a prosperous way. What things were like in the newer professions and in the vast business world—a chunk of society about whose social conformations we so far know amazingly little—I really do not know. Perhaps life was not so competitive for engineers, mine agents, sales representatives....

But death laid his icy hand on men of the new society as well as men of the old, and all of them would have to worry about their wives and children in the event of their premature decease. Investment in government securities, railways and real estate was no doubt how most men made provision for the worst; nothing then seemed as safe as houses. But how much could they save? It was repeatedly stated to the Commons' Select Committee on Income Tax in 1861 that only the most fortunate and best-established professional men ever made enough to be able to insure their lives for a worthwhile amount. In times when sons cost more and more to educate and daughters still had no respectable prospects but matrimony, a professional father's death could suddenly topple his family to equality with an artisan's.

Occupations and Incomes

But where did our mid-Victorians' money come from? One cannot do better than begin with a simplified version of Charles Booth's summary of his own summaries of his investigations into the occupations of the people as shown by the censuses. These gross employment figures at once say something about the dominant trends: the tremendous decline in the relative weight of agriculture, the very slight decline in that of manufactures (except in Ireland, where it was sharper), the slow but steady increase in weight of the building and transport industries, shopkeeping (for that is what most 'dealing' meant) and the 'public and professional service'; and a very notable difference between the experience of the three countries in respect of domestic service, truly suggesting, as the astonished Booth remarked, that 'servants are more numerous where poverty makes service cheap'. Thus were the contours of occupational distribution changing, within each national part of the UK and as between them. Such simple gross statistics suggest little about individuals' experiences but they do prescribe the economic limits within which individuals' experiences occurred. So do the gross figures of the distribution of national income between the principal industrial sectors.

It will be observed that the fastest-growing sector was that of 'income from abroad', the reward of that remarkable export of capital which reached its climax about the turn of the century; all of this money presumably went in the end to swell the incomes of the investing public. The fastest-declining was that of agriculture, etc., which more or less matched the decline in the proportion of people engaged in it.

The great defect of gross industrial and occupations figures like these, from our point of view, is that they are necessarily insensitive about *social* conformations. They tell us next to nothing about the social distribution of income and employments: how many persons were earning how much, at what levels of the hierarchy, and which classes or groups in the community were doing best out of the great mid-Victorian

Employment of the People of the UK 1851–81 as % of occupied population[7]

Occupations	ENGLAND & WALES				SCOTLAND				IRELAND			
	1851	1861	1871	1881	1851	1861	1871	1881	1851	1861	1871	1881
Agriculture	20·9	18·0	14·2	11·5	22·7	20·1	17·3	14·2	48·4	42·9	40·7	41·1
Fishing	0·2	0·2	0·2	0·3	1·5	1·7	1·8	1·9	0·4	0·3	0·4	0·5
Mining	4·0	4·5	4·5	4·8	4·0	4·5	5·1	5·0	0·4	0·4	0·3	0·4
Building	5·5	5·8	6·3	6·8	5·2	5·9	6·3	6·7	2·0	2·4	2·2	2·4
Manufacture	32·7	33·0	31·6	30·7	36·5	35·0	34·7	33·8	22·8	20·7	19·5	16·0
Transport	4·1	4·6	4·9	5·6	3·6	4·1	4·9	5·2	1·4	1·8	2·1	2·2
'Dealing' (i.e. Shops, etc.)	6·5	7·1	7·8	7·8	5·6	6·5	7·1	7·5	3·6	4·1	4·6	4·8
Public and professional service	4·6	5·3	5·5	5·6	3·5	3·9	3·8	4·2	2·2	3·7	4·3	5·0
Domestic service	13·3	14·6	15·8	15·7	10·5	12·0	10·7	11·1	10·4	13·3	15·2	18·0

Industrial Distribution of the National Income in Great Britain[8]
(as % of Total National Income)

Year	Agri-culture, Forestry, Fishing	Mining, Manu-facturing, Building	Trade and Trans-port	Income from Abroad	Govern-ment, Profes-sional, etc.	Rents of Dwellings
1841	22·1	34·4	18·4	1·4	9·6	8·2
1851	20·3	34·2	18·7	2·0	11·3	8·1
1861	17·8	36·5	19·6	3·0	10·4	7·5
1871	14·2	38·1	22·0	4·3	8·9	7·6
1881	10·4	37·6	23·0	5·8	9·9	8·5
1891	8·6	38·4	22·5	7·3	9·6	8·1

boom which took the gross national income up from an estimated £523 million in 1851 to £1,051 million thirty years
later; whether there was more than misery and envy to justify
the socialists' suspicion that 'the rich were getting richer and
the poor poorer....' It looks as if there was. The available
statistics have not made calculation easy even for experts in
that side of social science, but it seems certain that the wage-
earning classes (not at all the same thing as 'the poor', since
the top wage-earners were making up to £2 a week) did not
through our period increase their share of the national income
bill; which means that the working classes and the poor, taken
together, got a diminishing share of it. A. L. Bowley tried in
his classic *Wages and Income since 1860* (1937) to carry back
behind 1880 his tracing of the proportion that wages bore to
that bill. Between 1880 and 1913, he was pretty sure, their
proportion had slightly fallen. What was it doing between
1860 and 1880? It *seemed* (again) to have fallen by a few
per cent (although Bowley was so reluctant to place much
reliance on the figures that he said in conclusion: 'I do not
think that the statistics are sufficient for any fine measurements of income, earnings or wages prior to 1880; there is
indeed sufficient uncertainty after that date').[9] To that extent
—which is not necessarily what men meant when they said
that the rich were getting richer and the poor poorer—the
wage-earners were certainly not *as a 'class'* benefiting from the
boom.[10]

Middle-Class Incomes

The 'classes' above the wage-earners were more certainly benefiting. Measurement of their growth and stratification is not
much more satisfactory, but there are a few ledges and fissures
in the rock which a sturdy and determined climber (like J. A.
Banks, whose fine book *Prosperity and Parenthood* one must
use) can turn to good effect. There are for example the income
tax returns. The hope of abolishing that tax never died
through our period, but government persisted in costing so
much (£92m. in 1870: about 9 per cent of the gross national
product; cf. about 38 per cent in 1961!)[11] that it never could
be abolished, though Gladstone did get it down to 4d in
1866 and his disciple Northcote even got it down to 2d in
1875 and 1876. From 1842 to 1852, the exemption limit was
£150; between 1854 and 1875, £100 (with £100–150 incomes paying at a lower rate from 1854 to 1863); then the
exemption limit went back to £150 and stayed there till 1894.
The statistics of income tax tell us something about the earnings of people other than wage-earning manual workers who
by definition were below its inspectors' horizon (unless as
owners of houses of £20+ annual value they had to pay tax
under schedule A; in 1874 that meant 4s 9d on a house worth
just £20[12]). But the statistics do not tell us much.' For one
thing, the five schedules under which the tax was levied were
devised for the convenience of the tax-gatherer, not the historian; for another, plenty of nonmanual workers who might
have considered themselves in some sense 'middle class' (small
shopkeepers, clerks, dressmakers, commercial representatives)
lay also below the inspectors' horizon because their earnings
were no more than those of the better-paid manual workers.
Presuming however that anything that was happening to the
income-tax-paying middle classes was happening also to their
poor relations, certain conclusions can be drawn. Banks thus
sums up his scrupulous discussion of the question and all its
difficulties: 'we cannot escape the impression that the years
of mid-Victorian prosperity were marked by a more than proportionate increase in the number and incomes' of more or

less 'middle class' people. Again (p. 109) his general impression is that 'the middle class groups were growing far more rapidly than the rest of the population'.[13] Correlation of J. C. Stamp's *True Comparative Series of UK Taxable Income* with population figures gives us the following table:

Total Income Assessed (UK, including Ireland) and Total Population[14]

Census Date	Assessment Period	Incomes above £150	Income % Increase	Population % Increase
1851	1848–9 to 1852–3	£1,051·1 m.	—	—
1861	1858–9 to 1862–3	£1,299·1 m.	23·4	11·9
1871	1868–9 to 1872–3	£1,882·1 m.	44·9	13·2
1881	1878–9 to 1892–3	£2,506·3 m.	33·2	14·4

The earners of these incomes above £150 a year (alas! there is no means of knowing just how many of them there were; we know how many paid tax under each schedule, but not how many people paid tax under more than one schedule) were all in the general sense 'middle class' or higher: people with homes of their own and means to employ some domestic help. But how much more than £150 a year were how many of them earning? Was this a case of multiplication of lower-middle-class incomes or of higher incomes? Seeking to get beyond impressions, Banks painfully analysed the schedule which included none but individuals' salaries—'E', salaries of employees in civil service and local government offices, public companies, private firms and private individuals.[15] It has its shortcoming as a means of reckoning salary totals, since, as Stamp remarked,[16] the difference between 'D' and 'E' lay 'not so much in the character of the duties performed as in the constitutional character of the employer. For example, a clerk performing exactly the same duties at exactly the same salary may one year be under schedule D and the next under schedule E merely because the employing firm has become registered as a limited company; a Wesleyan or a Presbyterian minister is assessable under schedule E whereas a Baptist or Congregationalist is assessable under schedule D ...' The

uses of Schedule E are therefore even more limited than
Banks, with all his cautions and carefulness, allows. But they
are better than nothing, and they strongly suggest (what much
other evidence supports) that it was the incomes around the
lower levels of taxable income that were proliferating. All
levels of taxable income were increasing at a rate more rapid
than that of the population as a whole; but the middle middle
and lower middle class incomes were increasing fastest of all.
A table of Banks's,[17] to which I have added a less extensive
comparison of Irish figures (and some correction of his 'Occupied Males' and 'Total Population' figures, which are for
England and Wales only where they should be for GB), puts
the point clearly:

*Numbers of Taxpayers assessed at what levels above £200 under
schedule E*

£	1851 (GB)	1858 (Id)	1871 (GB)	1871 (Id)	% increase (GB only)
200+	8,885	664	17,529	1,024	97·3
300+	4,135	269	8,213	490	98·6
400+	1,993	109	4,092	226	105·3
500+	1,090	88	2,072	145	90·1
600+	603	48	1,253	75	107·8
700+	423	40	788	62	86·3
800+	293	35	624	48	112·6
900+	204	19	353	25	73·0
1,000+	1,125	60	1,832	98	62·9
2,000+	235	34	356	39	51·5
5,000+	58	3	80	3	37·9
All over 200	19,044	1,369	37,192	2,235	95·3
Occupied males (over 20)	5,423,000	1,539,900*	6,676,700	1,407,500	24·6
Total pop.	20,879,000	5,788,000*	26,158,000	5,398,000	25·2

*1861 figs

Banks's further analysis of the figures suggests that 'there was
a very extensive movement up the income scale over the
twenty years ... that over the twenty years many people had

received increases in their salaries and annuities of about £100 per head'. He is careful not to exaggerate the certainty of this but he concludes that 'quite possibly a large number of individual incomes increased by not inconsiderable amounts'.[18]

The Middle Class

How were these burgeoning middle-class characters making their livings? By far the greater part of them, of course, were involved in producing or distributing either the swelling volume of manufactures and raw materials which marked Britain's 'industrialisation' or the fast-developing range of consumer goods and services that met new wealth's demand for higher and more sophisticated standards of living. Most of them were urban. The rural population was shrinking during these years. The social composition of the countryside must indeed have been gently changing, as village craftsmen lost business to more 'advanced' operators from the towns and to agricultural machinery firms, as the fatty tissue of 'surplus population' continued to be sweated off, and as the 'monied' population of the countryside proportionately increased with the building of villas and purchase of bankrupted 'big houses' by men of means. But social change in the countryside was nothing compared with social change in the towns, where new streets and parades of houses and shops (each expressive of its class or sub-class of occupants) and combined operations of demolition and redevelopment in the old parts testified at once to the growth of relative wealth and to the number of people enjoying it.

One can to some extent measure and analyse this middle-class growth in gross by means of the celebrated reconstruction of the census data done by Charles Booth in the eighties (and already referred to: above, p. 98) so as to show what were 'The Occupations of the People of the UK'. Not all 'middle class' occupations can be neatly picked out, nor is any help given towards placing 'middle class' persons on the right level of their hierarchy; but the following figures, compiled by an acknowledged expert who knew at first hand the people and categories he was dealing with, must be presumed to be fairly trustworthy.[19]

What stands out most clearly in these figures is the steady gain in the proportion of persons engaged in education, 'literature and science' (mainly, I suppose, writers of every sort and standing), commerce and trade. The law men's failure to multiply I take to be more apparent than real; their clerks probably became increasingly classified under the 'commerce' category; lawyers usually make themselves so copiously indispensable! Men of commerce must by definition have been 'white collar' or cravat. The 'trade' category however is less straightforward. Booth's name for it was 'dealing' and he subdivided it into persons dealing with raw materials; clothing materials and dress; food, drink and smoking; lodging and coffee houses; furniture, utensils and stationery; and general dealers and unspecified (the second largest sub-group). Every one of those subdivisions, and *a fortiori* the generic category too, covered a social spectrum from the smartest Bond Street furriers down to the worst-shod street salesmen, from Dombey and Son down below Silas Wegg and Pleasant Riderhood; and there is no means whatever of winnowing them out. The

Growth of 'Middle Class' Occupations, 1851–81, in England and Wales
in '000, and as % of occupied population

	1851		1861		1871		1881	
	'000	%	'000	%	'000	%	'000	%
Professions:								
Law	32	0·4	34	0·4	39	0·4	44	0·3
Medicine	60	0·7	63	0·7	73	0·8	84	0·7
Education	95	1·0	116	1·2	135	1·3	183	1·6
Religion	31	0·4	39	0·4	44	0·4	51	0·4
Art and Amusement	25	0·3	29	0·3	38	0·3	47	0·4
Literature and Science	2	—	3	—	7	—	9	—
Commerce: clerks, accountants, bankers	45	0·5	68	0·7	119	1·1	225	1·9
Public Administration	52	0·6	64	0·7	73	0·7	82	0·7
Trade, wholesale and retail	547	6·5	674	7·1	838	7·8	924	7·8

Growth of 'Middle Class' Occupations, 1851–81, in Scotland[20]
in '000, and as % of occupied population

	1851		1861		1871		1881	
	'000	%	'000	%	'000	%	'000	%
Professions:								
Law	5	0·4	5	0·4	6	0·4	7	0·5
Medicine	7	0·5	7	0·5	7	0·5	10	0·6
Education	10	0·8	13	1·0	13	0·9	19	1·1
Religion	4	0·3	6	0·4	6	0·4	6	0·4
Art & Amusement	3	0·2	2	0·2	3	0·2	5	0·3
Commerce: clerks, accountants, bankers, etc.	8	0·6	11	0·8	19	1·3	34	2·1
Public Administration	6	0·5	7	0·5	9	0·6	10	0·6
Trade, wholesale and retail	74	5·6	89	6·5	106	7·1	123	7·5

Growth of 'Middle Class' Occupations, 1851–81, in Ireland[21]
in '000, and as % of occupied population

	1851		1861		1871		1881	
	'000	%	'000	%	'000	%	'000	%
Professions:								
Law	7	0·2	5	0·2	5	0·2	5	0·2
Medicine	7	0·2	6	0·2	7	0·3	7	0·3
Education	17	0·6	19	0·7	21	0·8	22	1·0
Religion	9	0·3	11	0·4	13	0·5	14	0·6
Art & Amusement	3	0·1	3	0·1	3	0·1	3	0·1
Commerce: clerks, accountants, bankers, etc.	12	0·4	14	0·5	15	0·6	16	0·7
Public Administration	5	0·2	5	0·2	8	0·3	11	0·5
Trade, wholesale and retail	109	3·6	114	4·1	117	4·6	111	4·8

growth of the shopkeeping populations is indisputable, but
to what extent it implied a growth of indisputable 'middle
class' citizens is not so sure; 'third rate shopkeepers', noted
the Bishop of Oxford in 1855 of an Oxford city incumbent's
classification of his parishioners, 'he classes with the poor'.[22]

Another of Booth's occupational categories however gives

us a surer grip upon the middle-class measurement problem: domestic service. Every family that could afford a domestic servant, it is safe to say, had one; the assistance of a char-woman or a pauper slavey marked a first step out of the working class; while no claim to true gentility could be substantiated without a preliminary qualification of servantry in the home—the basic minimum being three. The cheapest of pauper slaveys cost 2s a week (plus, of course, board and lodging). It is difficult to imagine any mid-Victorian employer of a servant not having some air of relative social superiority. The steady rise in the domestic servant class therefore—especially when you consider that servants' wages were, so far as they were moving at all, going up—seems one of the most reliable indicators of the growth of the more or less middle-class part of the population which supported it. (See table on p. 108).

'For the same periods', adds Banks, 'the total population increased as follows:

1851–61, 11·9 per cent; 1861–71, 13·2 per cent...'
and the number of separate families thus:

1851–61, 21 per cent; 1861–71, 12·4 per cent.[23]

By either comparison therefore the growth in the employment of domestic servants proves and in a general way measures the growth of the 'middle class'. Of what else it indicates about that 'middle class' we shall consider later, when examining the quality of life in mid-Victorian homes.

What kinds of middle-class people earned how much? The schedule E figures already given (above, p. 103) roughly indicate what proportion of salary earners earned what levels of salary. We want to know what jobs earned those levels of salary, and what levels of income came from what non-salaried employments. It is unfortunately very difficult to say. The manufacturing and 'dealing' worlds in particular are blanketed in obscurity. We know what civil servants got about the mid-fifties: established Chief Clerks (alias Principal Officers) started around £1,000; Senior (alias first class) Clerks rose from say £650 to £900; Assistant (alias second class) Clerks from say £350 to £600; Junior (alias third class) Clerks from

Indoor Domestic Service in England and Wales, 1851–1881 [34]

	1851	1861	% change 1851–61	1871	% change 1861–71	1881	% change
Females							
General Servants	575,162	644,271	+12·0	780,040	+21·1		
Housekeepers	46,648	66,406	+42·4	140,836	+112·1		
Cooks	44,009	77,822	+76·8	93,067	+19·6		
Housemaids	49,885	102,462	+105·9	110,505	+7·8		
Nurserymaids	35,937	67,785	+88·6	74,491	+11·4		
Laundrymaids	—	4,040	—	4,538	+12·3		
TOTAL	751,641	962,786	+28·1	1,203,477	+29·3	1,230,406	+2·2
Males							
Indoor General	74,323	62,076	−16·5	68,369	+10·1		
Grooms	15,257	21,396	+40·2	21,202	−0·9		
Coachmen	7,030	11,897	+69·2	16,174	+36·0		
TOTAL	96,610	95,369	−1·3	105,745	+10·9	56,262	−21·5

about £125 to about £300. The supplementary establishment clerks (a less numerous brood) never got more than £500; and temporary clerks of course much less. Civil servants were however not numerous. In 1853 there were about 42,000 all told, of whom only about 14,000 were of clerical and higher class.[25]

Of 'clerks', the most numerous class of salaried men, we know a good deal; partly because of the figures collected by the Civil Service Inquiry Commissioners in 1874,[26] partly because of B. G. Orchard's 1871 book *The Clerks of Liverpool*.[26] Junior clerks in quasi-professional offices like banks, solicitors, railway companies—i.e., young men of eighteen to twenty (not apprentice clerks fresh from school, for whom £20–25 a year was a common starting salary), generally began at between £70 and £80. How high they ever got would depend on their abilities and usefulness and on the extent to which the better jobs were reserved for better-class men. (E.g. that 'eminent firm of solicitors' which said that 'as a rule, the upper class of clerks is composed of men superior in ability and social position to the writing clerks'). He would have been an unfortunate and exceptional man who did not, in any of the rather classy establishments investigated by the Civil Service Inquiry Commissioners, rise to between £150 and £200 a year. The very highest to which clerks might aspire, in the legal and insurance offices, was between £500 and £600; but such cases were rare. One insurance office said that only two of its forty-one clerks made as much; one of the firms of solicitors reported twenty-one under £100, twenty-five between £100 and £200, six within the next hundred bracket and only two over £300. The Mersey Docks and Harbour Board, which employed about three hundred including apprentice clerks, reported ninety-six under £100, ninety-five between that and £200, twenty-three between that and £500, and only one higher. Orchard thought £300 was more than most clerks would dream of ever getting. These were figures for the early seventies, when salaries were certainly higher than they had been ten and *a fortiori* twenty years earlier; though by how much they were higher, I cannot reckon. In

1860 a reliable Lancashire statistician reckoned that the average salary of clerks in business in the Manchester district did not exceed £60 and that cashiers, men in really responsible positions, however routine-ridden, got £100.[27] Certain it is, that *most* 'white-collar workers' were earning little and perhaps no more than the best-paid skilled workmen, and that the differentials between them and the fortunate ones who rose to the top of the tree were very marked: just as marked as the differentials between those top skilled workmen and the unskilled general labourers.

One gets a glimpse of the spread of 'white-collar' and higher incomes from the statistician Baxter's works in the later sixties.[28] To an 'upper class' specimen he allowed £5,000 a year; to the 'upper middle class' 'professional man or tradesman (who) might live in a house at £50 rent and keep three women servants', £500. 'Lower middle class' he labelled the clerk at £99, 'living without any (resident) servant in a house at £15 a year rent'. A £15 a year house in London then would look very lower lower middle class indeed, and would scarcely guarantee respectability. £300 was cited as a 'small mercantile income' and as the average an average doctor might have left after deducting his £100 expenses from his gross earnings. £300 did not carry a family man far up the slopes of gentility. In industrial towns at any rate it would afford only two servants and a house of only about seven rooms;[29] and in London (where the stationmaster of St Pancras was only getting £265 a year in the mid-seventies) it would not stretch even to that.[30] By 1869, when the price-rise was near its peak, the experienced educationist, D. R. Fearon, was, in typical upper middle class vein, inviting readers of the *Contemporary Review* to shed a tear for the difficulties of the 'young married physician or lawyer' who, living in London 'with two or three children, and an income of £800 or £1,000 a year, ... is not likely to have more than one spare room' in which to lodge a governess.[31] His concern about the governess shows that Fearon had in mind only the most select and cultivated of physicians and lawyers. That was the big difficulty in all discussion of middle class incomes; whether they could be 'lived on' or not varied so much, according to the standard of living envisaged.

Lower-Class Incomes

To turn now to the lower classes: this period has been characterised by as eminent an historian as Asa Briggs as one of 'unparalleled working class progress';[32] yet if this was so, and so far as it was so, it cannot have been due entirely to wages relative to prices, for the progress shown in them is not all that clear before the end of the sixties. Many contemporary observers, and some later Victorian statisticians, believed in this progress (perhaps mainly because they wanted to believe in it) and thought they could demonstrate it. There was indeed some evidence for it but the shifts and falsifications they slipped in suggest the evidence was clear only to biased observers.[33] A historian no less scrupulous than Briggs, S. G. Checkland, has come from a close-up study of the same years with more qualified conclusions. On the one hand, he says, 'It is not in fact until the middle or later sixties that any really convincing aggregative evidence of rising real wages appears'; on the other, referring to the relative slowness of the rate of population growth in the fifties, he remarks that 'In this situation, workers' earnings at home were bound to improve'.[34]

That the early seventies in particular were years of heady wage rises, is incontrovertible. An 1850 worker's equivalent in 1875 (by when the peak was past) was unlikely to have less than 25 per cent more real wages and was quite likely to have 35 per cent more. Most of this increase would however have come since 1865, and—because 1867 and 1868 happened to be years of relative depression—would have seemed more recent still. The impression which so many middle and upper class mid-Victorians had of a rising working class standard of living through their period was, I reckon, no more than a 'common-sense' deduction from certain external evidence: the proliferation of the respectable working man, his unmistakable anxiety to dissociate himself from rowdies and 'roughs', the growth of his respectable working class side of the Liberal party, and Mr Gladstone's celebration of his virtues. The end (until 1865 anyway) of large-scale democratic movements and hence the suggestion to anxious propertied minds that the economic circumstances which had caused and even justified them in the thirties and forties had by now improved, combined with some consciousness of civic virtue in respect of public health and education and housing; it is by such ideas in the minds of contemporaries that I should seek to explain the often quite fervent claims made during this period that 'the working classes' were, right from its start, 'better off'.

Claims that some of the working classes were 'better off' even during the early fifties than they had been in the early forties need not have been unreasonable. But uninterrupted progress in some trades (e.g. engineering) was quite compatible with ups and downs in many and with real deterioration in others. Moreover an aggregate betterment among a swelling number of workers was not incompatible with a worsening of the situation of an actually increasing number. As one surveys the evidence for the latter possibility during our period—the still growing area of low-grade and overcrowded housing, the blooming persistence of crime and mendicity, the continuation of hard 'pre-industrial revolution' forms of labour and of casual labour, the reports brought back to civilisation by those explorers and officials whose business or mission it was to go among the streets and dwellings of the 'sunken sixth' (or 'submerged tenth' or whatever it was: see below, pp. 142–6)—as one sees this formidable evidence of a perhaps positively growing body of destitution and deprivation, the more one feels bound to exercise the utmost caution in making any general statement about 'working class progress', however much of it there may really have been; and the more one finds it necessary to insist on close attention to the circumstances of each individual case.

A London artisan with demonstrably rising real wages and shortening hours of work may still have been having to pay so much of his income for so persistently inadequate a home, and consequently losing so unnecessarily high a proportion of his infant children, that one would be hard put to it to say whether he was 'better off' or not. Even for middle class people, who typically rely on a single male breadwinner in a fairly permanent job, other factors than mere income—location and what we nowadays call 'fringe benefits', for example— can matter greatly. For working class people the father's in- come may be no more than one, and not even the most import- ant, of a number of factors determining his family's standard of living. Location mattered for him too; mattered probably more, since he almost always had to *walk* to work. Perman- ence of employment, regularity of work, were probably rarer in his experience; unemployment hit him more abruptly, sick- ness instantly lost him wages, severe illness was usually for him the end. On the other hand wife and children could work, and usually did. The hardest phase of a married working man's life was between the first baby's arrival (which might stop his wife working and would mean another mouth to feed) and the same child's becoming old enough to earn its first pennies. Thereafter, if family health held, and local economic conditions were favourable, relative riches would accrue, until the children began to marry and to found homes of their own. Fringe benefits could be important for others than farm labourers (who most obviously benefited); miners got free coal, railway workers cheap fares, shopworkers broken victuals, domestic servants cast-off clothes, etc. Another factor that often reduced skilled men's apparent wages by between a sixth and a quarter was their payment—because their work or their status demanded it—of a boy or girl helper. Some skilled men paid such, some didn't. One can never be sure, without microscopic inspection of individual persons and families, to what extent such factors mattered. I have become convinced that they mattered much more than hard-headed calculators of 'real wages' may imagine.

Real wages calculators have never been able to try to take into account any of these imponderables except unemploy- ment, and even that defies confident assessment during our period. My own study of the literature persuades me that no better summary can be made than Checkland's[35]: 'Taking the whole period from the forties to the later sixties it seems likely that there was a continuous trend in betterment, but so slight, and so often reversed in bad times, that the statisticians found real demonstration very difficult. From the later sixties the trend was markedly upward' to 1875; whereabouts our interest ceases. The increase between about 1866–7 and 1873–5 was conspicuous, incontrovertible; around 15–20 per cent. No major occupational groups missed it. Then, for sure, virtually all labouring men's and women's real wages rose (whether they had been rising or not thitherto). Yet—and this neatly emphasises the weakness of even quite firm real wages indices as indications of living standards—a variety of other evidence has made it seem to Eric Hobsbawm 'fairly clear [that] money [was] getting tighter for the working class household in the later 1860s'[36]. Real wages averages were so decidedly *not* everything that the reproduction here of any of the (more or less conflicting) existing tables seems more likely to confuse than clarify. The considerable 'working class progress' that we may correctly discern in most of the working classes from the later forties onwards did not rest wholly, perhaps for many not even mainly, on such increase of wages as may have occurred; its other bases—in the rising proportion of better-paid jobs, in improved environment, cultural provisions, shorter work hours, etc.—are scattered throughout this book.

Uncertainty about real wages movements and about their significance may deter us from a will-o'-the-wisp pursuit of their exact course. The spread and the levels of actual money wages may however be easily indicated and they are the more relevant on account of the tendency throughout our period for the proportion of skilled jobs to grow at the expense of unskilled. Differentials between skilled and unskilled were increasing too. The labour force was thus spreading itself out as well as thickening its middle-to-upper wages brackets. (Real wages statistics do not show this unless specially 'weighted' to do so, which they are not always.) Baxter's 1867 classification of wage levels conveniently indicates the working man's hierarchy and variety, besides what trades brought what rewards; the wages stated are those for men over twenty, working a full week, in England and Wales only.

The Hierarchy of Labour 1867[37]

Average Men's Weekly Wage	Occupational Group	Approximate Number	Average Men's Weekly Wage	Occupational Group	Approximate Number
35s	Scientific, Surgical and Optical Instrument makers	3,150		Building trades	387,600
				Shipbuilding trades	82,900
	Scale makers	1,150		Bakers' and Butcher's men	70,000
	Leather Case makers	2,200	25s	Seamen	100,000
	Watch makers	15,400		Warehousemen	15,200
	Jewellery makers	11,000		Watermen, Bargemen etc.	29,300
	Engine Drivers	9,300		Coach and Harness makers	30,000
28s–30s	Printers, Binders, etc.	28,350		Hairdressers	8,000
	Hat makers	9,000		Dockyard workers	12,470
	Ivory, Bone and Wood-workers	13,600		Gas workers	8,000
	Earthenware workers	20,300		Tanners, Curriers, Skinners	19,200
	Glass workers	9,700			
	Arms and Tool makers	44,250		Soap and Tallow workers	3,260
	Iron workers	91,700		Rope (and other hemp product) makers	11,300
	Cabinet makers, Upholsterers	39,000		Blacksmiths, Whitesmiths and Hardware makers	130,000
	Musical Instrument makers	2,200			

Average Men's Weekly Wage	Occupational Group	Approximate Number	Average Men's Weekly Wage	Occupational Group	Approximate Number
25s (continued)				Coalheavers	11,600
	Hosiery workers	20,000			
	Lace makers	6,700		Chimney Sweepers	4,300
	Linen workers	7,100		Servants	98,600
	Paper workers	12,000		Boot and Shoe workers	157,000
	Straw, Rush, Bark and Caneworkers	11,000		Brush makers	7,000
				Tailors	83,000
	Oilmen, Polishers, Japanners	8,500	15s–20s	Sailors	19,500
				Fishermen	50,000
	Copper, Brass, Tin, Zinc, Lead, etc., workers	50,000		Police	14,500
21s–23s				Coastguards and Militiamen	6,200
	Railway workmen	64,500		Civil Service Messengers, etc.	2,100
	Postmen	11,500			
	Coachmen, Cabmen, Carriers	81,700		Malsters, Brewers	25,000
				Glove makers	2,700
	Miners, all sorts	233,500		Straw workers	1,820
	Chemicals workers	15,000		Quarrymen	29,700
	Cotton, Calico, Fustian workers	143,000		Dock Labourers	29,500
	Wool and Worsted workers	95,000		'Messengers and Porters'	35,300
				Horsekeepers, Drovers, Gamekeepers	44,000
	Sugar Refiners workers	2,600	14s	Farm Labourers, etc.	880,000
	Millers	20,000			

Average Men's Weekly Wage	Occupational Group	Approximate Number	Average Men's Weekly Wage	Occupational Group	Approximate Number
14s	(continued) General Labourers	258,000	12s	Soldiers	56,000
				Chelsea and Greenwich Pensioners	17,400
	'Road Labourers and Scavengers'	10,500		Silk workers	34,500

Those tables list, I repeat, the average weekly wages in all major occupational groups of only *men* in England and Wales. Women's, girls' and boys' wages were lower; so much lower that Baxter spotted a 'curious fact, that in the great majority of occupations the average wages of a boy, a woman and a girl, added together, amount to those of a man'; the exceptions being certain light occupations requiring digital dexterity (e.g. lace-making) and domestic service. Baxter did not conduct a comparable analysis of Scottish or Irish labour. His gross figures for Scotland show, what one would expect of a generally poorer and socially less sophisticated country, that the proportion of jobs in 'higher skilled' groups was somewhat smaller than in England, but that the overall spread was much the same. Much poorer Ireland of course was utterly different, with an average income per head of only £14 against Scotland's £23 10s and England-and-Wales's £32. 'Higher skilled' jobs were twice as scarce again as in Scotland, and 'unskilled' jobs (which, with the usual unfairness, was allowed to include most farm jobs), which in Scotland and England were markedly fewer than the 'lower skilled', were in Ireland nearly twice as numerous.

The gross contrasts epitomise the dominant tendencies in the world of men's labour (not women or children's, with which I will deal separately: see below, pp. 119 ff.) during our period. Continued intense industrialisation in a dramatically enriching society as yet meant no slackening in the overall demand for more or less skilled workmen. There was indeed a continuing trickle of 'technological redundancy' as machinery became more refined and resourceful (e.g. in hosiery, fine textiles, coarse footwear, brickmaking) but its tendency to lower the status and earnings of skilled men was more than balanced, in the context of the whole labouring class, by the multiplication of skilled jobs: ever more skilled jobs of ancient kinds (e.g. cabinet and carriage makers, upholsterers, tailors, shipwrights, coal hewers) as well as skilled jobs of rather new kinds (e.g. engine drivers and signalmen, engineers and boiler-makers). These classes of workmen waxed and prospered throughout our period and the wage differentials dividing them from their industrial inferiors, the apprentices and the un-skilled labourers in their trades, are reckoned to have been steadily increasing. This elastic stretching of the labouring strata and relative thickening of its middle and upper layers (most markedly in England; least markedly in poor, industri-ally retarded Ireland) did not however mean an absolute shrinkage in the number of the unskilled. Still so abundant was the supply of men ready for any coarse and/or casual labour that it was not yet a major management concern to find labour-saving means to replace it. Docks continued to be dug out, embankments to be heaped up, mainly by spades, shovels and barrows; minerals (especially coal) and ballast were still heaved and humped by human bone and muscle; buildings were erected by means familiar fifty years before; except where the most go-ahead farmers invested in mechani-cal mowers and reapers, etc., or hazardously experimented with steam traction engines and wire ropes, horses hauled ploughs and men wielded spades and sickles in immemorial fashion. Few, if any, classes of unskilled labour absolutely diminished during our period, and some new ones appeared.

The style and proportions of labour, skilled and unskilled alike, must therefore be judged to have changed little before the eighties; certainly to have given little sign before then of that swelling of white-collar and 'technical' grades, that swing away from preponderance of manual skills and wage differ-entials which has become the mark of our twentieth century. The changes that mattered from our point of view were not so much in the style of labour as in its hours—to a smaller degree, in its healthiness and physical safety—and, in the seventies if not much earlier, in the ways women and children were involved in it.

Women at Work

Women and children first. Women (very different from ladies!) continued to labour during the fifties and sixties in much the same ways and proportions as they had laboured from time immemorial. Release of the materfamilias from the necessity of daily labour was still the goal of the socially aspiring; introduction into the home of a first pair of subservient hands still the sign that the upward social journey had begun—except in the land of King Cotton, where paid baby-minders were an economic necessity to mothers who had no blood relations to call upon. These totals and percentages, extracted from Booth,[38] show what was happening:

Women and Girls (of 15+) 'At Work', 1851–1881
to nearest '00, and as % of female population

	1851	1861	1871	1881
England and Wales	2,348,200	2,709,900	3,118,200	3,393,600
	= 25·7%	= 26·3%	= 26·8%	= 25·4%
Scotland	403,700	424,100	444,200	491,600
	= 26·7%	= 26·3%	=25·3%	= 25·4%
Ireland	832,100	794,800	816,200	765,300
	= 24·7%	= 26·8%	= 29·1%	= 29·0%

Women continued to work in the same groups of trades: domestic service principally, with textiles manufactures and what Clapham called the 'stitching' and 'washing' industries close behind them; machine-made outer clothing of the familiar modern kind was still very rare and indeed, for all but the roughest workers, *infra dig.* until after our period; mechanical laundries likewise appear only later. Wherever there was improvement in the conditions and hours of labour, as for example in textile factories and mines (see below, pp. 137–9), women shared its benefits equally with the men; and the number of women occupied in the coarser kinds of manual labour (e.g. brickmaking, 'dust-sorting', regular fieldwork) fell off in most of England and lowland Scotland and Ulster.

The number of working women thus affected was however small compared with the mass of them, the style of whose occupations remained just as bearable or unbearable as it had been earlier on. In retail shops, in milliners' and haberdashers' workshops, in tailors' sweatshops, in every kind of piece-work done at home (and there was still an enormous quantity of it), in Black Country nail-making and chain-making, in the Potteries and in all their domestic services whether done from within or without the household, our period witnessed no significant change in either the quantity or quality of women's work; and the scores of sentimental writers who enthused about The Home and about woman's place within it must not be understood to have been describing a domestic state that was anything like normal for most of the working classes. The leaders of the Women's Rights movement knew well enough what the facts were and denounced the particularly cruel humbug of talking about 'Women's Place being in the Home' while there was actually a surplus of women in the population and while between 26 and 28 per cent of them, unlucky or outclassed in the competition for husbands, had to strive to be independent. Their efforts (assisted by intelligent non-feminist philanthropists like Shaftesbury) were in these early years aimed largely to create a larger range of employments in which women might respectably earn independent livelihoods and to establish such educational institutions as might qualify women for them; and those efforts were beginning to bear fruit by the seventies.

The proportion of females employed in drapery and dress shops certainly rose much faster than that of males between 1851 and 1881; but in the latter year there were still twice as many males as females. Smart confectioners' and tobacconists' shops were usually staffed by attractive young women; whose business however was credibly reported to extend to more personal matters than sherbets and cigars. German governesses not yet having come into vogue, and French ones being often considered improper, British ones still had it all their own way; but the supply continued so much to outrun the demand, that the governess's bargaining position remained lamentably weak. Female doctors remained rare birds until the eighties; the two of them known to have been practising in the sixties were accidents. Some educated women wrote for a living and some smart ones ran businesses, but there was nothing new in that. A fast increasing number taught; Booth's summary showed an increase from 67,000 in 1851 (0·73 per cent of the total female population) to 127,000 in 1881 (0·95 per cent)[39]; but half of this increase happened in the seventies. It was the same with what Booth classified as 'commercial occupations'; clerks and book-keepers mainly, the meagre mid-Victorian equivalent of our modern typist-secretary syndrome; their decennial increase between 1851 and 1881 was (in thousands) 0·1, 0·5, 1·8, and 6·4. Nursing (which, outside the workhouse, was increasingly a middle class affair) occupied 38,000 women by 1881, but that was less than fifty per cent more than it had occupied thirty years earlier. Accurate figures for employment in 'the oldest profession in the world' are unfortunately not available (I wonder if Booth put them into 'General Labour' or 'Indefinite'?) but it is clear from every relevant contemporary account that they were very large, and that moreover there was much casual or part time employment in this field as in others. But no evidence that I know of suggests that either a higher or a lower proportion of women were driven or choosing to earn a living that way.

'Domestic Service' was by far the largest female occupation and it is, of all the main mid-Victorian occupations, the one whose importance may be made most difficult for a modern reader to understand, because it has so nearly disappeared from the homes of our own day. At the 1961 census there were found to be no more than 103,000 resident domestic servants in England and Wales:[40] a tiny percentage of the employed population. The figures for our period were startlingly different, and were in themselves huge. A steady rise took the estimated percentage of this corps of the British labour force up from about 13 per cent in 1851 to its modern peak in 1891: nearly 16 per cent;[41] after which it fell off, though

not by much until the First World War. Most of these domestic servants (and the indoor ones were by no means the whole
of them) were females. For the very well-off, the 'paraphernalia of gentility' (to use Banks's splendid phrase) required
men too; footman, butler, grooms, coachmen, full-time gar-
deners etc.; but the cost of their wages rose all the time and
they never spread much beyond the country house (where they
might be legion: the Duke of Westminster still had over three
hundred at Eaton Hall—including the ground staff—in the
eighties) or the showy town mansion in Belgrave Square.[42]
The difficulties of knowing how many there were of each type
are increased by the whimsicalities of the census, which seems
to have been at its most confused and unreliable in handling
this category[43] (some householders may have been anxious to
be credited with more servants than they actually had, persons
who were actually servants may have been anxious not to be
thought so) and which, for example, although capable of
nicely discriminating the occupations of 'Fossils and Coprolite
Diggers and Dealers', lumped in 'Footmen' with 'Domestic
Indoor Servants'. A small extension of Banks's figures[44] shows
this latter category of male servants diminishing thus in
England and Wales, while the number of 'Private Coachmen',
the least dispensable of the male part of the paraphernalia,
rose:

Male	1851	1861	1871	1881
'Domestic Indoor Servants'	74,000	62,000	68,000	56,000
'Private Coachmen'	22,000	33,000	37,000	(The figures for this year are, according to Booth, p. 323, im-possible to disen-tangle.)

These figures are impressive as evidence of the richness of
the domestic equipment with which the wealthy surrounded
themselves (all those absurd footmen in Du Maurier's draw-
ings!) but they are not in themselves particularly large. The

really large figures are those of female domestics and allied occupations.

'Female Domestic Servants' and allied occupations[45]

England and Wales Females Indoors	1851	1861	1871	1881
under 15	61,000	87,000	111,000	99,000
over 15	723,000	894,000	1,124,000	1,170,000
Total	784,000	981,000	1,235,000	1,269,000
'Extras' (washerwomen, charwomen, etc.)	187,000	233,000	251,000	276,000
Grand Total	971,000	1,214,000	1,486,000	1,545,000
as % of total population	5·4%	6·1%	6·5%	5·9%
as % of female population	10·6%	11·7%	12·8%	11·6%

We may sum up the quantities of domestic service with these figures of Booth's, which are not much different from those in Deane and Cole, and which are better for our purposes for separating the sister kingdoms:

Domestic Service as occupying a % of the occupied population[46]

	1851	1861	1871	1881
England and Wales	13·3	14·6	15·8	15·7
Scotland	10·5	12·0	10·7	11·1
Ireland	10·4	13·3	15·2	18·0

Indoor Domestic Servants as a class, male and female alike, represented in 1881 one out of every twenty-two of the whole population of England and Wales. The proportion differed, of course, in the different parts of the country. 'Thus in London the proportion ... was one in fifteen, in Brighton one to eleven, and in Bath one to nine ...' The Registrar-General went on to comment apropos of the Female figures, that:

'Of females above five years of age, one in nine was a domestic servant ... and of girls between fifteen and twenty years of age no less than one in three was a domestic servant. Such, at least, was the case according to the returns; but ... there is reason to believe that a considerable number of servant girls who are not yet fifteen years old represent themselves as having reached that age, so as to be more readily taken into service.'[47]

Of the life of the female domestic servant, one can only say that it could be as disagreeable or as delightful as the atmosphere and management of the household dictated. Employers as a class held the whip hand, no doubt of that; although it seems sometimes to have pleased them to talk as if they didn't. They complained endlessly about dishonest servants, incompetent servants, expensive servants; *Punch* in the sixties and seventies, as it moved from its initial perky radicalism to heavy reflection of upper middle class manners, had endless fun with the theme of the cheeky or pretentious or grasping servant, and Banks has conclusively shown that the rising cost of servants became a more and more formidable item in the socially aspiring householder's budget. But this was not so much because servants' wages rose, as because a rising middle class standard of life demanded more domestic assistance. Female servants' wages did not in fact go up to any noticeable extent. (Male servants' did, and by the seventies all but the really wealthy or the determinedly ostentatious were looking for ways to reduce them by substituting, e.g. parlour maids for men servants, or by hiring instead of owning carriages.) Female servants' wages certainly did not go up by any more than the national women's wages average, and may have gone up less. Banks's digest of advertisements in *The Times* suggests that in the course of the fifties and sixties, cooks' wages went up from £15 to something over £19; housemaids' from about £11 to about £14; nursemaids (a puzzling leap here) from £11 to about £17.[48] There was no limit to what might be paid to the most skilled and modish ladies' maids, the most reliable and honest housekeepers at the top end of the scale; nor was there, alas, any limit at the other end to what might (or might not) be paid to the 'maid-of-all-work', the skivvy, who, having usually no bargaining power at all, and no potential protector nearer than the magistrate, might be paid next to nothing and told she was lucky to have a roof over her head; as, of course, to some extent she was! Unmarried or widowed women and girls of the lower classes (we will not for the moment consider the married ones) had to get jobs and become self-supporting somehow or other. A few industrial occupations offered them a chance (see below, p. 126). But to go into service was even in the industrial areas a usual, and elsewhere almost the only, chance.

For some, it must have had its rosy aspects. The girl with any kind of social ambitions, no matter how modest, might well feel that there was objective truth as well as subjective self-congratulation in the upper-class axiom that a period of service in a well-ordered home amounted to a valuable education in domestic science, and that her prospects of making in due course a good wife and mother would be bettered. Her prospects of marriage itself might be bettered by removal from a humble home and restricted acquaintance to the busy servants' hall in 'the big house'. She would also have the chance, not generally available to unmarried working women outside the cotton counties, to amass those savings which might so powerfully attract offers of marriage. The same vital prospect must, however, have seemed improvable by more modest moves; and research by Banks suggests that it was no myth that country girls' marriage prospects were substantially better in the towns than they were down on the farm. There was thus some positive inducement to 'go into service' (expressive phrase!) as well as harsh necessity. During our period, however, and for many years afterwards, the necessity remained real; and it was that element of necessity in the situation which gave employers such a strong bargaining position. Older female servants became so to speak 'broken in' to the yoke, which was eased emotionally for them by a secular cult of duty and loyalty, and rationally justified by the fact that the employer, like a baron in feudal times, provided some guaranteed protection and support in a tough anarchic world. For the younger ones, who still hoped for marriage and wished not to become disreputable, life was just as hard or soft as the employer wished to make it; and the prudent girl had to take what she was given, because of the dread consequences of being sacked without a reference.

The manufacturing industry in which females were most conspicuous was the textiles industry. Here are the best figures I can get of persons of all ages employed in textiles factories in the UK, and persons of all ages occupied in any branch or kind of textiles (i.e. factory or domestic) in Great Britain.[49]

	Employees in Textile Factories in UK in '000										Textiles Total Employment in GB in '000		
	Cotton		Wool		Flax		Jute		Silk		Total			Total
	M	F	M	F	M	F	M	F	M	F		M	F	
1850	142	189	72	82	21	48			13	30	597	—	—	—
1851	—	—	—	—	—	—	—	—	—	—	—	661	635	1,296
1861	183	269	81	92	27	67			16	37	772	612	676	1,288
1871	—	—	—	—	—	—	—	—	—	—	—	584	726	1,310
1874	188	292	125	135	52	120			13	32	957	—	—	—
1881	—	—	—	—	—	—	—	—	—	—	—	554	745	1,299

Several points clearly emerge from these not wholly satisfactory figures. First, the evident decline in the quantity of domestic and workshop textile industry. Around 1850 less than half the total of persons of all ages and both sexes occupied in textiles was working within factories. By the turn of the eighties, factory work accounted for more than three-quarters. A smaller proportion of males, and a much smaller proportion of females, was occupied with textiles at home or in small, often quasi-domestic, workshop processes. Second, it was only in woollen textile factories that females were not strikingly more numerous than males; which meant that the normal pattern of domestic life was rather different in Bradford from what it tended to be like in Oldham, Belfast or Dundee. Third, the silk industry was in bad shape. It proved quite unable to compete with foreign competition in most lines, and remained 'backward' compared with the others: the least mechanised and the least concentrated, though Macclesfield and Coventry remained big names in it, and the east side of London continued to shelter a large population of ill-rewarded silk weavers. What these figures cannot show is the quite dramatic decrease after 1870 in the number of girls employed in these industries. The number of them (though not their proportion of the occupied female population) was slowly mounting through the fifties and sixties. Then—no doubt mainly in consequence of the English and Scottish Education Acts of 1870–2—it fell by a quarter during the seventies. Since the proportion of children (mainly girls) employed in the booming Belfast linen industry actually continued to rise till the nineties, the fall elsewhere in the British Isles must have been the more marked. Even in its most advanced industrial sector, where one might have expected it to be most like the rest of the UK, Ireland pursued a singular course.

The only industry (for so it should be considered) in which the decrease of female and child labour was at all noticeable before the seventies was agriculture; and there its decrease came in the context of that general reduction of its relative importance already noticed (above, pp. 98, 99). Of course agriculture remained a vast business even in England and Wales, where the shrinking of its share of the whole economy was most marked. Its share of their employed population was shown by the decennial censuses to be falling, fastest in the sixties, from something over 20 per cent in 1851 to something below 12 per cent in 1881. The numbers employed remained huge: subtracting the 'Farmers and their Relatives' from Booth's agricultural totals, there are as many as 1,388,000 in 1851 and 1,023,000 in 1881, actually recorded as occupied in one sort or another of work on the land. Mechanisation accounted for some small part of this shrinking: steam-engines came all but universally to replace older hand- or horse-powered methods of threshing, and, where the ground was firm enough to stand them, took over a little of the ploughing too; mechanical mowers and reapers and root-cutters multiplied in the dearer-labour districts. More significant was the growth of some concern for the efficient use of labour, which increasingly interested farmers in the midland and northern countrysides as their surplus population, basic cause of the chronic underemployment of the rural labouring population since the later eighteenth century, removed itself to the booming industrial growth areas, and as the competition of those areas combined with the first flush of rural trades unionism from the later sixties to push wages up; though how much that unionism was really responsible for the rise in wages, is matter for dispute. Hours and conditions of work remained for men what they always had been: long and rough, though intermittent. Labourers were not paid for workless days of winter or bad weather. Perhaps the main change in the quality of their working life that would have impressed itself on them, was that there were, through most of the year, fewer women and children in the fields. Here are Booth's figures for young males (under fifteen) and all female agricultural labourers and shepherds (in '000s).[50]

	England and Wales		Scotland		Ireland	
	Males under 15	Females	Males under 15	Females	Males under 15	Females
1851	106	144	11	5	62	144
1861	119	91	11	6	35	70
1871	98	58	9	7	42	71
1881	68	40	6	7	17	36

Only in Scotland did the number of women given to full-time agricultural work not absolutely diminish. Their absolute decline elsewhere and proportionate decline everywhere was presumably due mainly to the farmers' increasingly efficient use of their adult male labour force and, as the years wore on, to the lessening of the need for the womenfolk to earn money as the menfolk came to earn more. The decline in the number of young lads towards the end of our period was more the result of the progress of quasi-compulsory schooling than anything else. The nefarious 'gangs' of women and, in Lincolnshire and East Anglia, children, rightly attracted a lot of attention in the later sixties, but they were not quantitatively significant.

Despite this substantial withdrawal from agricultural labour, the condition of mid-Victorian working women is best summarised as practically unchanging throughout our period. Few of the forms of labour then or later thought unsuitable for women were during this period excluded to them. Their exclusion from underground mining was nominally accomplished in 1842 and I am not aware of their definite disappearance from any other major field of labour until long thereafter. Most of the 'unsuitable' occupations continued to engage them until later (*much* later, in the cases of sweated clothing workers and chain-makers). The numbers occupied in all the many sides of servicing middle and upper class households and places of resort only increased. Labour saving machinery and appliances during this period seem to have touched only one of the working woman's staple occupations during our years, and that was sewing; the sewing machine when used in bulk by large capitalists turned workshops (unregulated) into factories (regulated), and when used at home by those who could afford one presumably enabled a woman to get through her work less painfully; though whether she got paid any more for her time is another matter. The basic fact is, that work-necessitous women throughout the mid-Victorian years remained a reservoir of cheap labour, wanted for a limited variety of employments (most varieties of unskilled working men's employments were also, let us remember, normally oversupplied) and absolutely without organisation or bargaining power. Very few of them, I conclude, had any choice but to take what they were offered.

Children at Work

Of working children nearly the same might be said. Our period did not make as much difference in their lives as either the preceding or the succeeding ones. The great scandals of the early textile factories—the scandals which had to a perhaps unfair extent monopolised this side of public concern during the twenties and thirties—were done with, the worst evils of long hours and geographical isolation were brought under public control by the early fifties. Under-tens were barred from underground employment in mines by Ashley's Act of 1842. Most middle and upper class sentiment was

Industrial Employment of under-fifteens, 1851-81 in '000s

Occupation		1851		1861		1871		1881	
		England and Wales	Scotland	England and Wales	Scotland	England and Wales	Scotland	England and Wales	Scotland
Agricultural labour and Shepherds	{ m	106	11	119	11	98	9	68	6
	{ f	13	4	6	2	4	3	2	2
Nurserymen and Gardeners	{ m	2	—	6	—	3	—	2	—
	{ f	—	—	2	—	—	—	2	—
Mines	{ m	32	5	40	5	36	7	26	5
	{ f	1	—	1	—	1	—	1	—
Quarrying and Brickmaking	{ m	4	—	6	—	6	1	4	—
	{ f	—	—	—	—	1	—	—	—
Building	{ m	10	1	12	1	12	2	11	2
	{ f	—	—	—	—	—	—	—	—
Machinery and Toolmaking	{ m	5	—	8	1	7	1	5	1
	{ f	1	—	1	—	1	—	1	—
Metal Works	{ m	18	2	25	3	21	3	13	2
	{ f	4	—	5	—	3	—	2	—

Occupation	Sex								
Earthenware	m	6	—	6	—	5	1	4	—
	f	2	—	3	—	3	—	2	—
Wood, Furniture and Carriages	m	8	1	6	1	6	1	4	—
	f	—	—	—	—	—	—	—	1
Textiles	m	68	14	66	8	63	9	61	5
	f	81	17	83	15	90	17	66	10
Dressmaking	m	20	3	18	3	13	2	9	1
	f	30	2	26	1	23	2	20	2
Food, Drink and Tobacco	m	4	1	5	2	1	1	4	1
	f	—	—	1	—	4	—	1	—
Printing, etc.	m	2	1	3	1	1	1	5	—
	f	—	—	1	—	—	—	1	1
Ships and Docks [in port]	m	43	4	33	3	42	6	47	7
	f	3	—	1	—	2	—	1	—
Wholesale and Retail in general	m	10	2	14	2	18	3	15	3
	f	2	—	2	—	3	—	3	—
General labour	m	14	1	14	1	22	1	13	1
	f	—	—	—	—	—	—	—	—
Domestic Service, in general	m	8	—	11	—	10	—	10	—
	f	62	8	88	9	113	8	100	7

already by the thirties in favour of children going to school rather than to work until they were at any rate nine or ten years old; herein going against the views, so far as they can be generalised, of many farmers and many labouring parents. Thus much was, from the child-protector's point of view, solid gain; as was the growth of a rich vein of sentimentality in the ordinary respectable novel-reading mid-Victorian's heart. But neither this sentimentality nor the regulative precedents already laid down were of sufficient power to prevail against the demands of the market, the administrative problems of the next stage of 'state intervention', and all the moral and economic interests comprised by 'the freedom of the subject', until the later sixties; when at last a new spate of child-protective legislation occurred. The fifties and the early sixties therefore must be considered a rather black phase in the history of child labour; a period during which there was, as the demand for it called more and more children into industrial and domestic service, retrogression from the narrow bridgehead established by the pioneer 'factory reformers'.

On pages 130–31 is a digest of Booth's figures for the employment of male and female under-fifteens in the more important branches in England and Wales and Scotland.[51] (The Irish figures are not strictly comparable, but the extent and nature of their difference can be easily imagined.)

These are but clumsy indicators; nevertheless their general drift is unmistakable. In only four of these major categories of occupations—the building industry, printing and allied trades, the merchant marine, and domestic service in all its varieties —was there not a decided decline in the numbers of under-fifteens by the time the 1881 census was taken; which must mean, since there is no ground for supposing that the numbers of young teenagers declined, that the numbers of younger children fell off very sharply indeed. But that was only after the second spate of factory acts and the education acts of 1870–2 had begun to take effect. In some of these occupations the 1861 census, in others the 1871 census, marked the peak of absolute numbers of children employed. One cannot too much emphasise that the fifties and sixties were not in general decades of liberation for working children. Nor is there any ground for thinking that conditions of employment improved for children in any greater measure than did those of adults. Factories where textiles were spun or woven were under inspection and to some extent (no doubt varying greatly from industry to industry, process to process, and place to place) safer and healthier to work in from 1833 onwards; but such factories were in those respects unique until the sixties, and whatever improvement there may have been by 1860 over what conditions had been like in 1830, the factory inspectors were still in the sixties encountering grim and ghastly industrial accidents and diseases even within their strictly circumscribed domain. (See below, p. 139.) The only other industry where the government inspector ever appeared before the sixties was coal-mining, and he was not able to do much there. School attendance was during our period not compulsory for any children except those 'half-timers' employed in the already mentioned textile factories; for whom, while they were between nine and thirteen, part-time schooling was nominally obligatory under the Acts of 1833 and 1844. Anyone with influence over neighbourhood or dependants could 'encourage' school attendance; we know that some industrialists went to a good deal of trouble and expense to do so, just as many squires and parsons did in the countryside. But the effects of such influence could not be more than piecemeal (see below, pp. 172-3). Schools, like churches and chapels, were often under-used. The ethos of genuine or would-be gentility which prevailed among big employers, who thought of themselves as a sort of industrial equivalent of the landed gentry, could not be relied upon to spread any distance beyond them; and it was the small employers, like the small landlords, who characteristically did the least for those who made them, relatively, rich.

Moreover, only a really tough and progressive employer was able to thwart his generally conservative workpeople's desires to put their children to work at the earliest possible moment; often using them as a means of resisting mechanisation. 'Good' coal owners tried to enforce the 1842 prohibition of children going underground, but children were, so to speak, smuggled underground to do traditional chores for years afterwards. The so-called Children's Employment Commission, painstakingly charting the whole painful field during the middle sixties, found that throughout the 'earthenware' and all but the most up-to-date parts of the metal-working industries, and indeed most workshop and domestic industries, workmen still insisted on their age-old right to hire child-labour to do the running and subsidiary work for them. The commissioners unhappily came to the conclusion that 'against no persons do the children of both sexes require so much protection as against their parents'. Throughout all arable districts outside Scotland, and wherever there was no upper class interest in preventing it, children were put to bird-scaring, horse-tending, and so on as soon as they could toddle. Scotland was interestingly different. There, through the countryside and country towns, the convention seems to have prevailed that all children below about ten attended parochial school from October to May. Parents did not expect them to contribute to the family budget; farmers did not reckon on having their help; there was strong social pressure to give elementary educational opportunity to everybody. Such opportunity, parents of the English labouring class, rural or urban, did not expect; nor had the convention much life remaining in it in Scottish industrial areas. In every industry throughout the UK that still relied, to whatever degree, on homework, children were still worked in the immemorial ways just as soon as they could learn dexterity and keep more or less awake; the Children's Employment Commissioners learnt that four or five was the usual age for children to take up full-time employment in the domestic branches of hosiery, lace and plaited straw manufacture. They did not begin so young in the Black Country, but, as Clapham said in a fine passage,

'The fact that a child started to earn relatively late was no safeguard against ignorance, overwork, degrading conditions or excessive hours. There were the wretched little mould-runners of the Potteries, hurrying with their loads for twelve hours a day in and out of temperatures of 100 to 120 degrees...; the child nailers in their "private houses"; the savage children of the brick-fields; the chain-smiths' boys distorted by wielding hammers too heavy for their strength.[52]

'In the ribbon trade of Coventry [reported an observant contemporary] three hundred boys are employed in turning hand-looms. The incessant whirl has so bad an effect on the head and stomach, that the little turners often suffer in the brain and spinal cord, and some have died of it. In one scutching-mill near Cork, six fatal cases and sixty mutilations have occurred in four years.... There is no doubt that a great deal of quiet murder, perfectly appalling when attention is called to it, is continually going on among the juvenile population.'[53]

And there were still plenty of climbing boys: no less than two thousand, it was reckoned in the year of the Second Reform Bill. Kingsley's *Water Babies* was a book of the sixties, not the forties.

Into this still horrid scene of child exploitation, so little changed in essentials from that of thirty, or, for that matter, three hundred years before, Parliament again probed during the sixties. The basic facts had changed hardly at all since they were first publicised on Shaftesbury's enquiries of the early forties; but Parliament and public alike were now ready, as they had not then been, to do something about them; and more manufacturers could manage without children. (The twenty-year gap between full knowledge of the facts and the start of effective action is very like that in the history of public health.) It seems unlikely that heightened sympathy for children was the main cause of this change of mind. More probable were, first, prosaic factors of technological progress, making the use of regiments of cheap infant and female workers increasingly uneconomical and avoidable, and second, experience of the falsity of all those fears of economic disaster which had gripped so many otherwise not inhumane minds during the first phase of factory legislation. Shaftesbury, still the ostensible leader of the movement, now found former adversaries like Sir James Graham and J. A. Roebuck supporting him. Opposition came more from lobbies of particular interests, on point of detail, than from representatives of alleged general principles.

So, during the sixties and seventies, the so far unprotected child workers of Britain (i.e. all those outside textile factories and coal mines) began to be protected against the consequences of their parents' necessitousness or cupidity. The starting age for underground coal work was raised in 1860 from ten to twelve. The protections given to children by the textile factory acts of the forties and fifties (e.g. total prohibition of under-nines, and no more than 'half-time' for those between nine and thirteen) were circumspectly extended to cover bleaching and dyeing works in 1860; lace works in 1861; a group of trades discovered to be particularly hard on young children (fustian cutting, paper staining, percussion-cap and cartridge making, match making, and pottery) in 1864; a much larger group of trades (some were specified, and more were brought in by the act's self-definition as applicable to any premises where more than fifty persons were engaged in a manufacturing process) in 1867; and in the same year, all and any trades carried on in 'workshops', which were so defined as to include, in the case of children employed by their parents, the children's own homes. This latter act was in practice weakened by a multitude of exemptions and administrative ineptitudes, some of which remained after the next big act in 1878; but whatever the law's continued weaknesses in respect of women workers, its regard for children was by that decade complete; for Parliament in 1870 formally accepted, and was not long after prepared to enforce, the principle that every child under the age of ten should go to full-time school. In the countryside especially that was a difficult notion to bring home to people; but there too the law's new care for the welfare and literacy of young children was felt, in the 1868 act which prohibited the employment of under-eights in the worst sort of agricultural gangs.

Improvements in Working Hours and Conditions

While industrially occupied children were thus more frequently singled out to receive the benefits of Parliament's
increasing concern for the health, morals and literacy of the
next generation, during the same years all workers of both
sexes began to benefit from Parliament's cautious willingness
to enforce minimum standards of health and safety, and even,
in a few rare cases, maximum hours. The textile industries remained the leaders in this latter movement, and they were
able to do so for the same reason that they had begun doing
so in the thirties and forties; viz. that, because the factories
could not be run without great quantities of female and child
labour, the adult males were able to get shorter hours for
themselves (which they could not have done if that had been
their one avowed object) by means of getting shorter hours
for the women and children. (Which is not to deny that they
may also have thought that women ought to be prevented from
long hours for their own and their families' sake.) The twenty
years' campaign for 'short time' had won them a sixty-hour
week in 1850. Parliament lowered it to fifty-six and a half in
1874. In practice that meant ten hours' work (excluding meal-
times) from Monday to Friday and six and a half hours on
Saturday. The Saturday half holiday, when the textile operatives first achieved it, had been their possession alone; but by
the seventies the same working week was becoming the regular
thing in all officially inspected workplaces, while most skilled
trades were getting theirs down (mainly by means of industrial
bargaining) to an even slightly shorter one. Our period thus
may be said to have witnessed a reduction of the hours of
factory and skilled workers of between half an hour and an
hour a day, and the achievement for most—perhaps all—
industrial workers of the Saturday half-holiday, during the same
years as the hours of labour prescribed for children (by the
end of our period, ten to fourteen) and for 'young persons'
(by the end of our period, fourteen to eighteen) in factories
and workshops generally were brought within certain limits
and beneath the scrutiny of the Home Office inspectorate.

Further small but regular and irrefragable measures of relief from toil were extended, first to office workers and then to workers in most commercial and industrial premises, by the so-called Bank Holiday Acts of 1871 and 1875, which secured holiday status for Boxing Day, Easter Monday, Whit Monday and the first Monday in August.

In recognising these undoubted benefits we must not however exaggerate their spread. The smaller laundries and workshops (usually something to do with dress; but also certain traditional Black Country trades) employing women only were actually exempted from the great consolidating act of 1878, and could still be worked all hours, under any conditions. Shop assistants were totally without official protection (though voluntary agreements by the better sort of shopkeepers to close early on Saturdays—e.g. at 6 or 7 p.m.—had here and there been happening since the later forties). So of course were all domestic servants (as they still are) and so was all unskilled and casual labour, which might have to work very long hours indeed, when it had work to do. So also, of course, was all 'self-employed' domestic labour, which it is especially important to remember, because the pittances for which its characteristic workers (needlewomen, box-makers, furpluckers, etc.) worked could only be gained by excessive hours; a twelve-hour-day for such wretched people was light!

If reduction of hours of labour was one very clear gain to a part of the labour force at work in mid-Victorian Britain, some progress in health and safety standards may have been another. Whatever there was of it was neither constant nor irreversible. A lightening of the burden of labour characterised some few trades, but of others increasing strain or unhealthiness was the mid-Victorian characteristic. Dr William Farr, the great sanitary statistician, was as sober as ever when he noted, in the early eighties, that 'our progress in the industrial arts has been accompanied by hecatombs of deaths'.[54] By no means always did mechanisation mean the lightening of labour. Of this good economic historians are well aware.

'The more extensive use of machinery meant that for many people work became noisier, hastier and more monotonous,

with fewer interruptions to provide relief.... In some industries the mechanisation of most processes left a few still
to be done by hand in conditions that were more arduous
than ever because of the mechanisation of the remainder.'[55]

Clapham gives as examples 'stoking and coal trimming in a
gale, or in the Red Sea; puddling, and all the exacting work
of blast furnace and steel furnace; the long day, heavy with
responsibility, of the signal man or the engine driver; and
scores of laborious and often dangerous tasks in gas works,
chemical works and engineering shops.'[56] Neither the hours nor
the safety of the working day of the swelling army of railway
workers were in any degree improved; 767 of them were
killed and 2,815 of them were injured in course of their work
in 1875. Not less than a thousand miners were killed each
average year—let alone injured.[57] The Alkali Acts of 1863 and
1874 had in view not the health of those who worked in the
factories so much as the health and comfort of those who
lived or worked near them; and not until later than our period
can they be considered, any more than the series of attempts
to control smoke nuisance going back to even before the
thirties, to have done any good. 'Fossy jaw' remained a
likely fate of all but child workers in phosphorus factories
after the 1864 Factory Act. Indeed, it was only child workers
whose health and safety was certainly benefited by the factory
acts just listed, and that only because they were taken right
out of some trades and half out of others. General industrial
health and safety could hardly deteriorate and might improve
wherever the inspectorate penetrated—as we have seen, its
empire became much extended towards the end of our period
—and good-hearted industrialists certainly went beyond the
very minimal sanitary and safety gestures required of them,
to make work on their healthier processes of production as
healthy as it could be. But neither the goodwill of the 'better'
sort of industrialists nor the limited jurisdiction of the inspectorate could make, until after our period, any impact on
the fundamental causes of Death's continuing Dance around
the scene of labour: the proliferation of moving parts of
machinery (which workers *would* be careless about); the sheer

biological or chemical deadlines of so many processes, sometimes not fully understood and always 'essential' to the finished product; and, beneath all, the desperation that drove people to put themselves and their children to even lethal work, for the sake of the bread they could for a while gain. I do not believe Dickens was exaggerating when he summarised the stricken Shoreditch woman's attitude as 'Better be ulcerated and paralysed for eighteenpence a day, while it lasted, than see the children starve'.[58]

In only two big industries may our period perhaps witness a decisive improvement in health and safety: the merchant marine, and coal-mining. Samuel Plimsoll's celebrated campaign between 1868 and 1876 aimed rather to improve and enforce existing law than to press Parliament to embark on a new line of legislation. Had the comprehensive Merchant Shipping Act of 1854 been scrupulously observed by all shipowners and masters and the Board of Trade, Plimsoll could not have found much to complain about. But of course it was, like every other early and mid-Victorian government's early steps in the interventionary direction, evaded and avoided and ignored to the maximum extent; therefore positive improvement had to wait until the legislation that followed Plimsoll's campaign in the early seventies. Improvement came by similar stages into the working life of the coal miner, which was becoming increasingly hazardous as mines were sunk deeper (pumping and hauling machinery made that possible) and opportunities for accidents multiplied. Acts of 1850, 1855, 1860 and 1866 piled up good provisions, but such improvements as they made to mine health and safety (e.g. in ventilation; miner's asthma began to diminish after 1855) seem hardly to have kept pace with the unceasing deepening of dangers, and it was not until after 1872 that the tide turned.

Poverty and Unemployment

The assumption about the occupied persons spoken of in this chapter so far has been that they were fully supported by their labour in regular work, and able to live by it. We turn in conclusion to the variety of classes of persons who were not able to live by labour. Of these there were three main groups: those whose wages when in work were adequate or more than adequate, but who were out of work through no fault of their own; those whose usual work was so ill-rewarded or irregular that they rarely drew adequate wages from it; and those who, for whatever reason, never had much or any work to do. Evidently we here are traversing a broad social spectrum: at one end, the skilled craftsman of some education and of perhaps intense respectability, thrown by technological change or trade recession out of work and unable even by strenuous 'tramping' to make a subsistence wage; at the other, the 'work-shy' (our word for him) or the loafer (their word), the professional criminal, the beggar. If such characters actually met—as they may well have done, in the common lodging houses where poor travellers and vagrants had to put up—they could not have liked one another, but they might have been conscious of sharing that which justifies their common treatment in these pages: existence on the rough underside of the mid-Victorian economy, where there was chronic un- or under-employment, chronically inadequate means of subsistence, and, in the last resort, only the Poor Law or 'private' charity or crime between you and starvation.

How large was this depressed social area? We cannot exactly tell. We have to believe where we cannot prove. There are good grounds for believing that it was of formidable dimensions. I am not thinking particularly of the volume of contemporary complaint and comment about the quantity of vagrancy, crime, pauperism, unemployment and want, though there was plenty of it. The social historian's first serious lesson is that volume of complaint about a social phenomenon is no accurate index of that phenomenon's actual size. The early and mid-Victorian rush to establish institutions to alleviate or prevent destitution and suffering may have meant, not that there was suffering and destitution to alleviate, but that society was becoming more worried or compassionate about it. Comment upon the numbers of beggars and street traders and so on in the streets of the big cities, of such a style as to imply

that there were more of them than ever before, may only have
meant that such characters now offended eyes to which they
had previously seemed innocent; or that, with the growth of
the cities, the beggar and street-trading population, growing
no more than proportionately, had through staying in the
same central districts come to seem more concentrated and
hence conspicuous. We rightly look to (for instance) Dickens
for the most incisive impression of what a 'rookery' (see
above, p. 49), was like, but we must not expect even Dickens'
uncannily accurate impressions to be equivalent to 'scientific'
quantifications of the proportionate weight of such places in
the social scene. Nor (for reasons which I hope to make clear)
were the accredited official quantifiers of mid-Victorian England entirely reliable. The Poor Law ones in particular were
myopic and narrow-minded. But when all is said that can be
said about the inadequacy of contemporary statistics and the
possibly misleading character of contemporary expressions of
concern, far too much firm evidence and plausible hypothesis
remains for us to doubt that when, for instance, John Bright
—who feared them—talked of 'the sunken sixth' or 'the
residuum' that formed the permanent hard core of this fluctuating understratum, he was talking about something very
real. We must now try to measure it, and understand how it
kept alive.

No scientifically approved measurements of the amount of
poverty (at any rate urban poverty) were made until twenty
years or so after our period, and the big question is, how far
were the conditions *then* quite incontrovertibly discovered to
prevaïl, better or worse than, or much the same as, those prevailing earlier on? The measurements I mean were of course
those made by Charles Booth and his investigating team in
London, and by Seebohm Rowntree a few years later in York.
Booth, Rowntree and co. concurred in the conclusion that,
in York and in industrial London, in the nineties, nearly 10 per
cent of the inhabitants were stuck in such poverty that their
families' combined earnings could not win the minimum
necessary for mere subsistence, and that nearly 20 per cent
more were only just able to subsist, without any margin to

protect them against accidents, misfortunes, etc.

Ashworth[59] summarises the grounds for thinking that this total of nearly 30 per cent of the London and York population, in what Booth and Rowntree called primary or secondary poverty, may not have been fairly representative of national urban conditions: Booth may not have been justified in thinking that working class families with children of school age (the families his team sampled) were representative of the working class as a whole (because children below the earning line were a drain on resources); neither London nor York can be considered fairly representative of towns and cities as a whole. London must, for sure, be considered an exceptional case. Perhaps York is too; although it might well have represented conditions in all the smaller, older towns and cities, and perhaps also in all country towns whether new or old, in which I don't know how large a proportion of the working class lived. But Ashworth may be on shakier ground when he goes on to suggest that 'it is likely that the submerged tenth ... far from providing a surviving illustration of what had been general conditions earlier, had undergone some decline in their average material standards. There can have been few times when the lot of the very poor was more miserable than in the early years of the twentieth century.' Presumably he is comparing these years with the last quarter or thirty years of the nineteenth century, the years when real wages went up so unprecedentedly and by so much. Whether or not his comparison with that period is valid, I see no reason for supposing that the poor and the very poor, even in the early years of the twentieth century, were worse off than they had been during at any rate the years 1850–70. (The years 1870–5 *were* different: see above, pp. 111–14.) Coal, the indispensable means of healthy warmth in winter, may have been proportionately dearer by the early nineteen hundreds, and rents certainly were. But the quality of the cheaper foodstuffs consumed by the poor was liable to be low at both epochs, the work opportunities seem to me unlikely to have been significantly different, and the 'welfare' provisions of both Poor Law and philanthropy were certainly more generous and sensitive by the nineties and the early nineteen hundreds. Add to that the hard evidence of the real wages indices and Booth's own opinion that a similar survey in our period would have shown 'a greater proportion of depravity and misery than now exists, and a lower general standard of life',[60] and you are left with no firmer ground for supposing that the Booth and Rowntree percentages may not be taken as representative of *our* period than the feeling, natural in each successive generation of a developing and enrichening society, that 'this is so bad, things cannot have been worse earlier'. But the fact is that they can, and often were! Booth himself passed for a humane and considerate man, but what he thought tolerable for independent subsistence was already seeming almost intolerably low a generation later.

I conclude that there can well have been, through the fifties and sixties, at least as much rather painful poverty as Booth and Rowntree proved to exist in the nineties: i.e. affecting about 30 per cent of the population. And that is a sound start towards correcting the notion that the mid-Victorian years were to any great extent less hungry than the thirties and forties. Whatever rewards life could hold for the more fortunate of the labouring classes, the skilled and semi-skilled labourers (who comprised about three-fifths of the adult male labouring population), it only held them *in good times*; and there was at all times this permanent residuum beneath, for some of whom life was permanently hungry and brutish, and for others of whom life was, according to the ebb and flow of prosperity, intermittently anxious and deprived.

When however we seek to take the measures of that part-permanent, part-fluctuating residuum, we are met by great difficulties. The former was very largely, and the latter was partly, created by what we nowadays simply call 'unemployment', and of that there was then no accurate count taken; some figures exist, from which suggestive conclusions can be drawn, but they do not take one far. Similarly suggestive figures can be drawn from the rather unsatisfactory statistics issued by the Poor Law authorities and the exceedingly unsatisfactory figures put out by charity organisers, upon whose mutually supporting aid the victims of unemployment had to call. I shall summarise these figures as best I can but it is beyond my powers (and perhaps beyond anyone's powers) to magic them into the kind of firm significance that would make their meaning unmistakable.

For unemployment in our modern understanding of it there were no official statistics. One might almost say that there were no official statistics for it because officialdom and the prevailing social and economic orthodoxies refused to take it seriously enough to justify their collection. The persistence, for more than shortish periods of slack trade, of some painful quantity of unemployment among those whose will to work (if work could be found) was scarcely disputable, was a fact recognised and faced squarely by only two groups of people: socialists, who expected nothing better from capitalism; and unionised workers, who might or might not be socialists, but who knew from experience about unemployment and who took prudent steps to avert its calamities. Industrialists in trades subject to fluctuations, and farmers subject to the régime of the seasons, took it for granted that work and wages would rise and fall from time to time; but, for all their closer knowledge of the facts, they seem on the whole to have shared the assumptions of the propertied class in general: first, that the trouble with most of those who said they could not find work was that in fact they did not much want to find it; and second, that for those who honestly did want to find work, work was in fact waiting if only they would have the guts to get to it. In both of these assumptions lay much rigour, but neither was as inhumane or wholly unreasonable as the instinctive reactions of a sentimental modern welfare-state-beneficiary suggest. There is indeed no reason for supposing that the proportion of 'work-shy' was larger then than before or since, but Mayhew and his slumming emulators proved what longer-focused observers had long alleged, that the institutions and conventions of mid-Victorian society offered rich pickings to those who dared to operate without benefit of guaranteed legality. The myriad institutions for the relief of want and destitution could give at least subsistence to the hordes who, without going beyond the law, were ready to scrounge all they could. It was a constant complaint of the social policy makers of our time, as it had been of the period immediately preceding, that life was indeed harder for those of the 'poor' who tried to keep going independently than for those who, having less shame or weaker moral fibre, settled for 'sponging' on society. What this meant in terms of numbers and of proportions, it is absolutely impossible to say. Mayhew's ramified analysis of the classes of 'professional beggars' and 'cheats', and his collaborator Andrew Halliday's pages on the sub-class of writers of fraudulent begging-letters and advertisements, gives one's imagination something to go on. There is plenty of evidence that the Poor Law, far from being universally a thing of heartlessness and terror to the poor, was in *some* areas rather the opposite: an institution which could be relied upon, and not in hard times only, for at least subsistence and possibly for what was, relatively speakingly, luxury. Poor Maggie, Little Dorrit's protégée, who encountered such Elysian comfort and care in a public institution— presumably a workhouse infirmary—that she ever thereafter classified unusually nice experiences as 'hospitally', was expressing a truth.

But it was of course a truth of two edges, and the controlling oligarchies of mid-Victorian Britain gave themselves away by concentrating attention on only one side of it. What was the quality of life outside the workhouse and the sick-ward, if the workhouse and its sick-ward could seem so much more eligible? The policy-makers and public pronouncers thought too much of the 'moral weakness' which inclined sub-respectable people to rely upon the Poor Law etc.; they thought too little of what the conditions of life must have been, that made so many seem 'morally' so 'weak'. The same rigorousness, not in itself unreasonable or uncharitable but carried too often to an extreme pitch which made it so, underlay the other general assumption of the propertied classes, that work *was* available, somewhere, for all who truly sought it. Of course it was. But it was often at the other end of the country or on the other side of the earth, and it was often of a kind to which not every man or woman could easily adapt. Emigration, whether of Dorset labourer to Lancashire, Cornish miner to Northumberland, Highland crofter to Clydeside, Thames ship-builder to Tyneside, or the Englishman, the Scotsman or the Irishman to America or Australia, required positive moral strength and a willingness to do violence to all those traditional affections, loyalties, and attachments upon which the mid-Victorian moralist, in any other context, set peculiar binding value. Here, again, I find it difficult not to detect in the orthodox talk about emigration—of which there was a very great deal in our period—a kind of 'double-think' that may have been unconscious but was also rather convenient and comfortable. (I am not saying we are nowadays any better about this sort of thing.) On the one hand, the working man was encouraged to be loyal and trusting towards his employers and superiors, to love his locality and his country; on the other he was urged boldly to tear up his roots and get out of it when it (which may be to say, those who controlled its resources) became incapable of offering him the means of living by his own labour. That such large numbers of working folk did nevertheless tear up roots and emigrate to overseas (about 2,883,000 are reckoned to have left the UK between 1853 and 1880;[61] while the quantities of country folk moving into the town were of course enormous) perhaps says as much about their moral fibre as it does about their view of what life offered them if they stayed where they were born. Confronted with local unemployment—as indeed, with labour troubles of any kind—the orthodox at once recommended emigration, and accounted for there not being even more of it by some sort of moral feebleness in the unemployed. Therein they certainly tended to expect too much of the poor and ignorant. But they can hardly be held to have been wholly unreasonable; the grass *was* greener in the next field.

The prevalence and force of these assumptions about unemployment made the bulk of the propertied oligarchy incurious about its causes and character. It held them to the supposition that in normal times (and they believed that times were normally normal: anything but famine, whether of potatoes or raw cotton, was normal to the orthodox economist) anyone who could not for more than a short, perhaps 'transitional', period live by his own labour was lazy or incapable, and that society was under no obligation to do more than provide a minimal and morally bracing machinery for keeping such alive. Unemployment was however a much more serious problem than that! The trade unions knew it to be so, with their elaborate long-standing arrangements for out-of-work pay and for helping members in an under-employed part of the country to find work elsewhere. And in fact employers in seasonal or otherwise fluctuating industries knew it to be so too, and showed that they knew it by insisting, in the face of all the arguments and protests of Somerset House, on retaining throughout our period the use of Poor Law out-relief as a kind of dole to keep their labour force alive during lean times when that labour force had to be put on short time, or entirely laid off.

How much unemployment was there? Our only reasonably hard figures come from the records of certain well-organised trades unions which supported their members during periods of unemployment and kept careful account of what went on. Here is the latest recension of the figures of those which kept such accounts:[62]

1851	3·9	1860	1·9	1870	3·9
1852	6·0	1861	5·2	1871	1·6
1853	1·7	1862	8·4	1872	0·9
1854	2·9	1863	6·0	1873	1·2
1855	5·4	1864	2·7	1974	1·7
1856	4·7	1865	2·1	1875	2·4
1857	6·0	1866	3·3	1876	3·7
1858	11·9	1867	7·4	1877	4·7
1859	3·8	1868	7·9	1878	6·8
		1869	6·7	1879	11·4

For not many years are these figures of skilled men's unemployment severe. The question however is: to what extent do they, mere indicators, under-indicate the *total* quantity of unemployment? Their value as indicators is undoubted; when skilled men in a random variety of trades were out of work, other skilled men and most unskilled men were surely out of work too. One thing is certain; these figures grossly under-indicate the actuality. They must be allowed to serve well enough as indicators of the fluctuations from time to time, of the booms and slumps in trade (in particular, the peaks of employment in 1853–4, 1864–6, 1871–5). When these men were doing well, most employed men were likely to have been doing well. But even as indicators of nothing more than the rate of employment among their own kind, they are suspect. Clapham, for example, remarks on the Amalgamated Tailors, who never showed an annual average of more than 0.6 per cent unemployed from 1869 to 1886, and who showed for the trough year 1879 'the grotesquely cheerful figure of 0.46'.[63] One cannot but feel sure that the Amalgamated Tailors were misrepresenting the state of their trade! But none of these figures purported to show how much employment there was in less skilled and in unskilled occupations. Ashworth admirably sums up the inference: these figures, he says, take no account of the large number of casual workers, general labourers, petty hucksters, people of no regular trade, and domestic outworkers. When Baxter was calculating the National Income, he wrote

'None but those who have examined the facts can have any idea of the precariousness of employment in our large cities, and the large proportion of time out of work, and also, I am bound to add, the loss of time in many well-paid trades from drinking habits. Taking all these facts into account, I come to the conclusion that for loss of work from every cause, and for the non-effectives up to sixty-five years of age, who are included in the census, we ought to deduct fully 20 per cent from the nominal full-time wages.'

Other contemporary statisticians thought that his 20 per cent was far too big an allowance, 'but', concludes Ashworth, 'there can be little doubt that he was much nearer the truth than they'.[64] That his estimate was at once denounced as extravagant is not surprising. It presented believers in free enterprise and progress with suggestions about their system which must have been unpalatable. But such indeed seems to have been the condition of life among the lower-class inhabitants of at any rate the larger towns and cities. Overcrowded in their rooms and houses, unwisely or improperly nourished, spending far more on drink than was good for them, easy prey to illnesses and infirmities unending, prematurely ageing, and hampered in their efforts to find work by what was usually an inefficient labour market—what chance had they of getting or holding secure jobs?

Some of the chronically un- and under-employed formed the 'residuum' which social observers in the sixties joined in tracing at the bottom of society. That there was a great mass of residual poverty, a social sink into which every kind of incapable, misfit, wreck and malingerer settled, physically located in the most dingy and derelict parts of the towns and cities, was more common knowledge than was the heterogeneity of its actual human contents. Because some such were undoubtedly undeserving, others became unfairly branded as such. Those who spoke of 'the residuum' implied that all its members were worthless or useless. Many no doubt were. But not all the worthless and useless lived hard, and it was, alas, all too easy for the worthy and would-be useful to be forced down into the 'residuum'; where, being in it, they might become of it. Qualifications for membership were economic (inadequate or non-existent earned incomes) or moral (loss or absence of the power or will to be respectable) or both. Some of its members earned regular money that could, in the hands of a conventionally respectable person, have supported respectability: e.g. successful but socially unambitious criminals, unsteady artisans, the neighbourhood shopkeepers and the proprietors of its pubs and ginshops and saloons. Some earned regular money that could in no sense keep them alive, let alone provide respectability: e.g. the lower sort of washerwomen, slopworkers, outworkers for milliners, haberdashers, boxmakers, toymakers, etc. Some experienced bouts of good money alternating with bouts of no money: e.g. the coarser sorts of general and/or seasonal labourers and, one presumes, those much-talked of 'loafers' who decorated the rims and intersections of the criminal and sporting worlds, who mysteriously gathered wherever there was trouble or potentially profitable excitement and whose 'one economic virtue was that of being "on the spot"'.[65] Thomas Wright found a revealing cross-section of the residuum in 'Our Court', when temporary unemployment, demolitions for railways, and the necessity of living near a prospect of work forced him to take his family there, sometime in the sixties.

'Most of the men call themselves labourers; but there are a number of them who are never in regular employment, and who can do very little in the way of "odd jobs" of an honest character, as they do not generally rise till ten or eleven o'clock in the day, are to be seen loafing about street-corners during the afternoon, and in public-houses until a late hour at night ...'

They seemed to make some money by 'farmyard poaching', and their womenfolk and children by taking in washing, by charring, and (in the season) by hop-picking; but even so they all had an amount of money to spend on drink and tobacco and gambling that the would-be respectable Wright could not for the life of him explain. Then there were slopworkers, 'two prematurely aged, careworn women'; a consumptive dying tailor; two cheerful and shameless young tarts; and a 'wild Irish' family of what Wright called 'the "poor-but-honest" class, being hawkers, rag and-bone collectors, baked-potato sellers, and the like ...'. He summed it up as

'... a place of so pitchy a nature, that few may come in contact with it without being in some way defiled; a place where crime and misery jostle each other, and disease is rife; a place in which any latent disposition to depravity and vice in either man or woman, will be fostered and developed, and where childhood must be well guarded indeed if it be not corrupted. Yet, with all these drawbacks, a residence in it has not the single advantage which it might naturally be expected to offer—of cheapness ...'[66]

His four-room house cost him 6s 6d a week; or would have done, had he not let half of it. That he mentions only one Irish family suggests that his court was a relatively superior kind. H. M. I. Fitch provided this glimpse of the lowest, Irish, level of the Leeds residuum in 1870, living a 'life of indigence, squalor and hopelessness, which it is difficult for comfortable people to conceive. It is known that there are hundreds of families, whose average income from all sources does not exceed 1s per head per week ... There are rag-pickers, chip-sellers, and other persons of nondescript occupations; and there are hundreds of children in Leeds, the main preoccupation of whose life is to follow coal wagons about, with an old pail or basket ...'[67]

These last-mentioned were occupationally close to the tribe of 'followers-up' who trailed dustcarts. All these of the residuum, and all those above it who also suffered or were willing to admit that they suffered from inadequate or temporarily lapsed wages, had to rely for subsistence on each other, on charity, on 'crime', and on the Poor Law.

About the extent to which the destitute relied upon each other, there is little that can usefully be said. Superior class observers and historians of the social scene too often underestimate the importance of this factor, because it is the effect of a way of life rather alien to their own: the more communitarian, less calculating, some say more hearty and generous life-outlook of the classical close-living labouring class. It may indeed be thought that myth mixes with historical fact in this picture of proletarian virtue, and it is certainly an agreed point among both 'pro-' and 'anti-proletarian' historians and observers that none can be harder on the working class than the working-class man who has just managed to get out of it. Whether what is said is equally true of the agricultural and the urban working classes is also open to doubt. Both rural and urban mid-Victorian poor, when really hard pressed, sometimes showed a readiness to consign their, so to speak, family cast-offs—aged and domestically useless parents, crippled or imbecile children—to the care of the public authorities, which could shock superior class observers. Nevertheless there remain some reasons for thinking that the poor's willingness to help the poor was a significant factor in their means of living through our period. Sociological investigation seems to prove beyond all shadow of doubt that removal of the 'slum-dweller' (implying no moral judgment) to either middle-class respectability or (in modern terms) the open-aspect, low-density council estate, is found by those who experience it in their own persons and generation to exact a penalty of relative loneliness and isolation. Whatever the gains in social standing and self-esteem and economic opportunity, there seems often to be felt a painful loss of the mutual support and encouragement which belonged, with all its faults of non-privacy and roughness, to the tight-packed, open-doored street community life. This uncomfortable transition is felt and observed in our times, when such social movement is much more common than it was a hundred years ago. There being no reason to suppose that slum life was any different in quality then from now, and there being all too much reason to suppose that the quantity of people experiencing it was larger then than now, we could conclude that mutual support was a factor in the life of the poor by no means to be left out of account, even if we did not have several sorts of testimony to its vigorous existence. There is no more reason to doubt than to overstress the testimony of the novelists who made the mutual reliance of the poor upon the poor so common and admirable a feature of working-class life.

Philanthropy and Poor Relief

To distinguish between the 'unorganised' charity shown to one another to this unmeasurable extent by the poor, and the 'charity' that was organised to a more measurable extent by the less poor for the poor's benefit, may be morally indefensible but it is practically inevitable. No more than in earlier times could the mid-Victorian poor survive without the aid of charity. It had, in its innumerable forms, become part and parcel of their way of life and of their view of life. This was no more their doing than that of their social superiors. Through several centuries the better-off classes had developed and cultivated an ethos of what may, without disparaging intent, be called 'prudential charity'. They had put rather surprisingly large sums of money into the establishment of institutions variously designed to relieve the most unbearable and cruel pressures of poverty, to form in the lower orders a law-abiding and politically quietist frame of mind, and to open to the more capable or morally deserving of them some means of self-elevation: doles, food and clothing charities, almshouses, hospitals (in every meaning of that word), schools. ... The prudential element was clear but so were the philanthropic and christian ones, and it seems no more reasonable to depreciate the reality of the later element in the history of British philanthropy than to deny the presence also of the former. By the early nineteenth century the workings and, so it appears, uninterrupted growth of this impulse or convention of institutionalised charity (i.e. all the charity that was embodied merely in the passage of money or material from hand to hand) had covered the British Isles with a haphazard network of institutions, the more recently established of which were what the historian of English philanthropy identifies as charities of the 'associated' style. They were distinguished from the older foundations by the degree of active involvement required of the charitable, consisting typically of a governing board, council or committee which maintained a running interest in the institution (instead of leaving it to the law and lawyers), changed its policy if necessary and (usually) enjoyed prime rights of patronage to its benefits. To this pattern of charitable institution, which remained in full vigour throughout our period, evangelicalism had more recently added a still more personally involved pattern of charitable activity, which committed the charitable not merely to some standing managerial and financial responsibility but to personal charitable activity; to the expenditure of time and effort as well as, or even instead of, money. From its beginnings among the evangelically (I use the term loosely enough to include Quakers and pietists in general) affected religious public, this style of charity—herein following the course prescribed by its predecessor styles—became a standard one for the merely respectable as well as the distinctly religious, and moreover for the religious of all denominations; 'Tractarians' and other high church people practised it during our period as well as 'Evangelicals', and during the last quarter of the century one sees it practised by avowed agnostics and others whose motivation must have been completely different from that of its religious inventors.

Thus there was in the British Isles, by the middle of the nineteenth century, a great quantity of charity, if one may thus coarsely speak of it. There were endowed charitable foundations—schools, doles, alms-houses, etc., like Hiram's Hospital—which had become more or less petrified in forms generally unsuitable for nineteenth-century advantage, and were steadily being adapted for modern use by the operations of the court of Chancery and successive bodies of Charity Commissioners. There were 'associated charities', some (like the Foundling and Magdalen Hospitals) quite old, others (like Andrew Reed's chain of asylums for orphans and imbeciles) of contemporary foundation. And there were literally innumerable charities of the 'do-it-yourself' kind, from the tiny off-shoots of small independent chapel communities and country parochial hierocrats, to the highly organised branches of regional or national associations, with paid 'professional' managers. All of this charitable enterprise and generosity was meant to 'help the poor' and that it played a very large part in the lives of 'the poor' there can be no doubt.

How far it 'helped' them, and to what extent it was inefficient, were however questions that much bothered the mid-Victorian public, and that now bother historians. For one thing, this mass of charity had developed and become distributed unsystematically about the kingdom. It could be weak where most needed, super-abundant where most dispensable. The older the city, the likelier it was to own a comprehensive range of charities. The larger the proportion of middle- and upper-class citizenry, the more abundant the supply of men and women—especially women—with time on their hands and a desire—perhaps conscientious, perhaps not—to use it for charitable objects. While the newer and rawer industrial areas (e.g. the greater part of the Black Country, the Welsh valleys, the hosiery counties, the Durham mining districts, Thames-side below the Tower) managed as best they could by means of charitable self-help and whatever crumbs came from the sparse local representatives of the professional and landed classes, the City of London boasted an extraordinarily varied, ancient and opulent apparatus of charities, quite disproportionate to local need. So also the fashionable areas of prosperous cities produced battalions of the charitably minded, whose energies and aspirations could issue in little local utility and might issue in substantial local mischief. About the Dean Village, a picturesque slum within easy reach of Edinburgh's West End, we hear in the evidence offered to the Dilke Commission in the early eighties that it had been 'for very many years a favourite field for what is called missionary enterprise; all the churches have been attending to it . . ., but', concluded the witness, 'they did little or nothing for the physical condition of the locality . . .'[68] The poor of central and western London, it was universally acknowledged, were corrupted by the quantity of rather indiscriminate charity poured upon them. In an ancient cathedral city like Lichfield (where there was by the end of the century nearly £4,000 to distribute annually among the eight thousand inhabitants!)[69] or in an ancient industrial area like Spitalfields, which had been 'worked' and 'improved' by philanthropists for several centuries, the quantity of loaves and fishes waiting to be handed to the properly qualified (i.e. locally resident) applicant was vast. Spitalfields would have been no different in the fifties. Where such bounty could be had for the tactful asking, there seems never to have been any lack of tactful askers. Active reform-minded clergymen, making a clean sweep in such situations, regularly reported on the loss of communicants that followed the cutting-off of supplies traditionally distributed to same. The self-reliant artisan Thomas Wright commented adversely on the

'. . . many of the casually employed classes, and of the poorer kinds of regular labourers, and others who are not poor, who habitually prey upon charity, ordinary or special. To these pauper-souled cormorants the bread of charity has no bitterness, and they seek it with a shameless, lying perseverance. They are aware of the existence, and understand the intentions, constitution, and rules, of every local charity, temporary or permanent. They experience no reluctance or sense of shame in appearing before boards of committees, and tell their tales of woe with a glibness and detailed suitability to the resources of the particular charity invoked that *should* excite suspicion; and knowing 'the ropes', they resort to scenic effects if the agents of charity are sent to visit them in their places of abode ... It is these self-degraded dwellers on the threshold of professional mendicancy who in times of special distress among the working classes chiefly profit by the funds which a British public never fails to subscribe.'[70]

The most conspicuous of those funds during our period was the huge one of more than a million pounds raised to relieve destitution caused in Lancashire by the shutting off of supplies of raw cotton during the American civil war. Contemporaries then and historians since have agreed that it was on the whole honestly, humanely and economically administered. In those respects it would seem to have been unusual. Emergency and hardship funds, elicited usually by severe winters, especially slack trade and industrial disasters, were often credibly alleged to have been maladministered for the benefit more of the 'undeserving' than the 'deserving'. I know of no critical examination of one during our period that would conclusively prove the point; but we know more than enough about the analogous Mansion House Funds of the eighties and nineties! That sort of wholesale charity was, to use the Victorians' word for it, 'demoralising' in an obvious sense, and the imperceptive or careless lack of discrimination which made it so was under attack from the late eighteenth century onwards; but with no very marked effect.

The more deliberate sort of face-to-face charity typified by the conventional good works of the ladies of 'the big house' in the countryside could be considered 'demoralising' in another sense, which had equally been under attack from the time of Malthus. More likely to be discriminating, it yet encouraged subservience, docility and stagnation. I for one can hardly doubt that both the countryside ruling classes and all but the largest-scale, most successful employers of labour in the built-up areas instinctively preferred the system of low wages plus out-relief and charity to the idea of wages high enough to make the Poor Law redundant and charity dispensable; but that did not stop them adopting the language of individual self-reliance which only made complete sense if coupled (as in the United States it more nearly was) with high wages. So the British labouring classes caught it both ways. They were urged to be independent but denied the means of being permanently so, and charity was *in effect* (which is not to say, by conscious or discreditable intention) an integral part of the practical system of social subordination. The relief of destitution by means of charity (whether private or institutional) went along with the relief of it through the Poor Law, and so closely were the two sides of the operation connected in the Victorians' minds that it would be difficult to say that the latter held a more 'official' or 'mandatory' character in their thinking than the former. Whenever destitution was under discussion, it was *assumed* by all propertied parties that whatever might be the local deficiencies of the Poor Law (and its operations varied vastly from Union to Union), they would be supplied by local charity. The generality and depth of this assumption, which rested on and embodied the conventional ideal of the British christian citizen, independent-minded but socially responsible, is indicated by the fact that about 1870, after thirty years of 'New' Poor Law practice, there evolved, both within the Poor Law department and in the world of social theory and action without it, a 'revised code' of Poor Law operation by which the long-recommended cessation of out-relief was proposed to be rigorously enforced, and all of its recipients made over to an improved and efficiently organised system of charity. The attempt was only partly successful. Its central column broke on the same rocks of philanthropic free enterprise and competition which had foiled all attempts (e.g. Dr Chalmers's) to clean up the business earlier on. But it was very seriously made, and the Poor Law and 'private' charity were more closely associated after 1870 than before.

Just how much charity was annually dispensed—in what proportions, area by area—and with what social effect, are questions to which only the vaguest answers can be given. Estimates of the incomes and expenditures of the most conspicuous, the metropolitan charities, were often made but the same lack of co-ordination, the same free-for-all individualism, which frenzied the would-be organisers of *laissez-faire* philanthropy also effectively obstructed the enquiries of the would-be accountant. There seems no reason to doubt the figures produced by a Royal Commission on the *City* of London's Parochial Charities, showing that they had increased their collective annual income from about £67,000 in 1865 to about £100,000 ten years later; but they were a peculiar little lot.[71] One not implausible estimate of the sum devoted to charity in the metropolis *circa* 1870 was Hawksley's, of between five and a half and seven millions a year. A careful *Synopsis of Reports of* some *of the Metropolitan Charities* (excluding all the City of London ones, all the City Companies, and all strictly parochial ones, besides all whose accounts were nonexistent or unintelligible) calculated an annual income of just over two millions: two millions for the relief of want and suffering in London, 'independently of legal and local provision to an amount hardly calculable'.[72] The total is utterly incalculable. I do not see how the most zealously quantifying historian can hope for exact knowledge about more than the central core of open, advertising, 'associated' charities—the sort which was able to be examined in the *Synopsis* mentioned above. Countless little local charities carried on their business quite out of the public eye. The more 'private' they were in character or management, the less likely were they to invite or be open to critical scrutiny; the highly individualist Dr Barnardo's troubles epitomised a kind of problem and unpleasantness which was forever bothering charities dominated by particular individuals. The legion who made livings or parts of livings out of charity, and whose private interests were all against critical scrutiny, included not only the recipients (whose views were immaterial) but also the 'professional' administrators and organisers: secretaries, managers, visitors, missionaries and so on. There can be no doubt that participation in the running of charities was a useful means of livelihood for thousands of mid-Victorians, and that it was a lush pasture for the climber, the hypocrite, the incapable and the crook as well as for the genuinely businesslike and well-intentioned. And beyond this clouded world of more or less organised charity, the wealth and works of which we shall never exactly understand, there was the sometimes deliberately concealed charity of those 'little nameless unremembered acts of kindness and of love' shown by the better-off towards those who aroused their compassion. All one can say about the quantity of the incalculable side of charity is that there is no reason to suppose that it was increasing at any slower rate than the side which can be calculated.

By way of contrast, the sum spent on the relief of destitution, etc., through the 'official' channels of the English Poor Law is exactly known.

Gross Expenditure on Poor Relief in England and Wales, 1850–80 (to nearest '000) [73]

[including Metropolitan Asylums Board, 1867 ff.]

1850	5,400	1866	6,440
1	4,960	7	6,960
2	4,900	8	7,500
3	4,940	9	7,670
4	5,280	1870	7,640
5	5,890	1	7,890
6	6,000	2	8,000
7	5,900	3	7,690
8	5,880	4	7,660
9	5,560	5	7,490
1860	5,450	6	7,340
1	5,780	7	7,400
2	5,080	8	7,690
3	6,530	9	7,830
4	6,420	1880	8,000
5	6,260		

Such was the amount of public money raised (over 90 per cent of it, throughout our period) locally, by the poor rate. It was certainly less than the amount annually expended by charities; it may have been less than the amount annually subscribed by individuals to charities. Its increase during the later sixties (the 1863–4 figures were forgivably inflated by the Lancashire cotton famine), which stimulated much hysterical comment and twisting of statistics to justify a more economical and tough line, was in fact due not so much to an increase in the proportion of pauper population (see below, p. 167) as to the inevitable growth in its costs as it extended its social welfare operations. As the Poor Law Board said in its 1870 Report: 'it cannot be denied that the more humane views which have prevailed during the last few years as to the treatment of the sick poor have added most materially to Poor Law expenditure'. So much for the total expenditure. Now for the proportions in which this English and Welsh Poor Law money was expended.[74]

	'In-Maintenance'	'Out-Relief'	Maintenance of Lunatics in Asylums	Salaries, etc., of Staff	Buildings, Equipment & Service of Loans
[Averages]					
1856–60	17·6	52·9	7·1	11·2	11·2
1861–5	17·7	53·0	8·0	11·0	10·3
1866–70	19·7	48·3	9·0	10·7	12·3
1871–5	20·2	42·8	10·2	11·5	15·3
1876–80	21·8	34·9	12·4	13·0	17·9

The important shifts to be noted here are (1) the steadily rising proportion of total expenditure devoted to the maintenance of 'lunatics' in asylums (i.e. the county lunatic asylums, which took paupers at so much per head); and (2) the shrinking proportion spent on 'out-relief' after the middle sixties. This second shift was partly because of the economy drive already mentioned in connection with the movement to 'organise' charity, but it also partly sprang from the same wholesome tendency that transferred more and more lunatics to asylums, the creation (thirty or more years after the Poor Law Enquiry Commissioners of 1832–4 had recommended it) of specialised institutions to give special classes of the destitute the care they needed. Some of those specialised institutions were operated within the Poor Law structure: infirmaries, schools, isolation hospitals. Others however developed outside the Poor Law and so took off a small part of its financial and numerical burdens: reformatories, approved schools, and then board schools. But this relief would of course have affected both 'indoor' and 'outdoor' paupers. Before we go any further we must clarify the meaning of these two classifications.

'Indoor' paupers, by the Poor Law Board's unhelpful terminology, included all who were for whatever reason wholly dependent on public relief and who spent the night within workhouse walls. At one end it included vagrants or, as they became more often called through our period, casuals: homeless or itinerant poor who applied to the Poor Law authorities for a night's shelter. By contrast at the other end it included paupers who might be permanently resident: nonlunatic imbeciles, cripples and chronic sick, old folk, disabled persons. (Such might equally well be on out-relief—whether they were or not would depend on local and individual circumstances.) In between the most transitory and the most permanent came the great bulk of indoor paupers, those who were there, it was hoped and expected, for a while only: foundlings, orphans, children of adult inmates, adults who had been taken in (though they might very often have been given out-relief) because they were destitute through sickness, lack of employment, desertion, laziness. . . .

About these categories of 'indoor' pauper life it is important to observe, first, there was *not one* of them (except the certified lunatic) who might not equally have been sustained on 'out-relief' or by 'charity' or by a mixture of both. Each union managed its admissions in very much its own way. It lay under statutory obligations to relieve destitution of every kind, but how it chose to mix indoor with outdoor relief it considered its own business. The central authorities, disliking this, ceaselessly campaigned against it, but to no effect. Vagrants might be offered a place in the part of the establishment kept specially for such, or might be given just enough out-relief to enable them to buy a night's lodging in a common lodging house. Relations who could be persuaded to keep imbeciles at home could be subsidised to do so. The same went for the sick, the aged, the disabled, the orphan—for everybody, in fact, including even that 'able-bodied labourer' for whom the terrors of a deterrent workhouse were originally and expressly designed. No matter how much 'Whitehall' complained and needled, many unions both rural and urban—but especially urban, and of those especially northern—persisted right through our period in giving out-relief to the able-bodied unemployed. It was in effect used as a dole to keep both the wholly and the partially unemployed alive and available until the return of full-time work. Guardians stuck to this use of it, partly because it seemed to them to make better economic sense (why risk driving away or breaking the spirit of a good workman by compelling him and his family to come inside 'the House' when trade temporarily fell off?); partly because it was cheaper (the outdoor allowance could be pared down to what was judged necessary to fill the gap between the cost of subsistence and what the family as a whole could earn or scrounge); and partly, one may believe, because it was more humane to keep families intact and in their own homes, no matter how much less healthy and morally bracing than a 'well-regulated workhouse' those homes might be.

The overlapping of the 'indoor' and 'outdoor' categories is not the only reason why plausible generalisation about the mid-Victorian workhouses and their populations seems peculiarly difficult. Of the workhouses themselves one may safely say that most were new structures, built not longer ago than the later thirties and sometimes under construction during our period. So also can it be affirmed that most of them—the exceptions being, I believe, only the biggest urban ones—were of the character known as the 'general mixed workhouse': mixed, that is, in the categories of pauper maintained under the one roof, though not necessarily mixing socially with one another within the building. (The bigger the workhouse, the less was such mixing likely.) Mixed in that technical sense, they were also very mixed in character. An interesting vein of recent research makes it amusingly clear that 'the House' cannot have been the object of universal terror and dislike which the anti-Poor Law propagandists made it out to be. Some boards of guardians took great pride in their headquarters and, with one knows not what degree of ratepayer approval, embellished them grandly. The central board sometimes had to put its foot down to enforce architectural economy; as for instance when it refused, in 1869, 'to sanction proposals to introduce encaustic tile paving in the entrance hall, moulded Portland stone stairs to the chapel, an elaborate coffered ceiling to the board-room, decorated ceilings to the committee-rooms, Parian cement pilasters and other decorations in the covered way to the chapel, and Portland stone decorations to the front of the building'.[75]

Mid-Victorian workhouses and ancillary structures were not Bastilles of the type libellously alleged by Pugin in his early Victorian *Contrasts*. They were usually solid, symmetrical, hospital-like buildings, betraying no trace whatever of the prison-like; as a glance at any typical prison of the time at once shows. The northern industrial counties' workhouses seem to have been the most impressive in appearance and generous in management. Christmas Day in the workhouses of County Durham in 1852 was reported to have included dinners and free beer and tobacco at the expense variously of the chaplains, the clerks to the boards, the surgeons, the guardians, *and the Master*. 'Mrs Scawin and Mrs Monks provided cakes and fruit for all the children' in the Durham City house.[76] The historian of Poor Law administration in North-East Lancashire, Rhodes Boyson, tells us that for Christmas 1867 the Haslingden inmates received 'tobacco, oranges and apples from two local doctors, two brewers each gave a barrel of ale, and Mrs Pilling sang a few selections from the Messiah'. The Bolton workhouse children were taken on annual expeditions to flower shows, one of the Guardians gave them an annual excursion on the canal, and as soon as Blackpool's wonders were revealed the children were having trips there too.[77] The huge workhouses of those unions seem by his account to have been sensibly and humanely run, with proper separation for the sick and the insane, cheap but cheerful school arrangements, and what goes most sharply against the Bastille stereotype, no forced separation of members of families. Inmates regularly went out for visits on Sundays and took several days, even weeks, off at Christmas. (Even so intense an anti-Poor Law writer as Dickens allowed Plornish *père* liberty to leave his metropolitan grove of mouldy old men at weekends.) Dr Boyson's discoveries are conclusive about that part of Lancashire. That the Poor Law was managed on similar lines in the Manchester region is suggested by the splendours of the Swinton Industrial Schools, the 'Pauper Palace' set up by the unions of Manchester and Chorlton which moved Dickens to ambiguous raptures.[78] Liverpool's workhouse infirmary was already legendary by the sixties for its excellence, and one hears of thrifty respectable people with surgical problems wangling their way into it for free operations!

How far the same style of management occurred elsewhere, I dare not say. My impression is that rural unions, at any rate in the midlands and the south, had fewer attractive features; and most of what was officially reported about the Poor Law institutions of the metropolis inclines one to accept the appropriateness of the Bastille stereotype for *them*. A series of nasty scandals in the early sixties showed up horrors in their sick wards, and even nastier scandals marked the history of their handling of the hordes of children whom they had to look after. On the other hand one cannot deny that some metropolitan unions had a better record than others; some of their children's establishments won critical admiration; and their hospitals, new from the end of the sixties, at once became exemplars of excellence. Their out-relief seems to have been peculiarly unsystematic and unpredictable, and the policies of the guardians of the poorer unions were under constant attack in the columns of the press and the pages of the swelling host of publicists cashing in on Mayhew's theme. Yet the problems of pauperism in the biggest city in the world were vast and surely insoluble; it was not surprising that the Poor Law failed to relate to it to anyone's satisfaction. Humanitarians were dissatisfied because of the amount of cruelty and neglect that went on. Economists were dissatisfied because its cost kept rising: 1850, £741,900; 1855, £841,300; 1860, £896,400; 1865, £905,600; 1870, £1,465,900; 1875,

£1,588,700. Moralists were dissatisfied because of the amount of fraud and humbug that attached to it. And everybody was dissatisfied because, despite such expenditure, London's pauperism remained as voluminous, daunting, disagreeable, demoralised and demoralising as ever. It was at London in particular that Goschen's 'revised code' of poor relief, determined to cut down at least on out-relief, was aimed, and it was in London that a peculiarly tough new sort of labour test, the 'Popular test' for the able-bodied unemployed, was introduced. As the figures show, the object of reducing costs was achieved; but historians who have worked on this sector of social history have detected no substantial improvement in any aspect of the problem. London's pauperism was at the end of our period, as at its start, utterly beyond men's power to tackle it.

It remains to complete this sketch of the Poor Law's place in the lives of the poor by attempting some estimate of the extent of their reliance upon it. The task is made the more difficult by the idiocy of the official statistics which, like those of the census and I know not how many other standard official nineteenth-century reports, became quickly petrified into a mindless routine of details of diminishing utility. Pauper heads were counted twice a year during our period, on 1 January and on 1 July. Their primary classifications were 'indoor' or 'outdoor'. (Their other great concern was whether the recipient of relief was 'able-bodied' or not—a distinction which retained its importance in their minds and their statistics because of their obsessive fear of encouraging indolence.) The distinction between 'indoor' and 'outdoor' is less important than one might suppose if one did not know how little difference there might be in practice between paupers under either head. They may therefore be taken in aggregate as a combined index of the incidence of pauperism. But what do they show about the extent of pauperism? They show no more than the numbers of persons receiving relief on two not particularly representative days of the year. No more than any other official figures during our period do they tell us how long any other persons thus recorded remained in receipt of relief; an 'indoor' case might be there for only a few days before moving off—might indeed be there as a 'casual', for one night only; an 'outdoor' case might stay on the books for months. Mid-Victorian statisticians, intelligently aware of the difficulties, reckoned that something like the total number of persons relieved during each year (but they could not say 'relieved for how long a period') could be obtained by multiplying the official figures by three or three-and-a-half.[79] Here then, using three as a multiplier of the mean aggregate figures given by the Webbs,[80] are my estimates of the number of people assisted.

Estimates of the Number of Persons Assisted 'Indoor' or 'Outdoor'
by the Poor Law during each year, 1850–1880

Year	Number of Persons Relieved	as % of Population of England & Wales
1849	3,265,980	18·9
1850	3,026,100	17·1
1	2,823,950	15·9
2	2,747,030	15·3
3	2,659,090	14·7
4	2,593,850	14·1
5	2,693,060	14·4
6	2,751,250	14·7
7	2,655,030	13·8
8	2,726,660	14·0
9	2,596,340	13·2
1860	2,533,900	12·9
1	2,651,760	13·2
2	2,751,430	13·8
3	3,238,150	15·9
4	3,044,930	14·7
5	2,855,700	13·8
6	2,748,460	12·9
7	2,794,640	12·9
8	2,977,920	13·8
9	3,054,420	13·8
1870	3,098,400	13·8
1	3,112,080	13·8
2	2,931,600	12·9
3	2,651,060	11·4
4	2,482,340	10·5
5	2,429,740	9·9
6	2,248,430	9·3
7	2,159,850	8·7
8	2,186,620	8·7
9	2,296,365	9·0
1880	2,424,090	9·3

These figures are presented for what they are worth; but I do not pretend they are worth much. They are indeed worth more than the Poor Law Board's meaningless twice-yearly head-counts, because they get a good deal closer to the number of persons who, during each year, sought some sort of poor relief. But they say nothing about the period of time for which poor relief was given to those persons. As a measure of the quantity of destitution in any given year, they are quite useless, and are most sharply seen to be so, if one considers how absolutely they fail to tally with what we know about the ups and downs of employment, and with what Booth and Rowntree demonstrated to be the proportion of poor people permanently in need of relief from some source or other. The Webbs concluded[81] that the 'irreducible minimum of poor relief' bore 'little or no relation to pauperism', and that the official figures merely showed that the proportion of pauperism to population could be made to appear anything according to whatever policy of relief was adopted. We must therefore abandon hope of screwing meaningful statistics of destitution out of the Poor Law Reports. So much destitution (or pretended destitution) got relief from other sources, the published accounts and reports of which are even less penetrable to the scientific inquirer. We are thrown back upon 'impressions'; among them the impression that Booth and Rowntree's measurements may be taken as seriously for our period as for theirs.

3 : Education, Religion, and the Uses of Leisure

After 'work', what theme? Not 'play'. One might indeed thus entitle the corresponding chapter in a social history of a more modern period but it won't do for our mid-Victorians. Deliberate and frequent recreation was part of only some mid-Victorians' lives, and others who could have had it did not want it. Not 'culture', either. A familiar use of that word would sanction it as the chapter heading but it would be ridiculous so to ignore the effect, on the quality of their lives, of the occupations that filled, according to my calculations, between a third and a half of their waking hours. The title I have adopted is not ideal, but it is neater than: 'How they filled their non-earning hours'.

Education and the Social Hierarchy*

First, then, education; in respect of which the two leading characteristics of our period were an expansion of the proportion of the child population formally educated, up to the point when virtually every child was compelled to go to school for at any rate six years; and a sharpening of the 'class' divisions between and within the systems that conducted the process.

* A note on Terminology. Following modern, not Victorian usage, I prefer social and functional to legal or financial definitions. Thus I try to simplify the mid-Victorians' fourfold classification of 'private' (fee-paying and profit-making for private owner), 'proprietary' (fee-paying but not primarily profit-making in ordinary sense because corporately-owned, sometimes on joint-stock principle), 'endowed' (i.e. ancient, local or charitable foundations, sometimes resuscitated into new life as public schools) and 'public' (at the beginning of our period, only 'the original seven' of Eton, Harrow, Winchester, Westminster, Rugby, Charterhouse, Shrewsbury) into 'public' for schools new or old, proprietary or endowed, which were trying to become like Rugby and Shrewsbury so that their products should have some chance of holding their own in presence of Etonians; and 'private' for all schools neither in *that* sense public nor in any sense publicly financed.

I say 'between and within' because although on the one hand
one can not unreasonably describe most schools as either
'upper', 'middle', or 'lower class' ones, one must not therefore blink the fact that there were distinctions no less sharp
between this 'middle class' school and that one, between this
'working class' school and that one. Educational systems can
hardly help mirroring the ideas about social relationships of
the societies that produce them. In Chapter Four I shall comment on the complications of the British (and more especially
the English) social structure: how basic financial and hereditary criteria were criss-crossed by the multi-layered claims of
'respectability', vouched for with varying degrees of credibil-
ity (varying, that is, in the eyes of those to whom they were
presented!) on grounds of professional, industrial and commercial status, denominational membership, or whatever.
'Education' became, between the forties and the eighties, a
trump card in this great class competition. During the same
years that the quantity and intellectual character of it were
coming to be thought increasingly important from a political
and economic point of view, the social tone of it was coming to
be thought all-important from a social point of view. And so
the schools of Britain not only mirrored the hierarchical social
structure (as, in the absence of a strong government determined otherwise, they were bound to do) but were made more
and more to magnify its structuring in detail. 'The school you
had been to' mattered to not many men, I reckon, even in the
thirties. Peel and Gladstone indeed could not so smoothly have
risen to the social and political heights had they not been
made first-rate gentlemen at Harrow and Eton and then
Oxford. But Oxford and Cambridge mattered in the early
nineteenth century, to men anxious to raise their sons to indisputable social heights, more than the so-called 'public schools';
which were not numerous anyway. Nor was Oxbridge itself
all that coveted by men of the urban aristocracies; nor did you
have to go through 'public school' to get there. Some boys
came from grammar schools, some from what we would nowadays call private schools and 'crammers', some from private
tutors. By the forties and fifties, all that was changing; and

through the sixties and seventies it changed so fast, and to such effect, that by the eighties it was 'public school' that mattered more, among the wealthy and very respectable taken as a whole, than an 'Oxbridge' to which 'public school' (with 'preparatory school' before it) had become the standard approach; while all down the line of so-called public and frankly private education, the 'public school ideal' exercised an ever more potent magnetism, and groups like those Non-conformist urban aristocracies which earlier on had been able to ignore or even to deplore it, decreasingly chose or dared to do so. It was during our period that this great change occurred: a change momentous for the future, in that it case-hardened and extended within the English (not so much into the Scottish) educational system, the controlling axis of élitism it has only within the last twenty-five years begun to undo.

But that, though conspicuous, was not the only aspect of educational change in these years which was tending to sharpen, in the loose sense, class distinctions in education. The so-called public schools were, for all practical purposes, private schools; they owed their helpfully misleading name to the ancient endowments which had once enabled many of the old ones freely to educate deserving local or 'scholarship' boys; and the state interfered with them in our period no more than (mainly by means of the Royal Commissions known by the names of their noble chairmen, Clarendon and Taunton) to prod them publicly to consider whether they were using their wealth as well as, considering their vast influence, they should. With private schools *tout court*, schools without social pretensions or inherited endowments, schools that took fees for educating or otherwise taking care of children and asked for nothing from the state, the state interfered not at all; unless it was to insist, in exceptional cases, on minimum *sanitary* provisions, as I suppose it might have done in respect of some of the very worst, at the instance of particularly zealous MOHs or inspectors of nuisances. The HMIs had no warrant to go near them. But governments and Parliament were worried about the low educational quality of, apparently, so many of these private schools 'educating' at all levels from the middle to the lower low, that they took steps to reduce their potentiality to do damage. First, in consequence of the report of the Taunton Commission (1868), the endowments and constitutions of old grammar schools were begun to be refashioned so as to give middle class children a choice of something better (and, as it almost at once turned out, smarter) than those generally so bad private schools. Second, the state at last in 1870 accepted responsibility for placing an elementary school of reasonable guaranteed quality within reach of every child in the UK who could be attracted to it; thus, it was hoped, saving lower middle and low class children from the worst private schools. But none of this genteel campaign against bad-quality private education did anything actively to stop it. By common law it was as serious a crime physically to maim or kill a schoolboy or schoolgirl as to maim or kill anyone else, and that was the only legal protection schoolchildren had against the ignorance, folly or cruelty of their elders. If any school of the quality of Dotheboys Hall or Mr Wopsle's aunt's was closed by public authority during our period,[1] it can only have been because some child was known to have been beaten to death, or because (if the situation was urban) too many of the children had serious infectious diseases for the fact to escape public notice and reprobation. Private educational enterprise was interfered with by the state much less than private industrial enterprise; and the parts that were thus interfered with were not the small-scale concerns of lower social coverage but the larger-scale ones of higher.

So, during these years of general educational growth, the wholly private sector became increasingly prestigious and influential, and was helped by the administrations and parliaments of the time to do so, first by their admonitions to do better, and second by the facilities they provided for the refashioning of ancient endowments. We will more closely examine this sector later on. Now we must attend to what can hardly be called 'the public sector' but may be called the more public sector of education; the area of mainly primary schools within which the state played a sometimes quite strong part. Readers not already initiated into the mysteries of English education will perhaps be astonished to learn that there were few primary schools in England for which the state had full responsibility in 1850, very many for which it had no responsibility at all, and that its responsibility for the rest was shared with a variety of religious organisations. (This pattern remained unchanged until 1870.) The state had *full* responsibility only for the 520-odd schools run in whatever manner by the Poor Law (most of them within individual workhouses, a few very big ones financed by groups of urban unions); forty-odd army and navy schools; thirty-four prison schools; and the handful of superior specialised Schools of Design run under the Board of Trade, which were not primary schools at all, but are worth mentioning in order to emphasise how tiny the state's role was. The state had in 1850 no responsibility at all for whatever private primary school any private individual or individuals might care to run; nor did it have any voice in the running of the schools of those religious organisations which, as 'voluntarists', either denied its right to be involved (principally, the Home and Colonial School Society, the Congregationalists' and Baptists' societies and the Sunday School Union ((for Sunday schools were throughout the century considered part of the total educational provision)); but also many on the 'high' side of the Anglicans' educational society, the National) or which, acknowledging that right and longing for it to be helpfully exercised, could not or would not satisfy the state that they deserved it (many Roman Catholic, some National, and all Ragged Schools). Primary schools with the management of which the state had *something*, in 1850, to do, were either Factory Schools (established to satisfy the factory acts of 1833 onwards, and visited by the factory inspectors) or denominational ones, affiliated to one or other of the organisations that wanted financial help from the state and were prepared to conform to its requirements. These organisations were the National Society, the British and Foreign School Society, the Wesleyan Methodist Education Committee and the [Roman] Catholic Poor School Committee. The British and Foreign (non-denominational) and the Wesleyan were happiest about the state's requirements of minimum standards of buildings and equipment and a local management so constituted as to prevent both religious persecution (i.e. indoctrination of children whose parents could find no other school to send them to) and exclusively clerical control. Many National and a few Roman Catholic schools were able to satisfy these terms. They were then committed to receiving visits from the Inspector and to keeping their standards up to the level of his requirements. In return they could get financial subventions for building and extension and they would be better placed for getting a trained teacher paid partly by the state. These were solid and respectable advantages, in many managers' eyes well worth the loss of complete independence. Yet their independence was still very great. The 'managers' still effectively managed; more, indeed, during the fifties and sixties than during Kay-Shuttleworth's régime of the forties. The new race of trained teachers (Bradley Headstone and, he hoped, Charley Hexam),[2] at last certificated at the end of their gruelling course of apprenticeship and college, looked to the central office (the Committee of the Privy Council for Education; usually known as, simply, the Committee of Council) for support in their struggle for social recognition and professional independence, but they did not get it. Hiring and firing remained the managers' prerogative; more emphatically so after 1862 than before.

That was the 'system' of primary schools about the year 1850. It guaranteed educational quality only where the inspectorate penetrated, and that fine group of men—Matthew Arnold was not so outstanding among them as his admirers have supposed—had often to report that quality was low. The trouble was not with the teachers but with the parents and, to some extent, the economy. Poor parents might afford the fees for some of the time (twopence or threepence per child per week was usual) but they were habitually reluctant to keep a child at school after it became capable of wage-earning (at, say, ten years old on average), and they could, apparently, rarely resist the temptation to keep it away from school to help out in a domestic crisis or to take up some opportune temporary employment. When one considers what wages were in those years, and how necessary it still was for many labouring class families, throughout our period, that their children should win bread as early as possible, one cannot blame the parents for ₃not being keener on the children's getting an 'education' which, so far as they could judge, improved life's prospects hardly at all. Nor in fact did managers, teachers or inspectors generally blame the parents. They understood too well the facts of working class life; and unless they were prepared (as only some, mainly urban, educational campaigners were) to advocate that primary education should be free, there was not the slightest hope of making it compulsory. So attendance was poor, poor enough to take most of the stuffing out of impressive statistics, and it stayed poor until the seventies. Then for several reasons it improved: children were newly debarred from some industries (see p. 136) and the industrial demand for them was in any case diminishing; rising real wages helped families survive without infants' earnings; and, most important, it became an urgent concern of public authority to get every child to school and keep it there—for which purpose, attendance officers were invented. Attendance became universally compulsory between 1876 and 1880.

Did the quality of primary education improve much during the fifties and sixties? I doubt it. More schools did not mean —perhaps actually stood in the way of—better schools. Every Ragged School, many Roman Catholic and some National schools, remained below the qualifying level. Private schools varied as they always had done but I find no cause to conclude that the proportion of good ones grew. Perhaps the sector with the best likelihood of improvement was that of the voluntarist and independent educational organisations, like the Congregationalists and the secular Lancashire Public Schools Association. The religious voluntarists were on their mettle to prove that education would be better without state aid etc. than with it, but in any case their denominational schools, never numerous, scarcely touched the lower, poorer, levels; the 'secular' societies and groups (so-called not because they were necessarily un- or anti-Christian, but because of their conviction that all education would get along better if the 'religious' were separated from the 'secular' parts) were of their nature progressive, and certainly attracted and held fee-paying children of upper working and superior class. Inspected and grant-aided schools were continuously encouraged to raise standards, but only the ones able to exact relatively high fees of sixpence-upwards per week could easily afford to do so; and the inspectorate was virtually unanimous, along with most other informed opinion, that standards of everything but mechanical learning were depressed by the introduction of Robert Lowe's *Revised Code* in 1862; which stamped upon the state-involving sector a grimly utilitarian character not begun to be dispelled till at least the later seventies. 'Payment by Results', its mainspring, did not absolutely disappear till 1890.

My picture of the elementary educational world in the fifties and sixties is not a cheering one, nor am I herein making any different judgment from the best contemporary opinion. Men who cared about education agreed that England had too little of it. They might disagree about almost everything else—and it is notorious that they did so. Some universal and compulsory system, comparable to what much less wealthy and pretentious countries had, ought to have been established before the forties. Why was it not? Partly because of the 'religious' controversies of the period:—dissent versus establishment, evangelical versus sacramentalist, latitudinarian versus dogmatist, separator (of religious from secular instruction) versus integrator; partly because the dominant constitutional idea precluded firm guidance from the centre in any affairs that could, no matter how improbably, be brought under the umbrellas of 'religious liberty' and 'local self-government'; partly because —if this is not to put it too crudely—employers of labour in the aggregate were convinced neither that they could do without cheap young labour, nor that the adults would work better if educated (which, in respect of most unskilled jobs or traditional crafts, was I suppose true enough). These obstructions still stood in the way of elementary education through the fifties and early sixties. Political and economic events combined to clear them quickly out of the way between 1865 and

1870. Once the Second Reform Act had become law, in what at first seemed so threateningly democratic a form, the anti-democrats who had tried to prevent it could look only to education to alkalise its acids. About the same time British manufacturers, getting their first warning whiff of foreign competition, were advised by certain experts that education was the foreigners' secret weapon. The religious world was calming down. Most voluntarists had learnt that state aid and direction was, after all, indispensable. More and more Protestant Christians seem to have been understanding their faith in sentimental and undogmatic rather than doctrinal terms. Whatever the cause, it appears to be the case that throughout the urban world (by now, more and more dominant) there crystallised in 1868–9 a demand for some comprehensive solution of the problem. Men still disagreed over what form it should take, and were to go on disagreeing, often violently, for many years yet. But Forster's Education Act, in 1870, came in quick response to an unambiguous call that, after thirty and more years of dithering, the progress and the security of the nation should cease to be jeopardised by an elementary system of education so leaky and loose that scores of thousands of the children who most needed school's civilising (it was hoped) touch never got near it. None of the sensible contemporary estimates put the number of un-schooled children at less than a quarter of a million, and some put it higher. Attendance, up to thirteen, was not quite yet made nationally compulsory, but individual school boards, the new local education authorities, were empowered to make it so within their own districts, and most of the big urban ones had done so by 1875. After 1870 non-attendance, in both its absolute and occasional varieties, ceased to be as serious an issue as it had been earlier on, and the next big inquiry, the Cross Commission of 1885–6, found more cause to worry about the size of classes, many of which had become huge; the quality of teachers and teaching; and—still—that terrible 'religious difficulty', which was really so largely a social and political one.

We turn now to review that social stratification of schools which I indicated at the outset as a basic feature of the mid-

Victorian educational system's reflection of society. From bottom to top there showed a sharp and touchy social consciousness tending all the time to separate the social groups and sub-groups one from another and to issue, wherever circumstances made it possible, in 'single class' schools. We begin in the abyss: in the mean streets, courts and alleys of the old central and lowest industrial and commercial districts of the big towns. There were the bulk of the 'wastrels', the 'street children', the youngest wage earners of industry and commerce who, most helpless of all competitors in an overbrimming unskilled labour market, ran the errands, fetched the drink, carried the tools, did the cleaning and the clearing-up under the immediate command, often, of adults themselves unskilled and underpaid. These—but especially the rough and unkempt children, often seemingly homeless, who thronged the pavements of the business and shopping quarters, ostensibly selling matches and flowers, sweeping crossings, cleaning shoes, holding horses and so on but presumed to be on the fringes of the underworld—were the least school-going types who most worried the political public in 1868–9. Such experience of school as they may have enjoyed in the fifties and sixties was likely to be that of a Ragged School, an evangelical Sunday school connected perhaps with a City Mission, or (particularly in the Irish quarter) some Roman Catholic evening or Sunday school. The Ragged Schools, going strong by the fifties, did the most for the children of this lowest stratum; but they did it at the cost of cutting them off from all children whose parents had the remotest claim to 'respectability'. Ragged School children were by definition those so dirty, so verminous, so tattered, that even penny-a-weekers would not willingly consort with them. The children of the abyss had no choice but to undergo their schooling in Ragged Schools, unless they were given a lucky break by some (usually evangelical) emigration or industrial training scheme, or (in consequence of trouble with the police) perhaps a spell in a reformatory.

Between the abyss and the enviable plateau of independence rose terraced slopes where parental will to have children formally educated struggled with economic necessity in a hundred hurting forms. On these terraces existed the indescribable variety of private schools; the great mass of schools tied into the denominational and 'secular' educational societies, with those of the National Society, expressing the most self-consciously Church of England spirit, far outnumbering all the other non-private ones; and, especially in the more ancient towns, charity or endowed schools. Private schools, by definition, were fee-paying; the educational societies' schools were usually so; charity schools and endowed schools were usually free so far as fees went, but difficult to get into without local patronage. The quality of all of them may be said to have usually varied in proportion with the parents' expectations and readiness to pay for what their children got. The only important exception to that rule that I can think of, was in well-regulated rural areas where the expectations (and often payments) were not those of parents so much as of squires and parsons. Not, in general, of farmers; as a class they were always alleged to be remarkably indifferent, even hostile, to the education of the lower orders, and to be the least forthcoming of all potential patrons of schools. But where influential landowners and associated clergy insisted on villagers' children going to school, they usually went, whether the parents particularly wanted it or not. English rural areas could be educationally exceptional in another respect too. The children of even quite big farmers might be found sitting on the same benches as labourers' children. The fact when observed was usually thought worthy of comment, in the class-conscious southern and midland areas anyway, and held to be highly creditable to the local dignitaries responsible for it. The norm in most of the 'high-farming' areas, and in the urban areas as a whole, seems to have been that parents who could afford to pay something, preferred not to have their children consorting with those who paid nothing; and that parents who were willing to pay a relatively large sum—ninepence, say, or a shilling a week, at the best National, British, or 'Secular' schools—did not expect to find their children consorting with others less pre-eminently respectable or serious. So while 'working class' schools often took on the characters of the working-class sub-groups who patronised them, those of character superior enough to attract skilled men's, artisans', children (in places where artisans valued this sort of thing; as one cannot imagine, e.g., some of the Sheffield ones doing) would also be patronised by such of the lower levels of the commercial and clerical classes as did not shrink from what they might consider a common touch. But the same brand of school which, in this working class or socially mixed district, might thus take on corresponding social characteristics, could in a wholly 'petty bourgeois' district become a thoroughly 'petty bourgeois' school. Locality and demand were all. One cannot say, 'National Schools were of this quality, British Schools were that', etc. They could, though uniformly titled, be utterly different in social composition, community function, and educational quality.

Our survey, socially ascending, now reaches the urban middle classes proper: better-paid clerks, the soldier shopkeepers, professional men no matter how struggling and hard-up, retired and half-pay officers, genteel widows, commercial and industrial managers; from these and their like, upwards to where 'upper middle class' goldenly transmuted into undeniable 'upper class'—how were *their* children educated? As to the earliest years, the answer is quite simple: in private school or at home. No parents of this class, it cannot too much be emphasised, were under any compulsion to educate their children, let alone to educate them in any prescribed style. (The only legal compulsions, as distinct from moral or social pressures, were upon paupers, whose children had to undergo whatever instruction the guardians ordered, and upon factory owners, to provide part-time schooling for child-workers or to make sure that it was provided.) Middle and upper class parents were free therefore to educate their children at home if they wished, and many appear to have done so; how many, and what proportion, it is quite impossible to say. A father with time on his hands, an intellectual mother might undertake it themselves. Parents rich enough—they did not have to be very rich—to hire a governess or, more expensive, a tutor, could very easily do so; the supply of governesses was, considering the size of the market, literally inexhaustible, and for those who did not want or could not afford the best quality British ones, there was a fine imported range from France and Germany. Male tutors, often clerical or, increasingly, German, of course cost more, and presented peculiar dangers to families with daughters. One reads enough about them to be sure that they played an important part in at any rate the early stages of the education of quite a lot of well-off children; but one presumes that they became rarer as time went by, partly because they must have become increasingly costly, partly because the prep-school routine became less and less resistible, even to parents to whose moral sense it was repugnant. Governesses for girls were of course always more common, and remained so for much longer. Tuition at home must therefore be reckoned to have been a part, however incalculable, of the educational experience of the mid-Victorian middle and upper classes. But schools of some sorts were of course more usual; and very bad some of them were. The Taunton Commission discovered some real horrors, and I find no reason to be sure that it dredged the very depths. Matthew Arnold was only the most polished of the host of contemporary observers who remarked upon it as peculiarly lamentable that the English (*not* the Scottish) middle classes, having little experience of good schools themselves and no 'culture' worth speaking of, could not tell a good school when they saw one, had no idea that education was for its own sake worth paying for, and were more prepared to pay good money for schools that brought social advantage (relatively regarded) rather than educational. These denunciatory generalisations no doubt did injustice to many worthy and cultivated middle class characters at all levels. The parents who strove, by means of money or influence, to get their children into for example St Paul's or the City of London School, into the better of the old big city grammar schools like King Edward's, Birmingham, or High Pavement, Nottingham, or into fine modern foundations like Liverpool's, obviously cared about good schooling for their sons (it was the next generation that was to become equally concerned about their daughters), and must sometimes have been prepared to pay for it. Entirely private day schools could be very good, and were bound to cost something. 'A very good general education' was 'supplied at a moderate rate' at the Edinburgh Institution: 8 to 11 gns. p.a. for juniors, £13 to £16 for seniors. Two hundred and seventy boys were in attendance when the Argyll Commissioners visited; forty were learning German, over two hundred French. 'About ten or twenty only go to the university each year; the majority, when they leave the institution, enter offices, or become accountants or engineers.'[3]

After making allowance for these cases, however, I cannot but conclude that Matthew Arnold and co. were on the whole right; that the middle classes had in general grubby utilitarian ideas of education; and that the quality of the schools they sent their children to was generally low. Endowed, 'grammar' schools, where they were available for local middle class use, had so often gone to seed; while the quality of private schools was often just what you would expect, in a country where *anyone* could put up a brass plate and announce his establishment as a school.

From private schools proper we ascend to the social heights of the so-called public schools, which were in reality the most private of them all. Theirs is an astonishing story. Even by the end of the seventies they cannot have been educating more than a tiny proportion of boys of secondary school age (which then went higher than is usual now); yet already their great triumph was assured. The public school idea had broken through from its relatively insignificant pre-Victorian bridgehead to the point where that particular style of education was accepted as the only proper one for those who wanted to maintain or to attain irreproachable social position. Our mid-Victorian period was the crucial one in the public schools' achievement of this status, and the institution in the seventies of 'the Headmasters' Conference', an annual (not indeed at first; but it soon became so) get-together of the heads of the top schools, sealed their success.

The forces which produced the public school had, however,

been operating since much earlier in the century. Since when exactly, and through the operation of what forces, are not yet well understood. The whole topic is wide open to further investigation along lines indicated in the only really good book about it, T. W. Bamford's *The Rise of the Public Schools* (1967). Mr Bamford inclines to see it all starting in the years immediately after the Napoleonic Wars. Some might suspect an even earlier origin, and all might argue over definitions. We fortunately have no need to, for by the fifties the idea of a public school was well established and the great Victorian public school movement was in full swing. It was indeed not yet as buoyant, confident and noisy as it was to become during the years of its zenith, from the eighties to the First World War; apart from *Tom Brown's Schooldays*, first published in 1857, there was not much 'public school literature' before the seventies; nor was there, before our period, any notable amount of what one might call public school publicity and propaganda. The public schools' coming role in the heart of British government was prophesied or divined rather than proclaimed, by Thomas Arnold (whose reign at Rugby ended in 1842) and Nathaniel Woodard, who issued his trumpet-blast in 1847.[4] No one individual—certainly not Arnold, whose actual role was quickly misrepresented and misunderstood—was responsible for the public schools boom. It is best understood mainly in terms of social demand and response, and people like Woodard, Edward Thring and E. F. Benson, who constituted themselves its spokesmen and propagandists, were at most channelling a tide not of their own making. This demand, then, came from the classes who wanted education for their children beyond the age of fourteen: the age at which the lowest sort of private secondary schools saw most of their pupils going off to trade, articles, or apprenticeship. Parents who wanted more than that for their boys might have difficulty finding what they wanted at a price they could afford. If they (I speak for the moment of early Victorians) were fortunate in their place of residence, there would be an ancient local endowed grammar (or even, for residents of Rugby, Shrewsbury and Harrow, a 'public') school to send them to, on either a day or some variety of boarding system; or there might be a good private school or (favourite word then!) academy, of the sort which we know to have been plentifully provided through the later eighteenth and early nineteenth centuries. But many such parents were not thus fortunately situated, and were driven to look further afield for a satisfactory school; only a school away from home would get a boy away from socially lowering cousins and neighbours, besides, it might be hoped, putting him into socially useful company; while the number of parents potentially interested in the matter was of course growing through the whole of the nineteenth century, not just in proportion with the population increase but, because of the way the growing wealth of the nation was distributed, proportionately faster.

This merely physical development on the demand side must have been very important. It was however not the whole of the explanation of the boom from the forties onwards. One sees other factors in operation also; given here in what I reckon to be ascending order of importance. (1) Railways. From the forties it became much easier to send boys and their belongings to boarding schools; and by the same token it became easier to keep in touch with them once they had gone. (2) Examinations, both competitive and qualifying, were becoming more and more unavoidable at the points of entry to the money-making occupations deemed socially most eligible: i.e. for almost everything but 'trade'. The Indian Civil Service (run by the East India Company till 1857) imposed entrance requirements from about 1830. For the home Civil Service they were almost unavoidable after 1855; for the army, after 1857. The educational attainments expected of the clergy were rising fast; the foundation of the first modern-style theological college, Cuddesdon, in 1845, being an omen of future developments. Lawyers, like doctors, had to satisfy professional requirements. Some good education was of course obligatory for medicine and for many of the newer professions (e.g. engineering, surveying, architecture) but I must not make much of those because public schoolboys seem not to have been going in any strength into these professions till after the sixties. And on top of all, there were Oxford and Cambridge, becoming increasingly difficult for scholarship boys to get into. (There was no difficulty, in most colleges, for the titled or the rich.) So a training in preparation for these examinations was increasingly worth buying, in a world each year more full of young gentlemen than of good remunerative and respectable jobs for them to go into. (3) Social and moral distinction mattered at least as much as academic proficiency. This is where the seven old public schools, and Arnold and Woodard and co., their modernisers and plagiarists, came in. You might have got better instruction in more 'useful' subjects at a private academy; indeed you would, by modern standards, have got a better education at some such place in the early nineteenth century than even at Arnold's Rugby; *but would it be a gentleman's education?*

To such a fearful question (see Chapter Four) only the strongest-minded of non-Anglican urban aristocrats would dare to answer in the affirmative. It was not that the public schools were luxurious or particularly enjoyable. Notoriously they tended not to be so. Nor was it one of their attractions that they were ostentatiously costly. Private schools and academies (giving, perhaps, better educational value for money) could charge more; and some of the new public schools were as inexpensive as was marginally consistent with health and study. But they exercised a magic that the socially aspiring middle classes found increasingly magnetic. The public school idea, which crystallised during the fifties and sixties, comprised these elements: a self-contained society of boys partly self-governing, partly ruled by a Christian autocrat of a headmaster; a valuable political education in 'leadership' and the arts of social ascendancy, at first through submission to status and authority and then through the exercise of them; the practice of open-air pursuits (not necessarily, till after our period, mere athleticism) in classic English countryside settings; and, as the end product, the self-reliant cultivated Christian gentleman, a 'natural ruler' if ever there was one, and hand-made to take a place as of right in among the traditional socio-political élite of aristocracy and gentry. This public

school education was, if not wholly classical—for the more
examination-minded schools had 'modern sides', held to be
educationally inferior while economically necessary—at any
rate classical and generalised enough to be gentlemanly and
cultivated by Oxbridge and C of E standards, and to be
entirely unrelated to 'trade'. The more ambitious new schools,
not least the ones with 'modern' sides, shrank from the fatal
touch of 'trade', which would have utterly spoiled their hopes
of a place in the top league; it looks to me as if they only
took boys from the 'trade' sector on the implied understanding
that they were to be educated for something better.

The situation lower down the league was becoming, through
the seventies, more fluid. The progressive intensification of
public schoolery (from 'accepted' public schools, gathering
round the élite headmasters' conference table after 1869, right
down the line to aspiring grammar and private schools which
aped public school attributes) suggests that the badge of
belonging in that *galère* was becoming ever more valuable and
interesting for its own sake, and that any tinge of it which
could be imparted was socially worth while. But while the
growing number of schools acknowledged as superior (the
headmasters' conference ones) were busy consolidating and
sharpening their distinctions· and advantages as the schools
par excellence of what is perhaps best described as 'the
moneyed interest'—aristocracy, gentry, secure professional
men and 'businessmen' who were not too tradey; plus of
course the children of the public schoolmasters and the
Anglican clergy who served, not ignobly, as its 'chaplains'—
while the public schools proper were consolidating their ruling
class ascendancy, the inferior levels of secondary education
were perhaps moving in the opposite direction and becoming
less marked by class distinctions. Three years before Forster's
Act, permission was formally given to elementary grant-aided
schools to teach specified subjects at (in effect) secondary
level. This precedent was not long in being followed by the
more enterprising urban school boards. Bradford seems to
have been the first, in 1875. Others quickly followed in the
provision of what became known as Higher Grade Schools,

giving secondary instruction, by all reports doing it well, and presumably mingling working-class and lower-middle-class children. Working-class children could compete (under the usual disadvantages) for scholarships to the reconstituted grammar schools and might even aspire to rise from them to the academic heights of the chartered universities. Our period thus ends with the cautious erection of a new educational ladder by which merit might climb to the top; and to this ladder, with its openly competitive character, men could point in justification of the 'reconstruction' of the old endowed schools. Their productivity, it could fairly be said, had been increased; their benefits were now made available to a larger number of children *and* they were more 'fairly' distributed. This was fair comment insofar as the rising scale of examinations which made up the rungs of the ladder were 'fair'; which, from some working-class points of view, they might not be.

We have so far been considering solely the educational arrangements of England and Wales. Those of Scotland were very different: at no level more so than in secondary and higher education, where Scottish superiority was most apparent. The 'Parochial', elementary schools system, which had in earlier periods laid the foundations of Scottish academic prowess, and had since 1838 been supplemented by the so-called 'Parliamentary Schools', had not proved adequate to the demands of the cities. Ragged Schools, 'Dame Schools', low-calibre private schools, Industrial Schools and Reformatories came or were called into being north as well as south of the border, to maintain more or less inadequately the causes of literacy and civilisation against the same fearful odds; and when, at the time of Scotland's equivalent (1872) to Forster's Act, count was taken of the provision of elementary school places, they were found to be absolutely inadequate to the potential demand. But they seem to have been less proportionately inadequate than in English cities of comparable size; and at the secondary level, Scottish superiority was undoubted. The Argyll Commission, reviewing the whole of the Scottish educational field in 1867, reported that a higher proportion of children was receiving secondary education in Scotland than in Prussia—a much higher proportion than in France—while the comparison with England showed the Scottish proportion to be over six times larger! What share of this noble number was in what sense 'working class', I know not. Perhaps not many of these secondary pupils were from below the artisan class. Endowments being scarce, almost all parents had to pay fees. 'Scottish democracy' had a stronger basis in highland and rural than in urban facts. We do, however, know roughly what proportion of working-class students went to Scotland's universities. The Argyll Commission made some spot checks on the freshmen of the 1866–7 session and discovered that about 16 per cent of them were children of 'artisans and skilled labourers', about 3 per cent children of 'labourers' (including miners). We may assume that a few of the 'agricultural' and 'shopkeeping' categories were of no higher economic standing and therefore that at least 20 per cent of Scottish university students came from below the 'petty bourgeois' line: a higher proportion, certainly, than Oxbridge's. The commissioners themselves recognised this, remarking that the advantages of Scottish university education were 'not confined to a class, as in England, and, to a very great extent, in Ireland.'[5] But the difference went beyond that. In 1862 there were about 3,450 university students in Scotland, and a total population of just over 3 million; a proportion of 1 : 869. Whatever the proportion for England and Wales was, it can have been nothing like that.[5] The university was, if not certainly a more democratic, certainly a more familiar, even popular institution in Scotland than anywhere else in the British Isles. Oxbridge dons might sneer at its more juvenile manners and less sophisticated standards in classical scholarship, and might rejoice at the Scottish candidates' relatively poor showing in the new Civil Service examinations which they—the men of Oxbridge —had set. But they could (as yet) offer nothing comparable to either the breadth or the 'modernity' of curricula which had long characterised the Scottish universities and made them universal providers of fundamental philosophy, social science, language and literature, as well as rather expert providers of doctors, engineers, mathematicians, chemists, geologists, etc.

Cambridge and Oxford were not quite the only 'official' universities south of the border. London University had been awarding degrees since 1836 (internal ones; its external degrees began in 1858) and the faculties of its constituent colleges, University and King's, included from time to time scholars of distinction; but internal disputes—college against college, university against hospital—combined throughout our period to dim its lustre and depress its academic value. (Of *social* prestige, of course, it had none.) Durham, chartered in the same year as London, pursued the even tenor of its Oxbridgey way under the shadow of the cathedral. No other institutions were 'officially' authorised to award higher degrees until the seventies, but that formal blank should not obscure the realities of the progress in higher education through our period. The roots of the provincial universities of the seventies and later lay in the intellectual respectability and serious academic ambition of the fore-running provincial urban institutions which testified to the appetite for them and sometimes provided ready-made nuclei of staff and students. These included medical schools attached to city hospitals (as for instance at Sheffield, Leeds, Liverpool, Newcastle), Mechanics' Institutes (not all of which had gone soft after their first fine flourish), and technical colleges (like Glasgow's Andersonian Institution and Edinburgh's Heriot-Watt College). Then there were other institutions for the self-raising working-man (like Sheffield's People's College and Leicester's People's College, and university extension lectures, which got going in the later sixties), and colleges (usually at first preparing students for London external degrees) founded by educationally ambitious philanthropists like John Owens of Manchester, William Armstrong of Newcastle, Josiah Mason of Birmingham, and Mark Firth of Sheffield. Alongside such high-class institutions which might in course of time, and on the whole after our period, mature and amalgamate into universities and colleges, there buzzed in mid-Victorian towns and cities a variety of other means of higher education, which merged on their more popular side into means of entertainment. Provincial Athenaeums, 'Lit. and Phil.' and a vast range of historical, anti-quarian and scientific societies and such, offering library facilities and variously improving and educational lectures to well-heeled subscribers and their families; the ninety Art Schools under the Department of Science and Art and all the privately-run classes and courses, in or out of institutions, pre-paring people (presumably only males?) for the department's examinations in science which began in 1859; that brave army of evening and week-end adult educationists and mutual improvers so lovingly described by J. F. C. Harrison[6] (here fostered by church or chapel, there by secular ideals; often backed by Mechanics' Institutes, Friendly and Co-operative Societies but sometimes entirely spontaneous and self-helping); private schools, classes and lecture courses innumerable. It is difficult to resist the impression that the mid-Victorian public was streaked from top to bottom with strong urges towards educational self-improvement, which achieved satisfaction partly in home reading (see below, pp. 245–9), partly through attendance at this haphazard mosaic of institutions of adult and higher education; which may have been a hotchpotch, but which was full of moral and intellectual vigour, was closely adjusted to the needs and interests of its clients, and which may well have done something to atone for the current gross deficiencies in secondary education: the sector in which the mid-Victorians may be judged to have been, relatively, the most lacking.

Religion and the Social Order

In the cleverest religious satire in our language, Ronald Knox likened English Christianity to 'Israel's ancient creed' which 'took root so widely that it ran to seed'.[7] Of later nine-teenth-century Christianity something like that certainly seems to have been true. The decay or withering, whenever it began and under whatever forms, was itself a kind of tribute to the grandeur of the tree at its fullest growth; it had grown so big, been so successful, that in a world nevertheless imperfect and changing and irresistibly secularising it simply could not avoid some retrenchment, some decline. In or through what period Christianity was 'at its peak' in the constituent parts of the UK, historians argue and, happily, will ever do so. Was the period 1500–1650 more largely Christian than, say, 1780–1880? Was the nineteenth century meet to be called an 'age of faith'? Such questions are at once irresistible and unanswerable. By some criteria or other, indeed, they should be answerable; but what could those criteria be? Externals like church attendance are the more measurable, but they are not self-evidently indicative of internals—depth of devotion, seriousness of belief—which matter more and are in any case no more measurable than definable. Historians are driven back more smartly than usual upon their own 'judgment' or 'sense' when drawing conclusions from the findings of scholarship.

Facing now the question of religion in mid-Victorian Britain, and despite the providential assistance of the only religious census ever taken, the social historian is driven to rely more completely than usual on his own judgment. In this more than in any other field of social life, the essentials lie below the surface, often deliberately hidden. If a man regularly beats his wife, it is a fair presumption that his love for her is less than perfect. But it cannot be presumed that if a man goes regularly to a place of worship he perfectly loves God. There is too much reason for thinking that Victorians' motives for church-going were less than purely religious. Respectability prompted it, when religion didn't (see below, pp. 283–6); and mid-Victorian society (herein no different, I dare say, from most other societies) was not lacking in strong indications that its religion was less than total: e.g. commercial fraud and dishonesty, personal savagery and temper, personal and collective arrogance and insensitivity; for all of which unamiable traits one can find examples as easily as of their opposites.

But what makes a man really 'religious', anyway? To ask that question in a mid-Victorian context is to ask, what makes a man 'really Christian'?—for mid-Victorian religion was 'Christianity', save only for a tiny Jewish community concentrated in the metropolis and, I imagine, some covert scraps of religions of the Middle East and India. (Also, no doubt, much lingering paganism.) But what was 'Christianity'? We must make up our own mind about that, because some mid-Victorians calling themselves Christians were denied the right to do so by others with, they thought, better claims. The Christian world was then much more disunited and quarrelsome than it is now. The 37,000-odd English and Welsh Unitarians were thought sub-Christian by, it seems, the great majority of Trinitarians; Mormons, who counted about 18,000 attendances at their places of worship on that famous religious-census Sunday in 1851, were considered heathen by everybody else; 'high churchmen' and Roman Catholics tended to be dubious about the 'do-it-yourself Christianity' of the Protestant fringe; 'Evangelicals' whether within the established churches or without them tended to be very dubious about 'high churchmen' and papists; while 'high' and 'low' alike tended to be very dubious about the 'broad'. The 'liberal' or 'oecumenical' Roman Catholic was not yet even a utopian fantasy. Conscientious people in every group recognised some distinction between the genuinely devoted and the merely conformist, but found no sure means of distinguishing them; while reflective people in every group might see even in mere conformism some moral or religious advantages to society at large. Hypocrisy may after all be a tribute paid by vice to virtue; and social and political theorists might find something to say in favour of a religion which, through a thousand years, had so impressed itself upon a cluster of peoples, and adapted itself so comfortably to their social and economic development, as to make it socially unacceptable to admit to being as wicked as you perhaps really were, socially normal to give money to charity as a matter of unconsidered course, and as to impart to the minds, morals and habits of many who were certainly not believers the characteristics of those who were. We thus encounter a United Kingdom not 'wholly Christian'—what known body politic can seriously be said to have been that?—but officially, in outward forms and ceremonies, and in many significant inward aspects also, rather largely and noticeably so; and this phenomenon the historian seeks to explain, leaving it to the moralist and sociologist to inquire whether some congenital 'running to seed' may not be a price worth paying for 'taking root so widely'.

It was the custom of most mid-Victorian Christians (from now on I call all so who called themselves so) to proclaim that Britain was, essentially, a Christian country and that the British were a Christian people. Many Christians continued to maintain, in the face of 1829 and several millions of Irish-born Roman Catholic fellow citizens, that Britain was still a 'Protestant State'. That claim testified more to the strength of their feelings than to their logic. But the old maxim that 'Christianity is part of the law of England' still had some kick in it. Prosecutions for blasphemy did not cease to menace the plebeian and vulgar till this side of 1900. (Well-bred atheists who expressed technically blasphemous meanings in poetry, like Swinburne, or in intellectual prose, like John Stuart Mill, could however get away with anything.) National Days of Fasting and Humiliation were proclaimed in 1853 (cholera), 1854 (Crimea) and 1857 (Indian Mutiny). The state of the law regarding 'the Lord's Day' hardly altered during our period. The Sunday Observation Prosecution Act of 1871 put some much-needed limits on the powers of private prosecutors under a Sunday Observance Act of 1677, but there seems to have been no other perceptible relaxation of statute law, while the volume of public opinion that could be mustered to support Lord's Day Observance often outweighed that on the other side. Excursion and other Sunday trains were never statutorily suppressed, but Sunday postal services were strictly reduced (1850) and so was the playing of military, though not private, bands in public parks (1856). Theatres, pleasure grounds, and all other places of entertainment charging for admission remained as closed as they had been since 1781, and London's pubs and shops would have been in like case had not Parliament been intimidated by popular demonstrations in their favour (1855). Queen Victoria was a conscientious 'Defender of the Faith' who went to worship regularly on Sundays (Presbyterian in Scotland, Anglican in England; one wonders what she would have done if the Whigs had ever set up a papist establishment in Ireland!) and so severely discountenanced 'immorality' that anyone who had been connected with a divorce case was *ipso facto* barred from ever getting near her; but the court's Sunday laxities of conduct, extending even to the playing of chess, made many think that the royal family was not quite everything it should be.

Parliament daily opened business with prayers, and the beginnings and ends of sessions were solemn and splendid with religious ceremonies. Some members certainly believed not a word of it, and many presumably were no more willing than Lord Melbourne had been to let religion 'interfere with private life'; it is nevertheless a fact that Gladstone's administration in the early eighties was never more seriously embarrassed or endangered than by its attempts to help an honest and uncompromising atheist take the seat in the Commons to which the men of Northampton had elected him. As things were with the national representatives, so were they all down the line. I doubt if any noble family did not own at least one clergyman. Clergymen were called upon to add religious seriousness to every sort of public occasion, from prize-givings and cattle-shows to ratepayers' meetings and political protests. Urban clergymen were no longer, so far as I can judge, liable as in the twenties and early thirties to be met with menace and abuse from working-class secularists and radicals. More typical of our period, I think, was the cheerfully tolerant and essentially indifferent reception given to the evangelical clergyman at a secularist hall of science debate attended by Mark Rutherford:

'He was introduced by his freethinking antagonist, who claimed for him a respectful hearing. The preacher said that before beginning he should like to "engage in prayer" ... [beseeching God] to bless the discussion in the conversion 'of these poor wandering souls, who have said in their hearts that there is no God, to a saving faith in Him and the blood of Christ.' ... [The audience] listened with perfect silence; and when he had said "Amen", there were great clappings of hands, and cries of "Bravo" ...'[8]

Most people seem to have respected 'the cloth', although

many Protestants might not take it too seriously; perhaps a natural consequence of Protestant Christianity's protective adaptation to an anticlerical, acquisitive society in which the laity ruled the roost, no mistake about it, and had at least as many of the brains. And under these circumstances it was the most natural thing in the world for laymen (in some denominations, of course, there were no such people; all adult members being equal) to take prominent, even leading parts in Christian public ventures: evangelical and 'revival' meetings in school-rooms, hired halls, theatres, railway arches; missions to dockers, cabmen, costermongers, prostitutes; philanthropic organisations to mount and manage orphanages, specialised hospitals, emigration schemes, night refuges; associations to put up scriptural texts on every hoarding and to put down vice in every shopping centre. All this more or less religious activity had its effect, and foreign visitors felt it. The English (and *a fortiori* the Scottish) Sunday became during our period the fixed thing of amazement and terror to the foreign traveller it still to some extent is:

'Today is a Sunday [recorded a Swiss visitor to the Great Exhibition] and I ... walked down Cheapside which is quite a long street. I would have liked to have gone into a coffeehouse for a glass of ale or claret but all the shops were hermetically sealed ... Even the front door of my own hotel was locked and only if one knew the secret could one turn the right knob and effect an entry. Otherwise there would be nothing for it but to ring the bell. On returning to my hotel I asked for my bill as I have been accustomed to settle my account every day. But the innkeeper politely asked me to wait until Monday ... I got into an argument with a young lady who strongly criticised Parliament for allowing trains, omnibuses and cabs to run on Sundays. She explained that her own pious family always observed the Sabbath strictly. To illustrate this she explained that since her papa's funeral had taken place on a Sunday ... his hearse had been drawn by hired horses and not by the family horses.'

Such comments, coming from a respectable Protestant German-speaking business man, were more likely to be taken

seriously than those of Frenchmen like Taine or radical novelists like Dickens. We may feel inclined to take more notice of
the foreign observers; the more so, indeed, because of their
solicitude for the lower classes. Taine concluded in the later
sixties that 'compared with Edinburgh, a Sunday in London
is positively agreeable'.[10] What Dickens thought of London
and Edinburgh Sundays is made plain enough in Chapter
Three of *Little Dorrit* (1858) and in his ironic report from
Edinburgh, ten years later:

'You know the aspect of this city on a Sunday, and how gay
and bright it is. The merry music of the blithe bells, the
waving flags, the prettily decorated houses with their draperies
of various colours, and the radiant countenances at the windows
and in the streets, how charming they are. The usual prepara-
tions are making for the band in the open air, in the afternoon;
and the usual pretty children ... are this moment hanging
garlands round the Scott Monument, preparatory to the innocent Sunday dance round that edifice, with which the diversions invariably close.'[11]

It was also Taine, I think, who noticed what might have
been the British equivalents to those wayside crucifixes and
shrines which excited the grudging admiration of the Protestant tourist in Austria, Italy, Belgium and France. Besides the
texts on 'wayside pulpits' he noticed, with quizzical admiration, bibles provided on reading stands in main-line railway
stations, to help pious passengers pass the waiting time pro-
fitably.

The topography of the British religious world about the
time of the Great Exhibition is, fortunately, not difficult to
describe. At no other time in the nineteenth century can we
be as sure about at any rate England and Wales. (The Scottish and Irish situations are different: see below, pp. 213–15.)
The 1851 religious census of England and Wales, our unique
source of information, indeed had its faults and three recent
independent investigations make it very clear what those faults
were.[12] Those investigators nevertheless concur in concluding
that its muddles and obscurities are not such as to render it
useless for enquiries more particular even than ours. I may

therefore confidently use it and, with a deep sense of indebted-
ness to their essays on it, show the strengths of the denominations and their geographical distribution at the opening of
our period. About the changes in their numbers and distribution during our period we cannot, alas, be anything like
so sure; the idea of further such censuses was, for reasons in
part discreditable both to those who advanced and to those
who rejected them, effectively squashed, and the unofficial
counts or estimates that were made were partisan as well as
partial. Nor, even more regrettably, can we be very sure about
the social distribution of the religious public. Contemporary
assertions about it are not lacking and some of them seem fair
enough; but the refined research which will soon give us
'harder' information has only just begun. My account of the
formally religious dimension of mid-Victorian society must
therefore be lopsided; more complete and accurate for the
earlier than the later years.

What principally struck Christians who read this religious
census report or the periodical literature about it, was the
extent to which their countrymen had become (to quote the
reporter's own memorable word) 'habitual neglecters of the
public ordinances of religion': i.e. Sunday church parade. They
found themselves faced, as we who seek to understand them
are faced, with the gap between idea and reality. The idea was
as I have described it: a Christian people—more really Christian, some of them liked to think, than any other peoples—
suitably protected in its profound religious concerns by 'Christian' laws and conventions and (though Congregationalists,
Baptists, Unitarians and some Presbyterians disputed this
point) established churches. But what was the reality? On
the census Sunday, 30 March 1851, Midlent alias Mothering
alias Simnel Sunday, not less than 47 per cent but certainly
not more than 54 per cent of the population of England and
Wales of ten years of age and over 'went to church' (54 per
cent by the census reporter's dubious calculations; 47 per
cent by Pickering's 'maximum-minimum' count). That proportion is by modern standards impressive. By the standards
the Victorians set for themselves, it was humiliating. Reasons

were at once produced for why that Sunday's figures should have been unnaturally low. They do not convince us that it was significantly lower than it would have been on any other 'ordinary' Sunday. It would no doubt have been much higher on Easter Sunday or Christmas Day, festivals which then as now put many in mind of their Maker who normally neglect Him; but the moral certainty brought no comfort to a generation which valued the religious census, so far as it valued it at all, as a measure of the Christians who went to church regularly, as matter of course, and might therefore be presumed to be fairly 'real'.

It surprised men less, that the geographical distribution of that 47–54 per cent was unequal. For years it had been taken for granted as a general truth that church attendance was lower in cities than in the countryside. How much lower, and where in particular, was now revealed. But counties and regions varied too. Unpopulous Wales was found to be more 'religious' (by this test) than any parts of England except the small adjacent counties Bedfordshire and Huntingdonshire and wholly rural Wiltshire. 'The weakest areas', says Pickering, working up from the bottom, 'were London, Cumberland, Lancashire, Durham, Northumberland and Middlesex.' These ratings rested on county averages: ratios of the numbers attending worship to the populations of the counties. They conceal the figures for the provincial towns and cities, which showed some remarkable variations and proved beyond all doubt to those who had striven for years not to credit a story so unwelcome, that organised Christianity had 'lost' (so far as it had ever possessed, which is matter for debate) 'the urban masses'. It was indeed not absolutely true that church-going diminished in proportion as industrial towns (the crucial ones) got larger. Bristol and Wolverhampton were very big places with well over a hundred thousand inhabitants each, and their attendance figures were quite heartening: Rochdale, Wigan, Warrington, Huddersfield, Nottingham and Derby were in the same category. Leicester and Northampton were better still. But these instances of large or quite large urban areas with relatively high attendance figures were rather exceptional. There can be no doubt as to what was the general rule about industrial working class attendance, and it is best summed up by Inglis:

'All eight parliamentary boroughs of London are in this group [of towns with the lowest index of attendance]; and of the other twenty-eight towns in it, all except seven were within "chief manufacturing districts". Five of the remaining seven—Norwich, Macclesfield, Stoke-upon-Trent, Coventry and Carlisle—were centres of industry.... Even excluding London, the average population of the group was [very high]. It contained the four largest provincial towns: Liverpool... Manchester ... Birmingham ... and Leeds; and it included two other towns with more than 100,000 inhabitants: Sheffield ... and Bradford. These towns ... included every large town described in the general census as a cotton town, and the two greatest wool towns. The list also contains every large coal town (except Wolverhampton), the two great hardware towns Sheffield and Birmingham, and every large town in Lancashire except Wigan and Rochdale. Abstinence from religious worship was most common where the largest numbers of working-class people lived—in London and in many of the towns where the industrial revolution was wrought.'

We have so far been looking over the shoulders of recent investigators of the religious census to see where 'church attendance', undifferentiated, was high, and where it was low. The same investigations, read alongside that of A. C. Whitby,[13] enable us to measure and to some extent locate the strengths of the various denominations. Pickering's 'maximum-minimum' revision of the official reporter's figures gives us this table of persons present at the most numerously attended services:

	Persons present	% of persons of total population	% of persons 'at church' that Sunday
Church of England	2,971,258	17	47
Nonconformist	3,110,782	17	49
Roman Catholic	249,389	1	4
Sectarian	24,793	(·1)	(·4)
Total	6,356,222	35	100

The established church of England and Wales 'proved to be strong in those areas where total church-going was strong, which is roughly speaking from Cornwall to the Wash' (Pickering); except, notably, for Wales, where its following was negligible, and where the remarkable quantity of church-going was mostly Nonconformist. It apparently held the allegiance of more than a quarter of the population in Dorsetshire, Rutland, Huntingdonshire and Northamptonshire, and its following was, by the standards of the time, substantial in Somerset, Wiltshire, Oxfordshire, Cambridgeshire, Suffolk, Hertfordshire, Bedfordshire and Buckinghamshire. Inglis, using the official reporter's marginally dubious figures, finds that there were more Church of England than Nonconformist church-goers in Halifax, Kidderminster, Warrington, Wigan, Liverpool, and (though not by much) Birmingham and Wakefield, while in Salford, Blackburn and Walsall, they ran neck and neck. In those towns alone of the ones in the 'chief manufacturing districts' did the Church of England make a respectable showing. In some such its showing was lamentable. Pickering reckons that in Manchester and in Tower Hamlets—London's East End—it was frequented by not less than 6 or 7 per cent, but by no possible calculation, counting Sunday School attendances in with the rest, by more than 12 per cent of the total population.

Roman Catholics were strongest on English ground in Lancashire. In Liverpool and Wigan they certainly outnumbered Nonconformists; in Preston they almost certainly outnumbered Anglicans; in Manchester they comprised nearly a quarter of the church-going public. They comprised between 13 and 17 per cent of that public in Newcastle upon Tyne, Bolton, Salford and Walsall; nearly 11 per cent in Blackburn; about 6 per cent in Birmingham. Lancashire, the Tees-Tyne area, the Black Country and of course certain inner metropolitan slums were their strongholds; but the metropolis taken as a whole was big enough to sink them below the 3 per cent line.

At last we survey the mixed bag of Nonconformists, whose aggregate total of worshippers, however calculated, gave them approximate equality with Anglicans. About half this body (a body, it must be said, whose muscles and voice were stronger than its joints and nerves) were Methodists of one kind or another; slightly more than a quarter were Congregationalists; perhaps 20 per cent were Baptists; the rest, some sort of Presbyterian or 'sectary'. Except in Wales, which they dominated with nowhere less than 36 per cent of the church-going populace and in most places *much* more, their strength was spread more evenly than that of the establishment. They mustered between 24 and 35 per cent of church-goers in Cornwall, where Wesleyan Methodists were dominant and two Methodist secessions, the Wesleyan Methodist Association and the Bible Christians, conspicuous; in Monmouthshire, which had a peculiar concentration of Particular Baptists; and in Bedfordshire and Huntingdonshire, where the Particular Baptists again were concentrated, but where there were also quite a lot of Wesleyan Methodists. Pickering's third map shows that Nonconformity held between 23 and 12 per cent of the church-goers in every other English county except Cumberland, Westmorland and (what was rather significant in a still-industrialising England) Lancashire; Warwickshire and Worcestershire; Sussex, Surrey, Middlesex; and the metropolis. Nonconformity's weakness in London was indeed remarkable and, some considered, humiliating. In every part of London except the East End, 'Church of England attendances were higher than Nonconformist attendances, which were lower in London than almost anywhere else in urban England' (Inglis'; and among those metropolitan Nonconformists, Methodists were generally less numerous than Congregationalists, Baptists, and Presbyterians.

Methodists of every kind may have been embarrassingly thin on the ground in London; but they were, proportionately, thick on the ground in the rest of urban industrial England. It was perhaps Inglis's most interesting discovery, that 'Nonconformity owed what hold it had in large manufacturing towns above all to the efforts of Methodists', and most of its hold in the other large towns where Nonconformity was relatively strong; and that the Wesleyan Methodists, the main stem of the by now much fragmented movement, were by far the strongest in most large towns, whether manufacturing or not. This was especially interesting because most of us who till Victorian fields had been misled by the noisy claims of the early Victorian 'political dissenters' in their campaign against the establishment. The undeniable facts of Unitarian and Congregationalist eminence in industrial and civic affairs, and the undenied fact of the establishment's relative strength in the countryside, led to our assumption first, that Methodism was not all that important in the larger towns, and second, that the more 'democratic' and 'proletarian' methodist secessions, above all the Primitive Methodists and the New Connexion ones, must have done better than the Wesleyans wherever the working class was thickest. The overall picture is quite different! Wesleyan Methodist attendances were lower than those of other Methodist bodies in only these large manufacturing towns: Ashton-under-Lyne, Dudley, Gateshead, where the New Connexion flourished; Blackburn and South Shields, which were strong in Primitive Methodists; Rochdale, Wesleyan Association, and Wakefield, Wesleyan Reformers. The Methodist secessions were strong in some areas, but they made no better a showing than the non-Methodist Nonconformists in the larger manufacturing towns. That is not to say that they lacked special ties to industry, some major departments of which were based not on towns, in the normal use of the word, so much as on industrial villages or settlements, which might sooner or later develop into towns or conurbations but which might not. Many of the mining, quarrying and ironmaking areas were of this character, and so were some of the areas where domestic industry had not yet succumbed to heavy machinery. Some, perhaps much, of the Primitive Methodist strength in Shropshire, Staffordshire, Derbyshire and County Durham must have been 'industrial'. The same must apply to some of the Baptists (Particular) and Calvinistic Methodists who dominated the Christian world in Glamorgan and Monmouthshire; the Bible Christians in Cornwall; and the New Connexion in Staffordshire. But can the Baptists' relative strength in Northamptonshire, Huntingdonshire and

Bedfordshire really have been based on what were shrinking domestic industries of those counties? Must not most of the Calvinistic Methodists in North Wales have been agricultural? And what must have been the occupations of all those Primitive Methodists in Lincolnshire, the East Riding of Yorkshire, and Norfolk?

Knowledge of the occupations of church-goers would give us some idea of the class-composition of congregations. We can as yet be sure of neither. Perhaps there is nothing to be sure about. Generalisations sink like stones at the touch of fresh research. It was probably no less true then than now, that congregations tended to have some predominant class character wherever denominations were numerous enough to support more than one place of worship; the better-off were more comfortable among the better-off, the poor might feel uncomfortable in their company. But where geography and numbers bound members to a single congregation, the same phenomena would show in church and chapel alike: all social grades (except, I'm fairly sure, the residuum) could be found worshipping together, but policy would be directed by the wealthier ones. This seems to have been even more true of 'chapel' than of 'church'. An Anglican rector with a sufficient income from rents, endowments or (commuted) tithes, and a well-built church, could, unless he ran into real trouble in the vestry, run things very much as he wished and would not be bound to respect the interests or feelings of his richer sheep if he chose not to do so. Most Anglican country clergymen, I presume, did choose to do so, even if only on grounds of social and political preference. But some parishes would be entirely deficient in rich sheep; many urban parishes, especially the recently-formed ones, were of monotonously lower middle and lower class character; and in any case there seems always to have been a seasoning of radical or merely eccentric Anglican parsons who took advantage of their freeholds to espouse what they conceived to be the interests of the poor, and who might if they were persuasive or influential enough carry some non-poor with them. Charles Kingsley, the Hon. Sidney Godolphin Osborne, James Fraser who was made

Bishop of Manchester in 1870, are conspicuous examples of this attractive type in the Church of England, and the Church of Scotland had its equivalents in such as Patrick Brewster and James Begg. How many equally weighty Nonconformist ministers did the same, I do not know. E. P. Hennock's account of Birmingham Nonconformity[14] makes me suspect that the spell-binding George Dawson might have done so; but did R. W. Dale, at the city's premier independent chapel, Carr's Lane? Nonconformist ministers were more liable to financial dependence on their flocks—which of course meant the men with long purses and 'good credit'—because new chapels were rarely built, and old ones rarely enlarged, without a mortgage loan, the repaying of which became a major (and, sometimes, an insuperable) problem. That was equally true of Methodists and the rest. So far as incomes went, Methodist ministers were more fortunately placed than the rest. Their stipends were assured by Conference, and they did not have to mind their p's and q's so carefully. Ministers of every other non-Anglican Protestant denomination had for their own sake to work along with their more prosperous members, unless all their members were equally prosperous (as must have been the case with some of the smartest Unitarian, Congregationalist and Presbyterian chapels) or equally unprosperous (which must often have been the case too). And chapel communities could, we know, be either heterogeneous or homogeneous in social composition. It depended on several factors: antiquity and local tradition, location (chapels that followed their more prosperous members out to the suburbs became more conspicuously 'middle class'), sociological *raison d'être* (e.g. a small, isolated mining or fishing community might be as tight-knit in chapel as out of it) and so on. All sorts of combinations were possible. J. C. G. Binfield, who has scrutinised East Anglian Nonconformity with exemplary care,[15] points out that it included not merely the old-established 'urban aristocracies' and the new-rich industrialists like Sir Samuel Morton Peto (who built around himself the model olde-worlde village of Somerleyton) but also, in that region at any rate, an element of country gentry. This was not to survive the social pressures of the later Victorian period, when the upper strata of both town and country Nonconformity began to filter through the public schools towards Oxbridge and the Church of England; but in our period this diversity of social composition still mattered enough for us to beware of generalising too confidently about 'middle class dissent'. Any one Methodist, Congregationalist, Presbyterian or Baptist chapel might have been full of 'middle class' persons and none others; or it might not.

Are generalisations about the social character of mid-Victorian Nonconformity then impossible? No. Dissenting congregations might run from the edge of the aristocracy down to the rim of the residuum, but they were rather exceptional. A social spectrum of 'middle class', from well-established merchants and professional men down to small masters and the respectable artisans who could be so nearly indistinguishable from them, was perhaps less uncommon among the larger denominations than among the smaller ones. Unitarians (for whom Trinitarian Dissenters, especially when touched by evangelicalism, felt no particular love) and Quakers (who retained marked singularity) were felt to be socially superior, and were in fact so. Methodists did not yet think of themselves as Free Churchmen along with all the rest; they kept somewhat to themselves—as, being legion, they could afford to do; and while Wesleyan Methodists might come from any middle or working class strata, Primitive Methodists were more generally working class. It was a general assumption, and Binfield finds material support for it, that Baptists were of lower social standing than Congregationalists, although there was nothing to choose between the top men in either, and each was actually quite mixed. Presbyterians were, like Methodists, much fragmented; the famous disruption of 1843 and consequent birth of the Free Church of Scotland having been only the latest and largest secession of a long series. The Free Church gave itself excellent publicity and claimed to represent 'the people' much better than the establishment, but A. Allan MacLaren's examination of the social composition of the Aberdeen churches[16] (the only such known to me) only shows that the Frees were less dominated by the 'upper middle class'. There, at any rate, they do not appear to have brought any significant number of working class men as elders into the kirk sessions. There, as everywhere outside the established churches, the men who were in demand to run things or who by some process of natural selection became the runners of things were the solid citizens, the pillars of the community, who could most efficiently raise funds and inspire confidence. A church not founded on rocks was all too liable to run *on to* them.

Only the Roman Catholics in England seem to have been, in the lump, proletarian; even, lumpen-proletarian. That lump was leavened with finest social yeast, and I suppose that already by the end of our period certain Roman Catholic churches in Mayfair, Pimlico, Kensington, Bayswater and so on had as fashionable a character as did certain Anglican establishments in the same wealthy quarters. But the dominant characteristics of British Roman Catholicism were that it was mainly working class and mainly Irish. Wherever the Irish settled in numbers (Clydeside and Lanarkshire; Lancashire, Cheshire; Tyneside; the Black Country; and London) the church of their fathers made remarkable efforts to keep them faithful or, where habits of church-attendance had died, to reclaim them. This meant the provision of churches and—absolute necessity in the Roman Catholic scheme of things—schools; priests cost much less than either of these items; and most of the money had to come from the pockets of the immigrant Irish poor themselves, for that social yeast of old nobility and their professional men, thickened though it was by a succession of socialite conversions, could provide (even proportionately) little to match the financial support poured into the Anglicans' and Nonconformists' expansion programmes by their men of substance. Such moreover were the climates of opinion among both Protestants and Papists that there was no possibility of money flowing from one to the other. (Not that there are many possibilities now.) Money for missions being thus pre-eminently necessary for the Roman Catholics, the way was open for Protestant vigilantes to allege underhand tactics in getting it; and the Roman Catholic community (or communities; the Irish majority never mixed well with the English and Scottish minorities), pulling itself up by sacrificial self-help, became or remained as close and segregated a denomination as any in Britain. The strictest Particular Baptists, 'Plymouth' Brethren, or Scottish Original Seceders, were hardly more enclosed in their own religious and social worlds than the Irish Roman Catholics in England and Scotland, moving through inadequate church and school premises on the tightly-scheduled timetables that alone could give everyone the minimum of sacramental and sacerdotal attention necessary for salvation, and quite deliberately cultivating the sense of separateness which, in the case of the Irish anyway, also grew vigorously from strong economic and nationalist roots.

This great missionary campaign of the Roman Catholic church (on which little research has yet been done) was already moving ahead well before the fifties, but it was not publicly proclaimed, nor could it appear as official Roman Catholic policy, until the so-called 'restoration of the hierarchy' in 1850. To some extent it stimulated Protestants to counter-action. Protestant Evangelicals, especially Irish ones, got (and get) a peculiar kick from running missions to Papists, and the rest of the century was punctuated by smart offensives on both sides. But much more interesting from our point of view is the coincidence of this Roman Catholic campaign at least to 're-claim' lapsed Roman Catholics, with a general effort among the other Christian churches to reclaim and 'rechristianise' the masses in general. This, like the Roman Catholic campaign, was not new in the fifties; precedents, foundations, suggestions for most of it can be found even as far back as the twenties; but it certainly entered upon a new phase, a more strenuous and conscious phase, about the beginning of our period. For this spurt, the publication of the findings of the religious census was partly responsible. But they were not generally available until early 1854. I have the impression that sensible Christians already sensed the extent of (to use an official description) 'spiritual destitution' and were most affected by the census crystallising their ideas into brisk action. It hit impartially all Christians who cared to be more than sectaries, by making clear the extent to which neither 'church'

nor 'chapel' was succeeding in Christianising (or rechristian-
ising) the masses. The thirties and forties had been loud with
argument as to how this could best be done: most Anglicans
maintaining that only an established church and its schools
could do it, while Dissenters proper – not Methodists, who
kept out of the argument as far as they could and got on with
the cultivation of their own gardens—were maintaining by the
end of the forties that the 'voluntarist' principle was better
for schools as well as churches and that the masses (no one
worried much about middle and upper class religion) would
be more surely 'recovered' if there were no established church
at all. This extreme position, which Dissenters were bound to
adopt if they really meant the mean things they said about the
Church of England, was one about which some of them were,
one gathers, uncomfortable. Their claims seemed extravagant
from the start, and during our period were seen to be so
unjustifiable that some Dissenters, who had shouted loudest
for educational voluntarism in the forties, were recanting
through the sixties, as they faced the fact that, unless the state
undertook the provision of schools, there would never be
enough, and that the only way to get universal education without Anglican control of it was to sink their earlier scruples
about 'separating religion from education' and accept a common ground of secular instruction. This change of policy was
good politics (if only because it enabled them to turn the
tables on the 'national church' and to pose quite convincingly
as caring more for 'national' than 'party' advantage), but it was
also good sense because it offered some prospect of at any
rate 'civilising' those lower class legions whom the campaign
of the fifties and sixties had failed to 'Christianise', a failure in
which Dissenters and Anglicans alike were implicated.

The side of that campaign conducted by the religious education societies need not delay us. Mid-Victorian Christians
were of course profoundly interested in it. Whether the means
they adopted were denominational, inter-denominational, or
undenominational, they were agreed that no process of elementary education was worth the name if it did not include an
element of religious instruction; and their idea of the school-

child's week included Sunday school, upon which many school managers insisted. All this was important and cannot have been without effect. But our present concern is not with the part of the population that could be expected (and made) to go to school but with the larger part that could be expected to go to church, and could hardly be compelled to do so. Attempts at compulsion were indeed not unknown. Evangelicals and others who pressed for Sunday Observance were in effect willing to compel, and so was that side of the temperance movement which expected to diminish drunkenness by acts of Parliament. I know of at any rate two railway companies which expressed a desire that their employees should go regularly to some church of their choice, and I for one do not doubt the truth of the allegation often made, by secularists and Nonconformists, that very strong pressure was sometimes put on the rustic labouring population by some squires and parsons, to go to the church of *their* choice. But such compulsion, direct or covert, was certainly exceptional. Not compulsion but conversion; not direction but attraction, was the principle upon which the mid-Victorian 'rechristianisation' campaign had to be conducted.

The non-church-going masses had to be sought for, in language they could understand and by means that might prove attractive. This meant some deliberate popularisation, even (in no pejorative sense) vulgarisation of Christianity, and the realisation that nothing less would do meant more of an adjustment for Anglicans than for any of the others, and more of an adjustment for High and Broad Churchmen than for Evangelical ones. The Church of England's great effort during the early nineteenth century to recover the ground which it seemed to have lost, was based on the assumption that it only needed to provide church accommodation and staff adequate to the population for that accommodation to be made use of and that staff to be kept busy. The enlargement of old and the provision of new churches had by the end of the forties gone far. With funds and direction partly from 'the centre' (the Church Building and the Ecclesiastical Commissioners), partly from diocesan or single-city initiatives (the most active being Bishop J. B. Sumner in Cheshire and Lancashire, and Bishop Blomfield in the East End of London) the supply of church accommodation had, in some main urban areas, been brought near enough to the estimated potential demand. Sensible Anglicans had then to swallow the hard lesson that the urban masses had not absented themselves from the Church of England because there were no seats for them. They had stayed away, most of them, because they had no interest in the 'national church'; perhaps no interest in any church. Plenty of seats were available in Bethnal Green and Manchester by 1850, but not many of the working classes, the people they were primarily meant for, were sitting in them. Some were taken up by middle class people, an embarrassing number stayed empty. The lower orders would not come to church, therefore the church had to go out and get the lower orders. This was less of a change for Evangelicals than for other Anglicans because their tradition was largely built on 'evangelisation', and their practice included as much of it as was consistent with the decorum expected of the establishment. However, adventurous Anglican Evangelicals (ordained or lay) who had engaged in what was known as domestic or city mission work found themselves from the twenties onwards under censure for 'irregularity' in principle and for dangerous proximity to Nonconformity, which could engage in such popular evangelism without difficulty or scruple.

By the later forties this establishment starchiness was fast disappearing, as Anglicans of all parties were driven to try the same techniques that Nonconformists had always been free to use, and that some Nonconformists had pioneered. So we see, during our period, a new phase of Christian activity in which such popular evangelistic techniques as 'revivalism', for example, or lay private enterprise, or street-preaching, which had earlier been fought shy of by 'respectable' Christian leaders (Wesleyan and Presbyterian as well as Anglican), were more widely adopted. Of course, conservative Christians were still suspicious of such practices, and by keeping aloof from them or even trying to prevent them, implicitly expressed a preference that the masses should not be Christian at all rather than be Christianised like that! But the new mood was unmistakable. A few bishops dropped their dignity and mounted soap-boxes. High and 'ritualist' Anglicans conducted 'missions' just like Roman Catholics and Evangelicals, and justified liturgical innovations on the ground that the poor would not be attracted without them. The work of the 'city missions' —the undenominational London one being by far the biggest and best known—attracted new interest and respect, and the missioners' reports were given the attention they deserved.

Some Anglicans were moved by the evident success of some of these 'city missions' to suggest that the Church of England adopt their policy and carry the gospel to the working classes, not by its classical means of educated gentlemen but by working class evangelists and in frankly working class churches: a potentially radical line of thought from which stemmed in due course the safely controlled orders of Scripture and Lay Readers. The mid-Victorian impulse to mission also now began to prompt self-consciously middle or upper class urban congregations (Nonconformist and Anglican) to establish and finance *ad hoc* 'mission' or mission chapels in the lower class parts of their cities, hoping that the poor who would not come to a smart place of worship might go more readily to a humble one. Lord Shaftesbury sanctioned with his unique prestige the Anglican adoption of the Nonconformist evangelistic expedient of hiring theatres and music halls for popular religious services and programmed revivals: adaptations to urban *venues* of the originally American and rural camp meeting. And revivalism became quite respectable. A transatlantic surge of it in the later fifties hit Ulster in 1859 and was not expended before it had reached many less religiously excitable parts of the British Isles. Between that and the next major American impulse—Sankey and Moody in 1873— there was throughout the evangelical world a resourceful endeavour to, so to speak, institutionalise revival, to keep revivalist beacons burning for the guidance and inspiration of all the home and district mission work developing through the same years. Charles Spurgeon, the brightest beacon of them all, set up his pulpit in Southwark in 1854. William Booth, later to become General Booth of the Salvation Army, had already astonished the Christian world with his Hallelujah Band of reformed drunkards and wife-beaters before he pitched his tent on Mile End Waste fairground ten years later. The free enterprise sector of religion (then perhaps at its widest extension ever) provided innumerable parallels and imitators in city and village alike. Revival became familiar, even habitual, beyond the groups which had long enjoyed it, like the Methodist left and the corybantic sects.

But how successful was this mid-Victorian 'mission to Britain'? Did it, with all its dash and resourcefulness and, indeed, its popularity, achieve its object, the regaining of ground for Christianity among the British people—which meant mainly the working classes, so many of whom had abandoned its public observances, but also to some extent the middle classes, of the religious seriousness of many of whom there was reason to be doubtful? Hard figures are not available to settle the case one way or the other, but it seems most unlikely that the proportion of churchgoers in Britain was higher in the seventies than it had been in the fifties. Among Methodists (all sorts) this proportion (of worshippers to total population) slightly rose during the fifties and sixties and sharply fell from the seventies onwards. We know more about Methodist numbers than about any other denominations, partly because Methodists kept better membership records than the rest, partly because such good use has been made of them by Robert Currie.[17] Figures of the enlargement of church accommodation are plentiful enough, and quite impressive some of them are; but one dare not take them as meaning anything in real membership terms. Contemporary impressions of the membership situation throughout the period suggest that its hectic activity in missions, revivals, etc., produced no startling permanent increase. No one denied that revival, mission, and all kinds of special services often drew large crowds. Spurgeon, the most attractive of them all, was a sure-fire draw from the first of his preaching tours in 1855, and he drew 25,000 for his special service in the Crystal Palace on the Indian Mutiny day of national self-abasement. But were they not very often the same crowds? And were they not more 'bourgeois' than 'proletarian'? The air was turbulent with assertion and counter-assertion on these points, and all one can say by way of summary is that such successes as the mid-Victorian mission had on the British lower classes were local and temporary, leaving no significant imprint. The worshipping situation discovered by the social analysts of the later Victorian and subsequent periods was of the same cast as that revealed by the 1851 census. The pattern of drift away from dogma and the duties of regular church membership had become too deeply embedded in British society (though deeper apparently in English than in Irish, Welsh or Scottish) to be stayed at this late stage.

A good deal of what I have already said is as relevant to the social history of Scottish religion as to English; some of it will be relevant to that of Irish religion too. Scottish and Irish Christianity was institutionally different from English or Welsh in being less mixed: most church-going Scots were some sort of Presbyterian, and most church-going Irish were Roman Catholic. But similar ideals of national Christianity and Christian respectability dominated the Scots and the Irish too, and seem to have been more effective among the Irish Papists than their Protestant critics were usually willing to allow. As to the figures of church membership outside England and Wales, we are not well served. No religious census was ever taken in Ireland. The sun of statistics only begins to dispel the fog of surmise in 1861, when Irish residents were asked to state their 'religious profession'. I give the summarised results below. They show to what denominations men and women said they and their children belonged. Of course they give no clue as to actual attendance. But it seems reasonable to assume of so peculiarly intense a Roman Catholic country and society, with probably the most effective and influential body of parish priests in northern Europe, that profession of Roman Catholicism was equivalent to practice. After all, the shrewd and experienced Howie, taking the measurements of the Scottish religious scene in the nineties,[18] believed it was safe to make that assumption about the Glasgow Irish, although he would make it about no other denomination, not even his own Presbyterian. But might Irish Protestantism have been equally serious and sincere? It is at least possible. It has been (and it is) different from British in so many respects, it may have been different in that respect too.

Religious Professions of People in Ireland, in 'ooos

	1851	1861	1871	1881
Roman Catholic	no figures	4,505	4,151	3,952
Prot. Episcopalian	for 1851	693	668	636
Presbyterians	seem to be	523	498	486
Methodists	available	45	43	48
Others (excl. Jews)	,,	31	52	38
Non Roman Catholic total (excl. Jews)	,,	1,292	1,261	1,208

Variations among the denominations from decade to decade are for our purposes insignificant. Only 'Methodists' (all sorts) showed, over the twenty charted years, an absolute gain in numbers; which was almost wholly dependent on progress in Ulster. More significant, however familiar, are the regional distributions. Ulster, with dominantly Protestant County Antrim and Belfast city at its heart, was the Protestant province; only 20,000 fewer Protestants than Papists in 1861, about 40,000 more in 1871, grown to about 70,000 more by 1881. Presbyterians (all sorts) had little strength elsewhere. It was Episcopalians who made up the great bulk of Protestant numbers in Leinster; but even there they were only about one-sixth as numerous as Papists, whose preponderance was of course even more marked in the other two provinces.

About the numbers of Scottish Christians we are better informed; but not about 1851. The religious census of that year was held in Scotland too, but climatic conditions may have been worse; the census itself seems to have been much less (or, if you prefer it, even less) reliable, and no Horace Mann worked over it before it was published. It ended up a sadly imperfect document. This defect is to some extent balanced by the singular excellence of the Free Church Minister Howie's book, a work of extreme statistical carefulness, which floods the eighties with valuable light. The fifties and sixties alas remain obscure. Even Howie could not make much of them. Iain MacLeod's researches have however helped me towards a conviction that there was rather more church attendance in Scotland than in England.[19] Seven per cent more Scots than English were reported to have attended a place of worship that Sunday in 1851, and even if one allows for a larger margin of error in the Scottish figures, the Scots still win. The great majority of these were Presbyterians of one sort or another: established Church of Scotland, newly separated Free Church, more anciently separated members of the United Presbyterian Church, were the main groupings. Roman Catholics, heavily concentrated in the Glasgow region, made up about 7 per cent of the total worshipping population. By 1876, when Howie's searchlight was piercing the fog, the Roman Catholic proportion was more like 10 per cent: going up, while the aggregate Presbyterian proportion came down. Not less than 17 per cent of the Scottish population were, he reckoned, 'churchless'; utterly without connection with any organised church. That was from a Christian point of view a much more creditable figure than contemporary England could have provided, but it was an absolute minimum; Howie was sure the real figure must be somewhat higher, but how much higher, he could not be sure.

This review of the place of religion in mid-Victorian Britain may well conclude with an outsider's impression of its place in the lives of mid-Victorian Britons. This of course amounts to little more than an outsider's view of the outside of the mid-Victorians and tells us little about the quality of their religion, or of the degree of morality it may reflect. A post-Victorian observer will wish to consider how far a man may be 'moral' without being 'religious'; 'religious' (in Victorian terms) without being 'Christian'; and 'Christian' without being a regular attendant at public worship. Looking at church and chapel life simply as part of the social fabric, I see that for many church- and chapel-going Christians it obviously comprised a large, often no doubt the main, part of their social life. We cannot be sure about the proportion of apparent Christians thus involved. We do not know how many of those who went to worship on that famous Sunday in 1851 were 'regulars', how many 'occasionals'; nor can we tell you how many 'regulars' were devoted and committed members of congregations, how many were no more than 'adherents', Sundays-only Christians (not necessarily however an inferior sort). But even bearing such uncertainties in mind, one cannot help concluding that more or less religious activity filled many ostensible Christians' social lives. Sunday must often have been the busiest day of the week. Among Nonconformists at any rate it was not unusual to attend two services, and beyond that there was Sunday School which occupied many adults both as teachers and pupils. Men and women equally participated as Sunday School teachers; it was normal to begin during your teens, a senior position was quite prestigious, and the superintendent was a very important figure indeed. Examples of the numbers thus involved are given by Maclaren and Binfield respectively for Aberdeen, where the sixty-two Sunday Schools in 1851 engaged the services of about eight hundred teachers, and for a prosperous chapel in Colchester, Lion Walk, whose Sunday School was in 1860 keeping busy no less than seventy-seven teachers (that number being about one quarter of the chapel's membership). That their children should profit from Sunday School was, I believe, even more important for Nonconformists than for Anglicans, if only because infant dissenters would less usually get the 'right sort' of religious instruction at day school; hence the Nonconformist's readiness, by the later sixties, to settle for a universal 'secular' school system—they were already accustomed to doing the serious religious teaching on Sundays. But it is important to remember that, through our period, a considerable proportion of Sunday School pupils were above elementary school age and would be usually engaged in 'secular' as well as religious learning; many of the adults in Sunday Schools were simply catching up on the three Rs.

Sundays, then, were very largely given over to religious exercises by the serious religious public: more intensively by its dominant puritanical and evangelical parts, which tended to make a fetish of it, than by its latitudinarian and 'high church' parts where religious seriousness on Sundays was not thought incompatible with relaxation and refreshment. But the other days of the week could be filled with church and chapel activities too; not all of them devotional. That Lion Walk Chapel at Colchester had only 276 fully-committed members, but by 1860, Binfield tells us, it ran a Benevolent Society (presumably philanthropic, for visiting and relieving the needy), a Library, a Circulating Book Society, a Bible Class, a Ladies' Greek New Testament Class, a Psalmody Class (for sacred songs and solos), a Day School for 260 children, and the Sunday School already mentioned, which 'reproduced in miniature the societies of the mother church'; and, doing its bit in the 'home mission campaign', a Lay Preachers' Association running four missions each with its own Sunday School. Let its own honest minister, the great John Angell James, describe the state of Carr's Lane Chapel in Birmingham at the turn of 1859:

'We are not [he said] one whit better than some others.... We have now an organisation for the London Missionary Society, which raises as its regular contribution nearly £500 per annum.... For the Colonial Missionary Society, we raise, annually, £70. For our Sunday and day schools, which comprehend nearly two thousand children, we raise £200. We support two town missionaries, at a cost of £200. Our ladies conduct a working society for orphan mission schools in the East Indies.... They sustain also a Dorcas Society for the poor of the town; a Maternal Society, for visiting the sick poor. We have a Religious Tract Society, which employs ninety distributors, and spends £50 nearly a year in the purchase of tracts. Our Village Preachers' Society, which employs twelve or fourteen lay agents, costs us scarcely anything.... We have a Young Men's Brotherly Society, for general and religious improvement, with a library of two thousand volumes. We also have night schools for young men and women ... and Bible classes.... In addition to this, there are, in all our congregations, many and liberal subscribers to our public societies, such as the Bible Society, the Society for the Conversion of the

Jews, and all other objects of Christian zeal and benevolence...'[20]

Beyond these regular and formal group operations there were Sunday School outings (on Saturdays, I suppose) and the treadmill of tea-parties which occupied in ostensibly harmless style some part of middle class Christian females' ample leisure. It remains only to point out that important though necessarily irregular occurrences in mid-Victorian Christian life were the visiting star preacher or lecturer, often making propaganda and collecting money for a religious cause, and the mission or local crusade, which would excite some though not all local Christians.

It is quite clear that some part of this busy church or chapel social life was of a 'recreational' character; recreation, excitement and amusement (not to mention the contacts with the opposite sex which could lead to marriage) were available within all such religious communities as sanctioned them (i.e. all but the the severely puritanical) and were often ample enough to fill a member's time. Recreation was nevertheless elsewhere available, for those who wanted the non-religious kind, and to that we must now turn.

Society at Play

In surveying mid-Victorian leisure-time and the uses to which it was put, we are made more sharply than usual aware of the deepening gulf betwixt town and country. This was for the very obvious reason that town circumstances were changing fast while country ones were not. For significant new forms of 'recreation' appear in the mid-Victorian countryside. The already established pattern of holidays and fun-times (some immemorial, some quite recently introduced) persisted: occasions such as harvest home, shearing supper, Whitsun walks, agricultural shows, tithe feasts, markets and fairs—especially the annual 'hiring' ones at which farm labourers and domestic servants got fixed up for the coming eleven and threequarter months. The entertainments and wonders brought to the markets and fairs by travelling showmen reflected to some extent the developments of technology and communications; panoramas of the Wild West and the Australian gold-fields simply were not available earlier on; and the biggest round-abouts were beginning to be harnessed to steam-power. A slight widening of the countryman's horizon must have taken place; there was by all accounts a lot more drinking both on holidays and weekdays than there had been before the thirties; and, partly to counteract it, there were church- or chapel-organised entertainments (readings, lantern lectures, musical evenings, etc.) of a more systematic and deliberate kind than was usual before the forties. But I see none but minor, incidental changes in the pattern of rural recreation; which is exactly what one would expect in a countryside resting (through our period only; things were to change fast thereafter) on a stable economic basis and not yet much subject to depopulation.

How different was the town! These were years (as remarked above, pp. 81 ff.) when urban society was, so to speak, settling down: emerging from the uncertainties and emergencies of the first flush of industrialisation and discovering a way of life that offered security and satisfaction. Some citizens indeed got more security and satisfaction than others. One gathers that the way of life of the residuum did not improve much. Painful poverty, whether 'residual' or 'respectable', of course prevented its victims from enjoying all but the cheapest recreational offerings. Yet there were some such—e.g. 'penny gaffs' (very low, brief shows of melodrama or knockabout), and, for the more serious-minded, 'penny readings'—apart from the rough entertainments of the street-showman (Punch and Judy, songs, music, peep-shows, acrobatics) and the traditional fairground. The public parks and promenades which began to be opened (see p. 83) must have made life a little pleasanter for those with 'the key of the street', although the ragged were liable to be excluded. We see during our period, in every town or city of any size, wealth and concentration, the crystallising of a cultural apparatus providing for every level of the community. Not all of this cultural apparatus was new in the fifties and sixties. Many of its elements were inherited from twenty, forty, more than forty years before. But one broad category of elements was new during our period and it was a remarkable and significant one. The leisure patterns of modern industrial urban mass society now begin to take shape. There now develop in at any rate the larger urban concentrations of socially undistinguished people, certain recreational and cultural institutions characteristic of them alone; institutions called into being, it seems, by these common people's needs and interests (rather than by what benevolent superiors thought was their need and ought to be their interest), financed by their own payments, and for the most part made possible by the slightly more leisured existence many of them were experiencing (see pp. 137–8).

Conspicuous among these new recreational institutions, and representative of them, were the popular railway excursion, the music hall, (perhaps) the choral society, the brass band, and the association football club. Since these were especially significant I keep them for special treatment at the end of the chapter, remarking at this stage merely that despite the strong urge to fix a class label on them I find it difficult to label any but the brass band and the football club 'working class'; and there are ambiguities about even them. My impression is that it was no less true of these 'new' than of the 'inherited' recreational institutions, that although their coarser varieties (e.g. the low-grade saloons and pubs, the cheapest and smokiest proto-music halls, the most sensational and primitive dramatic productions) would be patronised exclusively by labouring and 'loafing' (see pp. 150–1) people of the rougher sort, their more respectable varieties would be patronised and supported by people of 'working' and 'lower middle' class character indifferently. Here as in most other social respects mid-Victorians seem to have made more of a distinction, and more explicit a distinction, between the respectable and the non-respectable than between (which is after all more our distinction than theirs) working and lower middle class. Rowdyism, beastly drunkenness (I do not say drink and conviviality), dirtiness, cruelty, uninhibited vulgarity—marks equally of those who cared not for 'respectability' and those who were too poor to care or even know about it—were shunned by 'respectable', 'decent' working people as well as by all of higher social standing save only those, sometimes of highest birth, who like to 'see life' and be thought 'fast', and who got some kind of kick out of the company of pugilists, horse-trainers, burlesque artistes and fashionable madames. Rich and poor, aristocracy and underworld, were never closer together than at the prize-fight, the cockpit, the rat-catching, the race-track, and the demi-monde saloon and casino. Extremes did not so nearly meet on the more respectable (not necessarily stuffy) side of the recreational world. There the natural tendency for people to keep to the company of those with whom they felt comfortable operated more freely. But there too was some—we cannot reckon how much—social mixture. We do not know for instance from what social levels came the members of those huge choral societies that, especially in the industrial midlands and north, became so notable a feature of civic life; but we may suspect that St Cecilia's net caught at any rate some 'upper working class' singers. Anyone who dressed decently and behaved decorously could use the public parks; and some who did neither might get in too (Hyde Park was already notorious). Theatres, we know, might be patronised by all classes; their accommodation and prices were often expressly designed to that end, and pit and gallery had long brought the mob close to the classics. Pleasure gardens—not as a species especially respectable, but very popular in our period—were open to all who cared to pay the entrance money, and all but the lowest 'music halls' would attract a mixture of patrons who, in their own homes and occupations, would not normally meet.

The recreational and entertainment side of the mid-Victorian town thus for the most part seems to defy strict presentation in terms of social or economic class; and my impressions of it—limited inasmuch as little good modern research has to my knowledge yet been done on it—are that, although it certainly had elements that were strictly class ones, it must have functioned to some extent as yet another of those common grounds for members of different social and economic groups which characterised social relations during our period and helped to keep them, relatively speaking, sweet.

Some mid-Victorian recreations were new, some were inherited and adapted; but common to many recreations in both categories was one factor which was simply not operative to any significant extent before the later forties: the railway. The railway can hardly matter more in any aspect of Victorian history than in its impact on the use of leisure. Of course I don't mean merely that people took pleasure in riding in trains—though there is plenty of evidence that they did! I mean that the railway suddenly made it quite easy for people, perhaps in great numbers, to do things and go places outside their own local community. The railway brought inland, extended, and speeded up the recreational revolution which had been started along populous banks of estuaries and navigable rivers by the steam boat. By the forties the Firth of Forth and even more the Firth of Clyde, the mouth of the Mersey and (most of all) the Thames from Chelsea right down past Greenwich to Gravesend, Margate and Ramsgate, were busy with steamboats, ferrying passengers from side to side, taking long-term holiday makers to seaside resorts and short-term ones to places of pleasure and interest. Now, from the early forties onwards, these and other delights came within reach of everyone near a railway. The special excursion trains—Thomas Cook's and others—which carried legions to the Crystal Palace from the midlands and the north may mark for us, as they did for contemporaries, the arrival of the railway in its newly-revealed recreational capacity. There is hardly one of the mid-Victorians' extra-domestic leisure activities in which we cannot trace its impact.

Railway excursions were the great novelty of our period. Prolonged holidays away from home were hardly yet dreamt of below, say, the middle middle class, but the day excursion and the weekend trip now came within the means of all but the poorest, and attracted all but those whose affluence or fastidiousness made the compulsory sociabilities of the excursion train avoidable or repulsive. The railway excursion should be thought of in its informal and everyday as well as its better known formal, festival character. Formal excursions were planned by 'private' firms or associations, by railway companies, and, with Thomas Cook in the lead, professional travel and tour agents. The two last-named called attention to themselves by advertising, and the 'private' excursions were often such big events in the local community that they at once achieved historic importance. Yet it may be that the facilities increasingly offered for informal, casual excursions and visits by the multiplication of stations and services, may have been no less significant. Without an amplitude of regular train services in Lancashire–Cheshire, the Clyde basin, the West Riding, the Tees–Tyne region, Derby–Nottingham–Leicester and the Black Country, and of course the greater London area, our period's momentous mushrooming of football and cricket clubs would not have been possible; nor would such diverse recreational activities as choral societies, brass bands and the Volunteer movement have flourished the way they did. Audiences and spectators could now easily assemble in numbers large enough to justify ambitious programmes as matters of course; teams, bands and companies could now easily travel ten, twenty, even more miles to compete with each other; and supporters could go too—with the same consequences for public order, public houses and private property that still perturb the peaceful and law-abiding. Sports-fans' rowdyism was not invented during our period. Far from it! Some elements of rowdyism and worse, had, time out of mind, hung heavily round race-courses, though some cleaning-up was now being encouraged by that influential sportsman Lord George Bentinck; the Derby at Epsom Downs seems to have provided an annual occasion for a most remarkable public saturnalia; and the quasi-legal prize-fight, even more notorious a focus of black-guardism than the horse-racing event, culminated in 1860 in the Heenan–Sayers 'international' in a field near Farnborough, to which most spectators travelled in regular trains. The football crowd during (as I reckon) the seventies began to present analogous problems: less pungent perhaps, less classy for sure, but much more widespread. Nor did the informal excursion as I define it matter only for events of organised recreational character. Crowds could now travel on Saturdays, Sundays and national or local holidays to enjoy prodigies and disasters farther away than they could ever have got to on foot. Stranded whales and shipwrecks, new parks and public buildings, collapsed warehouses and great fires and so on could now, if within reach of a local train service, be seen as well as heard of; with perhaps such unedifying consequences as occurred one weekend in April 1874 in Dukinfield, when the aftermath of a dreadful pit disaster drew a hundred thousand sensation-samplers from the neighbourhood, and diversified the tragic two-day burial ceremonies with vandalism, ribaldry, brutality and what sound like gang-fights between knife- and belt-wielding Manchester and Oldham men.[21]

Formal excursions presumably were less liable to anti-social accompaniments (though not less liable to accidents; the worst railway catastrophe to date, that in the Clayton Tunnel in 1861, involved London excursions from Portsmouth and Brighton). Railway companies seem to have lost no time in meeting the latent demand which was evidently very great, and was much readier to devote Sundays to excursions than Sabbatarians (who sought, with little success, to put them down) cared to admit. London was of course the mecca of the organised excursion. After 1851's demonstration of how easy it was, trips to London were offered on every special occasion (e.g. shows and exhibitions, visits of foreign monarchs, Crystal Palace concerts) on Easter, Whitsun and August weekends, and, by the seventies, on weekends throughout the summer. Excursions to London from Yorkshire and Lancashire perforce demanded the spending of at least one night away from home, and since many of those advertised in the northern press were of from two to eight days' duration, one wonders where people stayed; did many of them visit relations, or was there already a flourishing cheap hotel and lodgings business for the tripper to London, of the same kind as was developing fast through our period in seaside and inland resorts? Of course railway excursions went to the resorts too; my dips into Lancashire and Yorkshire newspapers show that special trains (I take the regular ones for granted) were by the later sixties provided for trips to places like Scarborough, Redcar, Saltburn, Whitby, Blackpool, Southport, Lytham, Windermere, Harrogate and Lincoln; besides sporting events like York and Doncaster races. But excursions promoted by railway companies, though probably the most numerous, were not the only ones to be formally planned and executed. Works outings, Sunday School treats, Trade Union 'galas' (stretching the Durham miners' term to cover analogous occasions), Friendly Society festivals (like that of the Durham Oddfellows to Redcar in 1869 when all were 'more or less depressed' by the sight of a drowned sailor on the beach),[22] even treats for workhouse children, like those day-trips to Blackpool which Rhodes Boyson found to have been arranged by the Burnley, Blackburn and Rochdale Guardians[23]—all such relied on the railway, and could not have happened without it.

During our period the railway was nearly as indispensable to the spread of the family holiday away from home. There was nothing new in the principle of this, as compared with the railway excursion; first coaches and then steam-boats had for many years put holidays within reach of all who wanted them and could afford them. Nor was it, humanly speaking, surprising that people should want them; though the gospels of John Wesley and hard work made their propriety suspect for respectable middle class males, and the general competitiveness and toughness of the lives of most wage earners kept many from ever daring to venture far from the home base. Nevertheless, it is perfectly clear from the growth of holiday resorts without more than temporary interruption throughout the century, that the holiday idea, in its seaside rather than its spa form, was pretty steadily spreading from the leisured and stylish down through the social order. Already by 1850 it seems to have become as common for the comfortably off in all levels of big city bourgeoisie as it or its inland equivalent had long been for gentry and nobility. The Kent coast resorts in particular throve on their mainly metropolitan clientele, which came by water (mothers, nursemaids and children by the week; husbands often for weekends only) years before the railway, and later inspired such musical jocularities as the songs 'What

Ho! She bumps!' and (a mildly risqué one) 'The Husband Boat'.[24] The Clyde and Ayr coast resorts and those along the coast of North Wales similarly sprang up before the railway age. But from the later forties onwards, it was increasingly upon the railway and no other means of transport that the destinies of holiday towns hung; and wherever the iron fingers reached, hopeful hotels and boarding-houses sprouted like jagged teeth on the cliff-tops, while promenades and even piers began to formalise the shore line.

But how far down the social scale had the seaside holiday habit penetrated by then? Not, I reckon, much below that sociological twilight-zone where the petty bourgeoisie can be seen as upper working class or not, according to the way you look at them; and perhaps not much within that zone either. It was a question of custom as much as cash. We may perhaps assume that very few families with children and an income below £100 a year dreamt of going together for more than a day-excursion to the seaside. Above that stratum, much might depend on whether you were 'white-collar', 'salaried', or, on the other hand, a wage-earner or self-employed. In the former category, you could be two degrees nearer a holiday than in the latter: your job would probably be more secure (therefore you could dare to leave it for a while) and you were much more likely to get paid while you were away. Mr Perkupp probably continued to pay his trusted clerk Pooter's salary during his holidays at 'Good old Broadstairs'.[25]

Periods of holiday with pay seem to have been virtually unknown among wage-earning manual workers before the eighties. But periods of holidays without pay were far from unfamiliar to significant chunks of the labouring masses. It was an ancient custom of the British workman to absent himself from the scene of his bread- and beer-winning labours at whatever festive times he felt strong or prosperous enough to do so. Domestic workers upset none but moralists when they thus took time off but men who worked on their employers' premises or sites, in factories, mines, signal boxes, workshops, breweries, gasworks, shipyards etc., presented a serious economic challenge. To 'discipline' and 'regulate' labour into predictable conformity with the time-clock and the power-plant was a major object of the captains and lieutenants of industry of the early nineteenth century. They were not wholly successful. Absenteeism, especially on Mondays and around recognised festive seasons (Whitsun the chief thereof), continued to be complained about by employers of the most strenuous and disagreeable labour: especially in the metal and mining industries. Thus some important classes of workmen, not the least well-paid, provided themselves (and perhaps their families) with leisure-time at their own expense and risk. But in the cotton countries a different leisure pattern established itself. There, where the battle for factory discipline had been fought first and fiercest, management had, as it were, made a deal with labour, and accepted the Wakes Weeks holidays (which by our period were staggered; which helped Blackpool etc. to cope with the numbers) around Whitsun in return for regularity at work. Into their Wakes Weeks the working folk of Lancashire and Cheshire concentrated the greater part of their holiday effort. Families saved strenuously for it and spent lavishly on it. Much of this money went to the traditional diversions of the season (fairs, sports, etc.) but with the railway came excursions, and unexpected transformations of small seaside towns and villages. The most remarkable transformation scene was that which produced, in Blackpool, the first sizeable town devoted wholly to the holiday and excursion industry. Its years of fastest growth were still to come, but the opening of its first pier in 1863 was a reliable portent of the shape of things to come.

Holidays away from home thus began to become feasible for working families, though no more of them than of higher class families (i.e. from petty bourgeois upwards) can one say exactly what proportion of those who theoretically could have taken such a holiday actually did so. The spectacle of the Yorkshire, Lancashire and North Wales coast resorts, slowly but steadily swelling through our period, suggests that it was the working classes of the most fully mechanised textile areas that were likeliest to get away; but how many more went on day excursions than for stays of one or more nights?

– and were the artisans of London (still, we must remember, the biggest industrial city in the country) forming a leisure pattern of the same kind? John Myerscough's pioneer researches[26] suggest that definitely non-bourgeois families first began to spend holiday periods of days at Blackpool sometime in the sixties. There is much work to be done all round this subject. Meanwhile, all we can be sure of is that, throughout the middle classes, holidays away from home were becoming more regular. The most affluent of them did as the nobility and gentry did. Nothing new in that! But here again, the railway from the early forties exercised its levelling influence. Jorrocks and Sponge could now with little effort pervade the whole hunting nation. Briggs ran the gamut of England's field sports before astonishing Scotland. Dombey and Bagstock had already patronised Leamington Spa, and Brown, Jones and Robinson gone on continental grand tours.[27] Thomas Cook took more serious tourists in bulk to France in 1855, and by 1878 had a large enough organisation to carry about 75,000 visitors to the Paris International Exhibition of that year. The Alps asserted themselves over the educated British mind and became obligatory for university dons seeking purity of soul. The seaside towns along the Belgian and north French coasts were discovered to be morally bearable as well as picturesque, and a good deal cheaper than the English resorts offering the desired combination of safe sea-bathing, rustic hinterland, and security from the gaze or, worse, conversational approaches of the vulgar: Worthing, Eastbourne, Folkestone, St Leonard's, Westgate, Cromer, Southport, Barmouth, Aberystwyth, Tenby, Weston-super-Mare, Ilfracombe, Torquay, Bournemouth.... Margate and Ramsgate seem by the seventies to have become roaringly plebeian; as had parts of protean Brighton.

'Sport', to which a survey of early twentieth-century use of leisure would probably allot pride of place, made momentous moves towards just this during the sixties and seventies. For one thing, it became *national* in popular but respectable forms. Horse-racing, hunting, pugilism and to a lesser extent cricket had for long commanded (largely through the medium

of the Sunday papers) a nationwide following of connoisseurs
and betting men; but that following, so far as it was respectable,
was hardly popular, and in so far as it was popular, was hardly
respectable. Now, about the fifties—and more because of the
railway than anything else—cricket began to develop its modern organisation: a fine-meshed network of local clubs, and
a focusing of local loyalties and talent on county teams, with
the stirring concept of All-England as the sun of the stellar
system. The essential qualities of the sport—its wholesome
country air, its aristocratic patronage, its metropolitan management, its near-unique combination of social deference with
manly equality—dated from the days of George III. There is
no denying cricket its pre-Victorian ancestry. But it needed
the diffusion of money and leisure and, above all, the railway,
to iron out local peculiarities and to make it more than a
specialised minority sport; which it had clearly ceased to be
by 1878, when the first visit by an Australian XI aroused
vast excitement throughout a national sporting public kept
up-to-date about its progress by sporting journalism, with
mail-trains and telegraph at its disposal.

By the later seventies football too had attained its majority
and a recognisably modern shape. Some of its growing pains
were parallel to cricket's. It had much more of a problem with
local peculiarities. First at Hambledon, then in the MCC,
cricket nourished from the start a potential legislator; standard
lengths, breadths, weights and rules were attained without
great difficulty. Football however grew without such a centre
and had to find one. By the time it did so (in the early
sixties) the tug-of-war between local peculiarities (excessively
strong in 'public schools') and the necessities of competitions
had bred two species of football, not one: Rugby Football,
and Association Football. For reasons that are not altogether
clear, the latter quite soon became established in England as
the more popular sport, while the former had from the start,
in England at any rate, a superior social tone. (Yet in South
Wales, Lancashire, and the Scottish border country 'rugger'
remained or became, I'm not sure which, much more democratic. But why?) 'Soccer' clubs sprang, like cricket clubs,

from local needs and energies, and about the same time. In their diverse origins they too owed something to the patronage and enthusiastic participation of public school type sportsmen. Most of the first clutch of soccer clubs which combined to form the Football Association in the sixties were of that character. But the upper class ethos did not dominate it for long, and the reasons are not far to seek.

Soccer was to satisfy a deep need of the industrial masses, and the weight of their devotion to it proved irresistible. The possibility of modern organised sport (i.e. 'leagues' of teams permanent enough to play each other regularly) in the industrial areas hardly existed before about 1850. Only about then, with the privations of the thirties and early forties giving way to better times, the Saturday half-holiday steadily spreading, and—of course—the railway, did the right conditions begin to form. Soccer suited the purpose admirably. Ancient varieties of it, often of alarming barbarity, were already familiar to many towns and villages. Through our mid-Victorian years teams and clubs crystallised around such heterogeneous nuclei as schools, Sunday Schools and other church or chapel groups, boys' clubs, cricket clubs (seeking winter occupation), pubs, institutes, industrial concerns. Elements of patronage and philanthropy were in the early years present locally as well as in the national legislator and organiser. Grounds, equipment, perhaps fares had to be found; pillars of the community would often be pleased to help working men fill their new-found regular leisure with recreation that was healthy and harmless, and satisfying to local patriotism. By the eighties however the game had almost entirely shed the mixed social character which cricket so remarkably preserved. The masses had taken over and made it their own. The 'gentlemen's clubs' of the home counties and the soccer playing 'public schools', which shared the Football Cup between them through the seventies, began in the early eighties to meet stiff northern competition; 1883, when the Old Etonians lost to Blackburn Olympic, was felt to mark the turn of an era. By then all the main features of the modern game were present: 'leagues' of teams visiting each others' grounds; charges for admission;

'professionals', bred by the clubs' desire to compensate their best players for financial losses incurred in club service, and by their growing need, as their scale of operations and overheads rose, to keep the fans coming; and, in the wake of the fans, roughs and vandals.

No other sports mattered as much as cricket and football, the rapid development and organisation of which are significant of that easing of circumstances of urban and industrial life that all but the residuum of society began to encounter from the later forties onwards. These games were of course played in the country too, but it seems unlikely that there they had any part in promoting or reflecting a major change in the quality of common life. In the towns they did; and the swift spread of these relatively humane and civilised sports made it clear, by the end of our period, that they were the true representatives of the dominant popular sporting interest rather than pugilism, badger-baiting, rat-catching, dog- and cock-fighting, coursing and other brutal survivals from a less squeamish past; which however survived vigorously enough, both in the countryside, among the more isolated industrial groups, like miners, and throughout the sub-respectable entertainment world of the big cities. No so-called 'sport' was too cruel and beastly that you could not find it, no lust to bet or gamble too self-destructive that you could not indulge it, in mid-Victorian London or Liverpool; and from the ease with which you could find anything you wanted in those unusually large cities, I presume that things were in proportion in smaller places. London might be considered exceptional but I don't see why Liverpool should be particularly so.

'Sport' was part of the recreational apparatus with which mid-Victorian urban society made life more bearable or interesting; but it was by Victorian definition an all-male affair—by climatic necessity a seasonal one—and by virtue of human variety a less than universal concern. The rest of that recreational apparatus, available to both sexes and to families, must have been much weightier in terms of both numbers and cash. Means of enjoyment became readily available. The modern entertainments industry took giant strides forward, and for its history the mid-Victorian years matter as the time when regular mere enjoyment, unintellectual and (in the contemporary sense) unimproving, became more or less 'respectable'; and when an urban mass-market began to demand satisfaction. That people should wish for entertainment and should get it must seem a risible platitude to any post-Victorian reader, but to the early Victorian governing classes it was no laughing matter. Part of the many-tiered problem they saw in the masses gathering in the industrial areas through the early nineteenth century was, what would and what should the workers do when they were not at work? It was clearly desirable that they should be at work most of the time (there was no special class-unfairness in that; *all* respectable early Victorian citizens were expected to fill six days a week with work) but there were the evenings and Sundays and holidays.... *Education* was the early Victorians' prescription for these vacant hours: catching up on lost schooling, technical instruction, self-improvement in secular as well as religious respects; the merely amusing or relaxing, the utterly uneducational, was deprecated as morally feeble, while the coarse, the brutish and the drunken was, understandably, deplored. 'Rational recreation' (their favourite phrase for it) was ardently recommended. The seeds of this strenuous gospel fell on soil not wholly unreceptive. Plenty of working men and boys were ready to respond ascetically to what one of them called 'the sacred cause of self-advancement', and not more before our period than during it; it was in 1851, at the opening of a Mechanics' and Apprentices' Library in Liverpool, that the zealous adult educationist J. W. Hudson, a man by no means lacking in human sympathy, looked forward to its users:

'... receiving cultivation, not in reading the latest accounts of misdemeanours and local calamities [i.e. the local proletarian weekly press] but in imbibing instruction and high gratification from the perusal of select and valuable works whether they lead him with the traveller across the pathless tracts of ocean, or cheer and console him with moral sketches of human nature.'[28]

The continuing prosperity of such reading-rooms, of Mechanics' Institutes, of more or less educational public lectures and displays, and of mutual improvement groups, testified to the staying power of the idea that leisure should be devoted to self-improvement, not self-indulgence. But, whatever had been and whatever remained its appeal, it was by the fifties losing out to the demand for mere entertainment. Working people for the most part would not, after ten or more hours' labour through the week, flog their intellects till bedtime through the *Penny Encyclopedia* and manuals of political economy, or quit their firesides to go only to lectures on geology or to missionary meetings. Dickens quite understood the situation.

'The English are, so far as I know [he expostulated] the hardest worked people on whom the sun shines. Be content if in their wretched intervals of leisure they read for amusement and do no worse. They are born at the oar, and they live and die at it. Good God, what would we have of them!'[29]

The lust for relaxation and amusement *would* be satisfied. Educators and philanthropists learnt the hard way that the best they could hope for was to slip in some instruction with the amusement and to accept the merely respectable as a substitute for the 'rational'. With varying degrees of reluctance and regret they observed the inexorable growth of a lower class leisure pattern based rather on the pub, the pleasure garden, the dancing saloon, the music hall and the Working Men's Club than the reference library, the singing class, the lecture-hall and the Mechanics' Institute.

Public lectures indeed flourished abundantly, across the gamut from religion to ribaldry (combining them in the case of the 'No Popery!' specialists); they were given by societies and institutions, by itinerant celebrities and professionals (possibly working through agencies of some kind) and by local worthies. Music-making, always before the nineteen-sixties understood to be a peculiarly virtuous form of recreation, flourished among the lower as well as the superior strata, with brass bands booming from the mid-forties (they were soccer's musical counterpart in every respect), choral societies recruiting (one supposes) not only from church and chapel, but also from choirs and classes trained for service in that interesting war between the supporters of the Nonconformist Curwen's tonic sol-fa system of easy singing and of the Anglican Hullah's more traditional system. Public libraries multiplied, a few of them run by municipalities under local acts or Ewart's Acts of 1845 and 1850 (only about sixty such by 1875), untold others run by local institutions of philanthropic and educational character for the benefit of readers below the subscribing circulating library level; and plenty of working-class readers used them, but, librarians reported, what they usually read was fiction, and not the heaviest kind at that.

While rational recreation thus survived, paying some price for popularisation, facilities for pure enjoyment proliferated. Most of them were of a traditional type, and the one important innovation of our period, the music hall, was new only in the classic perfection it had attained by the end of it; none of its ingredients was new, and all of them survived independently. Pleasure gardens still drew crowds on warm dry days and evenings, as they had done for ages. Vauxhall, most famous of them, adapted to the changes of fashion and a lowering of class of clientèle successfully enough until its closure in 1859. Cremorne Gardens in Chelsea, just upstream from Battersea Bridge, seems until 1877 to have offered a range of entertainments and relaxations like those of Copenhagen's Tivoli Gardens. Rosherville—established like Cremorne in the thirties, on the promise of the Thames steamer traffic—was a more countrified version of the same, just to the London side of Gravesend. The Crystal Palace Company at Sydenham, easily accessible by rail from 1856, had a gigantic pleasure garden of a peculiarly edifying and educational kind as well as a range of delights peculiarly characteristic of the 'period, including refreshment rooms, music, paintings, sculpture, tropical trees, architectural models, and 'Science and Philosophy teaching their sublime truths in a geological illustration of the Wealden formation'[30] complete with life-size bronze dinosaurs. There were countless lesser pleasure gardens in and around every city and conurbation. Wherever streets and houses lay thick, it was worth someone's while to set up a vista of Arcadia. Most such places had little staying power. The Crystal Palace was a pike, Cremorne a trout, among minnows. The multitude of little pleasure gardens, counting on pedestrian or bus-brought patrons, often lay right in the line of the speculative builder's fire, and were likely to succumb to it. The thrill of even the most elaborate ones began to wear off once the popular seaside resort came into full blast, during the eighties and nineties, and they either had to turn like Bellevue into funfairs (where a stiff pace was set by the International Ex-hibitions) or sell out.

But there was another way out for the pleasure gardens, a way that led straight to the music hall. They could beat the speculative builder to it and build themselves, improving their indoor entertainments at the expense of their garden ones. From the pleasure gardens that took this course came those charming early Victorian hybrids, the saloon theatres, of which the Eagle Tavern in the City Road was the best known exemplar until it began the usual series of shifts and adapta-tions that culminated in its sale to the Salvation Army in 1879. Most such had either succumbed to the site-developer or become real music halls long before then. Into the music hall proper flowed other tributary streams: pantomime, 'vari-ety', tavern concerts, all-male 'singing assemblies' or 'song-and-supper rooms' of the tribe headed, in the West End, by the Coal Hole, the Cider Cellars, and Evans's Late Joys. His-torians of the music hall find it more difficult to distinguish its sources than to date its birth. The sources seem compli-cated partly because of the confusions, deceptions and illogi-calities introduced or enforced by the laws governing licensed premises, theatres and other places of public resort, and partly because so many developments were heading in the same direction through the forties and fifties. There is about its flowering an unmistakable air of socio-economic determina-tion. The conventional date given for its decisive arrival is 1851; the place, the (New) Canterbury in Lambeth, today about where the lines from Waterloo go over the Westminster Bridge Road; the presiding genius, Charles Morton, who moved north of the river ten years later to found the Oxford and so to start that rivalry with Weston's which opened what its historians call the great or golden period of the music hall, when it asserted artistic equality with the theatre. The Canterbury under Morton offered to *mixed* audiences splendour and luxury (crystal, gilt, glass and plush ad lib; not to mention a picture gallery!), programmes of vocal entertainment by singers of *both* sexes (from opera excerpts to the latest comic or pathetic 'pops') under the direction of a chairman-compère, and food and drink while you heard them. The Oxford in Oxford Street and Weston's (later the Royal) in Holborn marked advances only in the even greater display of splendour, the more spacious bars and promenades, the more dazzling displays of barmaids and promenaders, and the beginnings of that gradual withdrawal of refreshment facilities from the body of the hall which by about 1914 had assimilated the lay-out of music-halls to that of the 'straight' theatre.

For mid-Victorians however, that development lay in the future. The music hall as they knew it was a place for eating and (more) drinking while you savoured the songs and studied the stars. It is for our purposes more interesting than most other recreational institutions, because it shows the Victorian city—which had, goodness knows, dark sides enough!—at its brightest and best. It strongly suggests that for many of its humbler denizens it had rewarding aspects as well as grim ones, and that the two were taken together in the stride of a lively popular culture. Popular it certainly was, in most relevant senses. Its songs came straight from popular experience or aimed straight at the popular heart. Whether they were about figures of fun (mothers-in-law, courting couples, lodgers, dominating wives, curates, swells, foreigners ...) or aversion (rate-and-rent-collectors, puritans, foreigners, bullies, snobs, seducers, hypocrites ...), or of pathos (the heartbroken, the destitute, the abandoned ...) or of admiration (royalty, heroes of the day, Jack Tar, Gladstone ...); whether they were self-consciously patriotic or noble-hearted or virtuous or tragic, they were always on themes familiar and interesting to ordinary people. Its artistes seem virtually all to have had humble origins, and typically to have begun singing in bars, laundries, factories, shops. Its songs were the pop songs of the day, their topics could be highly topical, its stars became folk heroes and heroines. And it must be judged popular on account of numbers too, though no one seems yet to have studied this aspect seriously. The specialist newspaper's enumeration of music halls in 1868[31] says there were twenty-nine of the larger, ten of the smaller sort, in London; ten in Sheffield, nine in Birmingham, eight in Manchester and Leeds; over the United Kingdom as a whole, excluding the London ones, about three hundred. That number must be minimal. The London list apparently omits at least one large hall (the Bedford) and draws the defining line so as to exclude the small and the professionally questionable. Since the big ones held up to two thousand people, the music-hall-going public must have been large, even if many patrons went more than once a week. A few things about that public are however fairly certain, and intriguing. It was popular in the sense of 'common', ordinary: working class and petty bourgeois, with some top dressing of bohemians and 'men about town'; it was noisy, demonstrative, emotional and on occasion severe; it was not deterred by the charges of sub-respectability which attached to it; yet the moral tone of the performances at the big, better-known halls anyway (evidently the tone varied in proportion with locality and clientèle) seems not to have been worse than, in part, 'racy'.

There can be little doubt that the lower varieties of music hall—varieties so hybrid and artistically negligible that the music hall's historians count them out—went beyond partial raciness. They were part of the mid-Victorian city's leisure apparatus and that apparatus had plenty of low and primitive tastes to cater for. Just as you could find any low 'sport' you wanted in the biggest cities, so could you find any low or underground entertainment you wanted. London of course provided the widest variety, of which Michael Sadleir's novels *Fanny by Gaslight* and *Forlorn Sunset* are documentary reconstructions. Less familiar will be the contemporary observer Hugh Shimmin's observations of Saturday night life in Liver-

pool in the mid-fifties. The only thoroughly respectable show
he found was the philanthropically-subsidised Saturday evening concert, where a pit full of operatives and side galleries of
people 'by common consent or courtesy called "the middle
class" ' watched a quite cultivated two-hour show of social comment and satire that provoked both tears and mirth. He could
hardly say what was his least respectable encounter, so appalling did he find most of what he saw in the dance halls, taverns,
concert rooms and cheap theatres. He thought that the expense of a music hall charging 1s 6d admission, and the sight
of a policeman by the entrance, would guarantee respectability,
but the only respectable thing about the interior was the social
class of the men consorting with the tarts and good-time girls
in the promenade thoughtfully provided. The lower grade
places presented really obscene songs, *poses plastiques* (then
as now the nearest a public performance could get to a strip
show) and sexy dances, one of which sounds like a can-can.
Even at the less blatantly improper dance halls he saw packs
of prowling wolves, seeking shopgirls whom they might devour.
The attractions at a fairground-cum-funfair at the junction of
Roe Street and Lime Street included a 'Royal Shooting Gallery', where you could pot at Victoria, Albert, Wellington and
Napoleon III; a cosmoramic show of the 'Destruction of
Nineveh'; 'the most elegant lounge in Europe', in a converted
chapel; and a wild and obscene laughing-gas demonstration
by a 'medical galvanist'.[32]

The theatre (broadly defined) spanned no smaller an extent
of styles than the music hall (vaguely defined), but it was
preserved from the grosser impurities by the law which, from
1843, firmly tied theatres to theatrical entertainments and
nothing else; i.e. kept them from becoming also places of
public resort and refreshment. Puritans might continue to
entertain prurient suspicions of what went on in the private
lives of theatre artistes; they had little occasion to denounce
what went on in the mid-Victorian theatre. So unintellectual
and virtuous had it become that theatre-going seems to have
become legitimate for much more of the religious public than
had dared indulge in it earlier on. Respectable people of course

went only to the bigger, costlier theatres, to behold purified and, whenever the producer had thought it necessary, brightened versions of the classics; 'musicals' might not be an unfair description of the run of them. Not all contemporary productions were extravaganzas, 'spectaculars', and pantomimes, prominent though such were; especially during the winter, for family outings. Contemporary authors wrote plays about contemporary society as well as domestic farces, costume dramas, and cribbings from the French. The bulk were wordy, melodramatic and sensational—'stagey' in the most basic sense— but Tom Taylor's *Ticket-Of-Leave Man* (1863) was a serious tackling of a crime and punishment problem, and T. W. Robertson's plays at the Prince of Wales's from 1865 introduced a new, *un*-stagey note into contemporary drama which jerked it a good bit nearer Ibsen and Shaw. Dublin and Edinburgh and the big provincial cities might expect to see these plays. The smaller ones could hardly hope to see them done properly. Indeed they could hardly hope to see anything done, and the smaller the theatre, the more purely popular its style was likely to be, for there would be no middle class patronage to encourage it to aspire above raw melodrama and slapstick. Yet the moral tone of all theatre above the level of the 'penny gaffs', the cheapest and lowest of theatrical shows, seems to have stayed high. I give as an example that of the Little Theatre in North Shields (which happens to have been carefully studied and which I have no reason to believe unrepresentative of its modest kind), where the advertisement for *All That Glitters Is Not Gold*, or, *The Factory Girl*, in 1854, said:

'It portrays in strong colours, the inestimable blessings which flow from Education, Industry and Honesty. To the humble and lowly it plainly shows that rectitude of conduct and industrious perseverance will never fail to raise them in the estimation of all good men, securing them more real respect and admiration than will fall to the lot of titled indolence. While those who move in the higher circles may learn that Pride and Arrogance, though backed by Riches, may frequently render them objects of ridicule; while kindness and condescension will secure them the love of those whom Fortune has placed beneath them.'

What improving lessons it drew from *Sweeney Todd*, who got there ten years later, I unfortunately cannot discover.[33]

The important leisure time institution that remains to be discussed is drink. (Not that it wholly lacked connection with work; pubs and their wares continued well into our period to be used for paying certain classes of labourers: particularly navvies and dockers; and 'drinking customs' lustily survived in many trades, though the proportion of working men and boys observing them was probably smaller than it had been earlier in the century.) In the history of drink in Britain our period stands out because it saw the alcohol consumption per head of population momentously rise to its all-time peak about 1875. In that year the official figures of spirits consumption in the UK (and of course they will have missed illicit spirits, which were known to be plentiful in Ireland and the Scottish highlands and islands) showed that each national individual had consumed 1.30 gallons of spirits. 1876 was the peak year for beer, with each same individual consuming 34.4 gallons of the stuff. (The early seventies was also the peak period, before the Second World War anyway, for consumption of wine: 0.53 gallons per head.) These are staggering figures.[34] It is not difficult to understand contemporaries' concern about this scale of alcoholic intake, when one considers that this statistical individual drinker was the product of a calculation including all ages, both sexes, the teetotal and temperate as well as the convivial and the truly alcoholic. Obviously those who *did* drink more than a little or occasionally, drank immense quantities, and spent immense sums on it. Nothing more disheartened the Victorian worker's friend than the calculation of how much money went on beer and spirits that might have been put to 'better' uses: housing, clothes, savings, schooling, better diet, improving books, etc. When one considers further the quantity of immediate misery and violence resulting from drunkenness—every single source of evidence agrees that it was awful, though (given the wholly unsatisfactory nature of the crime statistics) it defies the objective quantifier—the historian's open-minded resolve not to be 'superior' melts into a more sympathetic attitude towards those mid-Victorians who sought, by free means or forced, to reduce the scale of, as some of them called it, 'the drink problem'.

For us, as for them, it seems to be mainly a lower class problem. No upper bourgeois home was complete without its wine cellar, no men's club imaginable without drinks at all hours; farmers rode home tipsy from market-day dinners; the bottle was perhaps more than nowadays a standard recourse for those sunk in pain, misery, loneliness or boredom. But when all allowance has been made for consumption by palpably non-labouring people, it remains clear that the bulk of the expenditure on beer, and much of the expenditure on spirits, came from labouring people. Since there is a strong case for believing that drink brought them, in the aggregate, wretchedness as well as comfort, and also a *prima facie* case for wondering why more of them were not capable of realising this, it becomes important to distinguish the causes of this amazing addiction. Suggestive advertising was not responsible. Brewers and distillers and their retail outlets did not need to press the virtues of liquor and of those who drank it upon an otherwise-minded public. Non-alcoholic drinking habits (tea, coffee, even cocoa) were spreading throughout these years, but the whole weight of tradition and folklore was on the side of the liquor drinker; beer was 'manly', no doubt about it, and (what was more true of the non-adulterated article than anti-drink analysts then knew) beer was 'strengthening' too, while spirits (much more weighty in Scottish and Irish consumption than the English) were palpably warming and exhilarating. It was the anti-drink propagandists who had to do the advertising. Their main enemies were certain characteristics of lower class existence; the quality of work, home and neighbourhood; habit, conventionality and ignorance. Licensed premises—public houses, beer shops and gin shops or, in the more splendiferous instances, 'gin palaces'—were amazingly plentiful; one per 186 of the English and Welsh population in 1861, one per 255 of the Scottish; and their density was greatest wherever poverty

was worst. This fact was morally deplorable but socially un-
derstandable. Where homes were least homely, work most uncertain or disagreeable, people least able or willing to save,
pubs or other drinking places naturally become social centres.
This tended to be the case in all but the most consciously
respectable working-class areas—in all labouring strata, in
fact, up to where they began to meet the competition of the
club, which might meet in a pub or might not—and was
perhaps especially so in rural and semi-rural areas (like most
mining ones); but it was statistically demonstrable that the
deeper the poverty, the denser the pubs.

Addiction to improvident and (from all rational stand-
points) excessive drinking in those black areas was not unintelligible. What the philanthropic and elevating found less
intelligible was the hold that drink had upon the not-quite-so-
poor and the not-really-poor-at-all: the lower skilled workers
in Baxter's classification (see pp. 115–16) and the higher skilled
workers. The explanation seems to lie along these lines. Their
work was often arduous, exhausting and unpleasant; they
drank in the course of it to keep them going (literally so, in
infernos like furnaces and gas-works) and they drank in the
intervals and aftermath of it to help them get over it. The rest
of their existence was often hard and—especially perhaps for
the women—physically painful; drink helped both sexes to
forget or not to notice. Their homes and work places were
often cold and draughty; drink helped to warm them up. They
drank a great deal at home; beer might be a normal drink at
any meal and although the quantities thus absorbed cannot
have been very intoxicating, they added up over the week to
a big item in many household budgets. It was moreover so
normal to drink and, however absurdly, to embellish so many
common social occasions with drink, that the man who would
not drink might find himself disliked and despised. Drinking,
even more then than now, was the subject of a great deal of
nonsense to the effect that you were not 'manly' unless you
drank and that you were not a 'good chap' unless you engaged
in carefree giving and receiving of drink with groups of other
men. The workman who tried to be temperate, let alone tee-

total, often ran into trouble: e.g. ostracism, victimisation, and which might be worst of all, loss of the foreman's liking.

Drink was, to sum up, still very much a part of working-class life, hardly yet beginning to be sapped by alternative beverages (though the twentieth-century eye can discern the foundations of the triumph of tea) and by the growth of *practical* alternative lines of expenditure: house purchase (though that was beginning in some artisan communities, especially in London, Yorkshire and Scotland), consumer durables (not much for working folk to buy until after our period), holidays (just beginning but not yet gone far: see above, p. 226), and so on. Drink therefore flourished throughout our period and proportionately mattered more for weal or woe among the working classes than ever before or since; and the pub and its relations attained the splendour of plush, brass and decorative glass which makes the well-preserved one an eminently worthwhile *objet d'art*. Whether that vast liquor consumption which went on so largely in and around the pub resulted more in the happiness and welfare of the working class as a whole than in their misery and deprivation, can only be estimated in the light of personal values. The jolly sight and sound of those pubs and all the feelings of *camaraderie* therein engendered, do not, to *my* mind, efface the spectre of undernourished, underclad and undereducated children, or deaden the sound of blows. That a well-known later Victorian ballad began 'Please sell no more drink to my father', may seem funny now but was not funny then.

After recreations outside the home, recreations in the home. What was new or characteristic about mid-Victorian domestic leisure? Only, I suggest, two things: the increased quantity of it, and the immensely widened range of reading matter that helped fill it.

Of the increase of regular leisure time, nearly enough has already been said (pp. 137–8). Most wage and salary earners had more regular leisure by the seventies than they could have known in the forties. Factory and shop workers had at any rate their half-day a week. Most domestic servants, one gathers, could bargain for as much or more. Hours of work must have been diminishing for many. The *mores* of the business community were relaxing; work was still work—a very serious matter—but the insidious doctrine of 'all work and no play makes...' was seeping in (Query: was it part of the influence of the public school?), although it was not till after our period that it became openly admitted. Whether the paterfamilias accompanied them or not, the rest of the bourgeois family was going away whenever it could for a summer holiday each year. In these ways the institutions of society permitted or enforced more leisure than in the (recent) past. But the aggregate of leisure time may have been swollen also by the growth of the social proportion of leisured or relatively leisured people. I don't know how this could be demonstrated (the census and income tax returns are not, through these years at any rate, adequate for the purpose), but it seems likely that the number of people living (mainly) on investments or rent was going up fast, as industrial and commercial families moved into the second and third generations, and money continued in its usual way to make money for those who already had it. I have an overall impression that the social proportion of people living partly or wholly on 'unearned income' was higher between the eighteen-eighties and 1939 than it had been earlier (or than it has been since); and if that impression is indeed correct, then the phenomenon must have been building up before the eighties and perhaps during the sixties and seventies. But apart from that, the very increase in the number of servants betokened an increase of leisure possibilities both in the families which employed them and in their own upper echelons. Few Victorians who could get a servant to do work for them would for preference work themselves; every early or mid-Victorian that I have read of (except for the few devoted to an ascetic religious life) hired servants the moment he thought he could afford to do so (and sometimes before he could really afford to do so!); and as soon as a hierarchy of servants was established in a big house, the upper ones made as easy a life of it as they could—until, in the smartest and wealthiest establishments, the butler and the housekeeper, the head groom and head gardener would be putting their feet up and relaxing to an extent that would have turned most GPs, bank clerks and curates green with envy.[35]

We turn in conclusion to the question of how leisure was, domestically, occupied; and at once we run into literature: new quantities and qualities of it. I see no other significant novelty in the mid-Victorian family's mode of entertaining itself within doors, and this one is is significant mainly because of its scale. Domestic recreation continued to be a matter of indoor games, music, art, handicrafts and reading. The range of indoor games extended and acquired a new category of 'scientific' devices, especially optical ones (stereoscopes, etc.); more people may have been prepared to play games (cards were earlier taboo to many of the 'pious', but they became increasingly played as standards relaxed) and more people must have been able to afford them; but none of this was new in principle. Music likewise; cheap upright pianos came within the means of a much larger group, but the bourgeois desire to own one and have the girls perform on it had already been a joke for Rowlandson; the cost of sheet and album music fell for reasons common to the whole publishing world. The case was the same with painting, drawing etc., except that no major item of equipment cheapened particularly. Hours and hours weekly, even daily, continued to be devoted to needle-work in all its varieties by mothers and daughters with any pretensions to gentility: ornamental, strictly *useless* needlework for the most part; the *useful* stuff, the men's shirts and women's dresses and underwear, was done by working women. In none of these departments of domestic leisure appears any qualitative change from earlier or, indeed, later; the number of ways members of a family can pass time indoors is, in any culture at any time, strictly limited! But in the quantities and kinds of literature consumed, something more like a significant change is seen.

The ground had been trembling for many decades, but now came a real earthquake. No single cause can be alleged. Fiscal changes in 1855 and 1861 had some importance. In 1855 the 'newspaper tax', which had in 1836 been reduced from 4d to 1d, was abolished; six years later the excise duty on paper, which had kept the price of all publications from sinking to its open market minimum, was abolished too. But these acts are more sensibly viewed as responses to, or products of, deep shifts in public opinion and consumer demand, than as themselves initiators of change. The fact is, that by the fifties a large and still enlarging middle-cum-working-class public was ready to read all the cheap literature it could get. (*Mutatis mutandis* the same was true of the public for not-so-cheap literature; but that led to no important innovations.) Reading was no problem for most working people. R. K. Webb has concluded that between two-thirds and three-quarters of the working classes could read in the eighteen-thirties, and he has found (what one would anyway have expected) consistent evidence of improvement in those approximations through the succeeding decades of educational effort.[36] The workman who was so illiterate that he had to be read to (one may in any case suspect him to be rather a mythical figure, since it was more often the expensive rarity of newspapers and the cost of lighting that led to their being read aloud to a group in a pub or club, not the majority's total illiteracy) was becoming rare by the sixties. Weightier factors were the cost of reading-matter, opportunity to read it, and of course inclination. Opportunity to read increased for reasons already given, ability to afford to read did not diminish in the fifties and certainly increased from the sixties onwards; perhaps the will to read increased also, with a generation which added to the usual human search for amusement and diversion a stronger than usual valuation of self-discipline and the acquisition of knowledge.

Whatever the causes, the results were clear enough: the decisive creation, during our period, of a mass-market for cheap literature, and an unprecedented explosion of the newspaper press. Not all that was cheap was trashy. Some publishers now specialised in low-priced cheap editions for lower class and casual use: mid-Victorian equivalents to our paperbacks. They covered everything. I give the random example of Hickling's Cheap Book, Music and Paper Warehouse in High Street, Coventry where, by 1849, you could buy for 7d, 8d, or 9d, hundreds of 'Standard Books', including Jenks's *Family Devotion*, Buffon's *Natural History*, Lawson's *Complete Farrier*, *The Hunchback of Notre Dame*, Brown's *Concordance*, *Memoirs of Mrs Rogers*, *Amelia* by Fielding, *The Conquest of Mexico*, *Fatherless Fanny*, and Sherlock on *Death*.[37] Then there were the books by cheap instalments. A shilling per monthly part was quite a painless way to get most of Dickens, Surtees, Thackeray and Trollope; not to mention Newman's *Apologia*. About 1860 the part-issue succumbed to the monthly shilling magazine, which gave you serial novels, and other reading matter. *Macmillan's Magazine* ran *Water Babies*, *Tom Brown at Oxford* and *Chaplet of Pearls*, while the *Cornhill* delivered *Romola*, *Framley Parsonage*, *Armadale*, *Wives and Daughters*; not to mention *Culture and Anarchy*. Work of equivalent quality could also appear in even cheaper serials; Dickens's *Household Words* and *All the Year Round* cost twopence a week, and included his own *Hard Times*, *Tale of Two Cities*, and *Great Expectations*, Wilkie Collins's *Woman in White* and Mrs Gaskell's *North and South*, besides much else – fiction, documentary and general interest – of extraordinary quality considering the price.

The great novels just listed as masterpieces of the part-issue and magazine-serial *genre* strike our attention because of their subsequent staying-power, but they were no more than a tiny proportion of the great mass of fiction published in these serial forms. It was of every level of art and learning, right down to the spicy melodrama of the mass-circulation Sunday papers, *Lloyd's* and *Reynolds's Weekly News*. Between Sunday papers and weekly periodicals there might be then, as now, little difference. Together they made perhaps the most significant block of cheap literature now coming into all but the poorest or more isolated homes. For every one reader of the consciously cultivated periodicals (i.e. from *Cornhill* and *Macmillan's* upwards into the intellectual heavyweight layer of the *Fortnightly*, the *Contemporary*, the *North British*, *Fraser's* etc.) there were dozens reading the popular (in the broadest sense) weeklies; decent 'family papers' like the *Family Herald*, *London Journal*, *Cassells's;* deliberately religious family papers like *Leisure Hour*, *Christian World*, *Christian Herald*; Sunday newspapers, some just above or hovering on the line of respectability like the *Observer* and the *News of the World*, some definitely below it like *Lloyd's*, *Reynolds's*, the *Weekly Dispatch*, the *Illustrated Police News*, etc.; sporting papers like *Bell's*; humorous papers like, pre-eminently, *Punch*; pictorial papers, of which the *Illustrated London News* was for long the undisputed leader. To get some idea of this pullulating variety of periodicals (excluding newspapers) Michael Wolff extracted a sample from the list of those published in London at the end of October 1864, the ones with titles beginning with 'A'.[38] There were twenty-nine of them The names of six may still be familiar: *ABC*, *All the Year Round*, *Army and Navy Gazette*, *Army List*, *Art Journal*, and *Athenaeum*. A few were wonderfully characteristic of their age: the *Artisan*, the *Appeal* (a halfpenny monthly of evangelical religion aimed at the heart of the servant girl), and the *Anti-Tobacco Journal*. The total circulation of non-daily London-published periodicals in that year was reckoned by a trade expert to be: 2,203,000 weekly newspapers (more than half being of the *Reynolds's* sort); 2,404,000 other weeklies (a third being predominantly religious and/or educational); and 2,490,000 monthlies *nearly two million of which were religious*.[39]

The daily newspaper side of the periodicals press showed the same rapid swelling, both in circulations, and in numbers of papers in circulation. *The Times* at last met competition worth speaking of. Still selling at 4d after 1855, 3d after 1861, its circulation remained impressive; 60,000 or more daily through the sixties and into the early seventies. But quite quickly it lost that brute quantitative ascendancy which had supported and partly justified its arrogance. The respectable penny papers now caught it up. First the *Daily News*, then by the early seventies the *Daily Telegraph* overtook it. The story was the same in the provinces. In 1846, when *Mitchell's Directory* first appeared, there were no dailies outside London, which had fourteen, and Dublin, which had two. By 1880 there were (counting evening ones too) ninety-six in the English provinces (including Monmouthshire), twenty-one in Scotland, four in Wales, and seventeen in Ireland. Circumstances conspired in the fifties to boost the provincial press to hitherto undreamt of activity: the newspaper tax gone, the telegraph to hand, express trains, news agencies, provincial vigour and independence—all of which they needed to beat the lightning competitiveness of W. H. Smith's, who by the later seventies were getting the five a.m. editions of London-printed daily papers to subscribers in Bristol soon after nine, York by ten, and Newcastle by noon. For the time being—for many years, in fact—the provincial newspaper press was safe. Small and feeble indeed was the town that did not boast at least two papers by the seventies. Big provincial cities would have handfuls. May's *British and Irish Press Guide for 1874*, for example, lists for Newcastle upon Tyne five dailies and five weeklies; for Cardiff, two dailies and four weeklies; for Dundee, two dailies and three weeklies; for Plymouth, two dailies and two weeklies; for Cheltenham, seven weeklies; for Driffield, three; for Peterborough and Trowbridge, two each. In the London suburbs too, with their strong community feelings and buoyant commerce, there occurred the same phenomenon. When Mitchell started his Directory, he could find only one suburban paper, the *South London Press*. By 1880 there were a hundred and four. The mid-Victorian's appetite for newspapers was, like his appetite for other inexpensive periodicals and for cheap books, insatiable.

4: The Social Order of Mid-Victorian Britain

Sir John Clapham's reference to 'the mid-Victorians, living in a world which was demonstrably getting more comfortable and running without too much friction',[1] may stand as representative of the terms in which many historians have summarised British (and even, to a lesser extent, Irish) social relations during our period. They have taken their cue from a gush of contemporary comment beginning about 1850. Most of the friction and some of the hunger of the thirties and forties seemed to have gone. The fifties, sixties and early seventies were said to be relatively happy and harmonious decades; an epoch 'when the great man helped the poor man, and the poor man loved the great', decades socially happier and more harmonious by far than the more anxious and turbulent decades which preceded and followed them. Chartism, in so far as it had been a working-class movement fired by working-class consciousness (and it had been only partly so), had thriven on sturdy suggestions that the interests of great men and poor men were not so comfortably compatible, and that a just social order could not be attained without radical reconstruction. Socialism, when it revived in the eighties, was to make even stronger suggestions even more emphatically. The revival of mass radicalism in the mid-sixties perhaps had enough of these suggestions in it to break the long calm. W. L. Burn, who memorably christened that calm 'The Age of Equipoise', thought so. But Burn too believed in a mid-Victorian calm. It seems indeed very difficult not to believe in some kind of calm through at least the years 1850–65.

This sense of safety after storms seems to have set in between 1848 and 1851. The unprecedented celebrations of the latter year (a year, wrote Macaulay, 'long to be remembered as a singularly happy year of peace, plenty, good feeling, innocent pleasure and national glory')[2] included a rich vein of national self-congratulation on social and political grounds as well as economic ones. Not only did Britain unmistakably lead the world in commerce and manufactures, she was held to lead also in setting an example of a harmonious and orderly modern society that needed no, so to speak, 'external', imposed-by-government military or police power to keep order, but kept order of its own accord. Beneath many peaceful social exteriors, such internal checks and controls may or may not be working. A distinguished American sociological historian refers to the ' "day-to-day repression" of ordinary society'.[3] To a modern mind ambitious for free expression of individuality and fearful of the powers of Leviathan, that 'repression' (to use a word already loaded) may seem a sad or bad thing. To the respectable mid-Victorian mind, which gave it a different name, it seemed admirable. To the Newcastle Commissioners about 1860, for instance, it seemed that there was:

'... a material difference ... between the political and social circumstances of our own country and those of countries where the central administration wields great power over a people but recently emancipated, habituated to the control of a searching police, and subjected to the direct action of the government, without the interposition of a numerous landed gentry and a multitude of great employers of labour ...'[4]

The 'direct action of the government' (what a revealing phrase!) was something the ordinary Briton hardly knew and did not like the idea of; the influence of landed gentry, employers of labour, clergy and other professional men, and the operation of conventional notions of religious duty and constitutional propriety, on behalf of or in lieu of 'government', was something the ordinary Briton believed he perfectly understood. Mid-Victorian British society seemed (a small exception made for the new police) to have hit upon the secret of keeping order more or less of its own accord: a sort of constitutional equivalent to the law of perpetual motion.

Through the clatter of clichés on this theme could be clearly heard great gasps of relief at the national good fortune to have discovered (over the past two centuries or so) so safe and prosperous a middle path between military despotism on the one side, and what was so often called 'red republicanism' on the other. Contemporary Europe was regarded as a well-stored magazine of examples of both extremes, and it would be a great mistake to assume that, because none of the social-ist experiments of 1848–9 succeeded, the British propertied public did not take them seriously. A danger did not have to be practically imminent for mid-Victorians to get worked up about it; as their somewhat hysterical anxieties about Popery sufficiently prove. The 'red' scare' of the same period, al-though it throve among only a section of the citizenry, was similar in intensity and fancifulness. Macaulay, than whom no representative statesman of the period stood more four-square 'against the encroachments of despotism and the licen-tiousness of democracy',[5] thus let himself go on the subject of 'red republicanism' at the close of the second volume of his *History of England*, published early in 1849 :

'Doctrines hostile to all sciences, to all arts, to all industry, to all domestic charities, doctrines which, if carried into effect, would, in thirty years, undo all that thirty centuries have done for mankind, and would make the fairest province of France and Germany as savage as Congo or Patagonia, have been avowed from the tribune and defended by the sword.'

By the close of the Great Exhibition of 1851 it was clear that the fairest provinces of Britain were safe from becoming another Basutoland or Hudson's Bay. Until as recently as that exhibition's opening, its managers—a representative group of the ruling classes—had continued to fear that the working classes would make of it an occasion to exploit class ends and to embarrass and humiliate their superiors. A proposal to engage a committee of working men in the planning of the exhibition was cautiously declined. Many responsible persons thought the opening ceremony should be private, lest Chartists or foreigners should make trouble. Once the Crystal Palace was open, however, these lingering fears vanished like morning dew. The sun of social harmony seemed to rise bright in an unclouded heaven. Well-behaved working folk from all over Britain flocked to the palace on its shilling days in such vast numbers, and behaved so well there, that it became quite the thing for adventurous upper-class ladies and gentlemen to go on shilling days as well, to enjoy the unaccustomed—perhaps, in an urban context, unprecedented—sensation of mingling with 'the people' on a ground of common interest. *Punch* on 14 June 1851 neatly hit off this mood of astonishment and relief: a working-class family facing a West End one, smiles on both sides, and the legend, 'Who'd have thought of meeting *you* here?' When it was all over, *The Times* noted that more than six million tickets had been sold and that one day the number of visitors had been as huge as 109,915. It drew the lesson of the year:

'When it is remembered that these extraordinary figures, which can be thoroughly relied on for accuracy, illustrate popular movements that only a few years ago would have been pronounced on the highest authority most dangerous to the safety of the state, we have the more reason to wonder that they should have taken place not only without disorder, but also almost without crime.'[6]

The hungry forties and the radical thirties suddenly seemed remote. The mid-Victorian calm was announced and enthusiastically acclaimed; the leaders of the most recently disturbed part of provincial society hastened to communicate the healing message to their (I use the word in no merely parliamentary sense) constituencies. The language at the dinners and meetings in Leeds, for instance, exactly echoed what Prince Albert and Henry Cole and co. were saying in London; no other object but social reconciliation seems to have lain behind the Oldham Lyceum Exhibition of Works of Industry and Art which the leading industrialist of the town, James Platt, and colleagues mounted during the summer of 1854. The Earl of Wilton at the opening spoke movingly of his conviction that its main result would be the 'strengthening and drawing closer those kindly feelings and offices of amity which ought to subsist and be reciprocated between the employer and the employed'. The *Oldham Chronicle*, after writing in the usual vein about enriching mental culture etc., looked forward to all 'the kindly feelings, the generous sympathies, the lofty philanthropic aspirations, which the genial intercourse and association of classes, *inseparable from the operation of such an agency,* cannot fail to foster ...'. (My italics.) Platt himself, when introducing a lecturer whose commentary on the art exhibits would help to divert local minds from the 'animal and vicious' to the high and the pure, spoke of his exhibition as an 'agreeable re-union of all classes of the people of Oldham'.[7] Resolutely deaf to the sirens of socialist theory and radical agitation, masters and men would sail triumphantly together across a calm sea of social harmony.

This calm, in so far as its foundations were more than economic, rested on a common acceptance by (as it seemed) the greater part of every articulate social group, of a hierarchical social order, and on the wide diffusion of a common cult of personal qualities known as 'respectability' and 'independence'. Respectability and independence in practice tended to amount to much the same thing, but their sources—the former rather religious, the latter more economic—and calibrations were quite distinct. The pecking order in that overriding social hierarchy was determined by factors different again. A social position unassailable according to the canons of respectability and independence was all too likely to be placed lower in that historic hierarchy than its possessor thought his due. Much anguish followed. Nor was that anguish of mortified self-esteem the only kind of grit in the social machine. There was also (and how should there not have been in a complicated society so full of religion and religiosity?) much endemic moral disapproval; there was a lot of drunkenness, violence, harshness and selfishness to disapprove of ; there was some plain Marxist class hostility; and there was at least one major race problem: the Irish. The Irish tended to keep together and wherever they occurred were likely to excite hostile comment and worse; many, perhaps most, of the really big public disturbances of our period had Irishmen willy-nilly at the bottom of them. But notwithstanding these inner strains, and despite the persistence of inequalities and deprivations which might have been expected to exacerbate them, harmony, not dissonance, was the dominant characteristic of British society during our period; though why it should have been so, and to what extent it was more apparent than real (i.e. how far it depended on the bottling up rather than the dilution of bad feelings), are questions that seem unlikely ever to be answered to everyone's satisfaction, and for which I can propose only provisional answers.

It was that very superior observer of his mid-Victorian countrymen, Walter Bagehot, who put into general circulation[8] the two terms which historians nowadays find irresistibly appropriate in describing the mid-Victorian social order; and it was the dominant politician of that period, the irresistibly popular aristocrat Palmerston, who was their foremost populariser. The terms were 'deference' and 'removable inequalities'. Bagehot in 1866 was quite explicit in his use of them. Palmerston did not, I think, explicitly use either term, but he was a master in the expression of the substance of at any rate 'removable inequalities'. ('Deference' he no doubt took for granted.) His somewhat surprising summary of it in his famous *Don Pacifico* speech of 25 June 1850 is very well known but so classic and concise that it may be cited again:

'We have shown the example of a nation in which every class of society accepts with cheerfulness the lot which providence has assigned to it; while at the same time each individual of each class is constantly trying to raise himself in the social scale, not by violence and illegality, but by persevering good conduct and by the steady and energetic exertion of the moral and intellectual faculties with which his creator has endowed him.'

If he had said that in 1855, it would have seemed less surprising, for by then it was the standard claptrap of patriotic boosters. Palmerston was well to the fore of them by saying it in 1850, because the past half-century of British history in fact demonstrated exactly the opposite! Only since 1848 could a prudent man have confidently made out a decisive turn of the tide. Presumably it was, however, exactly what Britons wanted to hear; and Palmerston, who can only have gained from saying it in 1850, went on saying it for the rest of his life. I cite another (and by contrast an unknown) speech of his from fifteen years later, given in April 1865 at the prizegiving of the South London Industrial Exhibition;

one of the myriad little local exhibitions of industrial and art objects which trickled on for years after the great international one. It is in itself such a remarkable text, that the report on it merits citation in full; since it so clearly expresses the common creed of the fifties and sixties: [9]

'In the course of his speech, Lord Palmerston remarked that such an exhibition as this, and the various works performed by so many of the industrious people of London in their leisure hours, were extremely significant of the happy influences of the constitution under which we have the good fortune to live; which opens to every man having talents, energy, perseverance, and good conduct any honours and distinctions which his turn of mind and attainments may qualify him to aspire to. We live, pursued his Lordship, under a constitutional monarchy, and of such a monarchy an aristocracy of wealth and an aristocracy of rank are essential ingredients. It is true that aristocracies of wealth and rank exist in many other countries, but, unfortunately, there are almost impassable barriers separating them from the rest of the nation, while no such barriers exist in this country. With regard to the aristocracy of wealth, the medals distributed today have inscribed on them the names of a great number of men who, starting from very small beginnings, attained, by their talent, their industry, their perseverance, and their good conduct, the very highest positions of social merit and distinction. Many more might have been added to that list. And you must all have seen in your own experience men starting from the smallest beginnings who have in this very city realised princely fortunes. In the manufacturing districts examples of this kind are abundant, for no man can go, even for a few days, into those districts without hearing of great wealth, acquired by men who started with little, but, by their talents and genius, raised themselves and their families to opulence. Then, again, does the aristocracy of rank in this country consist simply of those who can count in their pedigree generations of noble ancestors? Look at all the great men who have figured in public life. Look at your Army, your Navy, your Law, your Church, your statesmen. You will find in every one of those careers men who have risen to the highest points, who have either themselves started from the smallest beginnings, or whose fathers began with nothing but their talents, their industry, and their energy to aid them. I do not mention the names of any of these, though, for the men themselves and for their families, it would be a most honourable roll; but you are all conversant with names renowned in the history of the country who belonged not to noble families, but who founded noble families; springing, many of them, from the very class which I have now the honour of addressing. Does not this afford even greater encouragement than the prizes just distributed to all of you who have cultivated the talents with which nature has endowed you? Wealth is, to a certain extent, within the reach of all; but be assured of one thing, that, even if you fail in gaining those summits of ambition which I have indicated, there is no greater source of private comfort and of individual happiness than the exercise of intellectual faculties and the enjoyment of domestic affection. The exercise of the intellectual faculties, to which the exhibitors here show that they have devoted themselves, must make them happier men; must contribute to raise them, not only in their own estimation, but in the estimation of all who know them, and must lead to the noblest of all exercises, of all pleasures—the cultivation, improvement, and development of the human intellect. I may be told that the examples I have cited of men who attained great wealth or distinguished positions are few, while the competitors are many, and that to the bulk of those who struggle to arrive at such goals the effort must be hopeless. I would ask whether many of you have not gone on a fine bright day, in the beginning of summer, to that great seat of amusement, Epsom racecourse, and seen horses run for that celebrated race, the Derby? Three or four hundred horses entered for the race, but only one won the prize. All the rest failed to obtain the object of their ambition. But those luckless horses that did not win the Derby won other races. If they were good for anything they all won something. And thus the training, the industry, the pains, and the expense of those who had fitted them for the competition in which they were to take part were eventually repaid. And so I say to you—you are competitors for prizes. You may not all become Generals or Admirals; you may not all become Lord Chancellors or Archbishops; you may not become members of the Cabinet; but depend upon it, you will, by systematic industry, raise yourselves in the social system of your country—you will acquire honour and respect for yourselves and for your families. You will have, too, the constant satisfaction of feeling that you have materially contributed to the dignity of your country, to its welfare, to its prosperity and greatness, and that you have been worthy of the nation to which you belong. I beg again to express the extreme pleasure I have derived from what I have witnessed today; and I trust that hereafter these exhibitions may be even more successful than the present, which I am told has exceeded that of last year. Go on, ladies and gentlemen, and prosper; and depend upon it that the blessings which you will confer upon yourselves and your families will be proportioned to the industry you display, and to the cultivation which you give to those noble faculties with which Providence has endowed you.'

In that comprehensive rhapsody is movingly embodied the social theory of removable inequalities; with the emphasis placed rather on the 'removable' than the 'inequalities', as was appropriate at a prizegiving for, in the main, clever artisans. The inequalities needed the less emphasis, inasmuch as they were so familiar. Palmerston could take them for granted in addressing an audience of exemplary self-helpers dedicated to removing them. Men who really found the inequalities of their society removable or who at any rate believed them to be as much so as was reasonable in an imperfect world, were not likely to be dangerous radicals. Nor were men (now we return to Bagehot's other invaluable term) with deference in their bones. One can scarcely imagine a less 'Marxian' industrial working-man than a mid-Victorian artisan who won a prize at that exhibition and who also felt instinctive deference towards the notables gracing it with their presence. The deferential was, so far as social order went, the more important of these two ideas of Bagehot's because it *was* the more instinctive and because it induced the same sort of acquiescence in the social order in the most unequal people, whether their inequalities were removable or not. The mid-Victorians of course had no historical monopoly of deference. But deference does seem to have been remarkably strong in their time, and Bagehot was its Darwin:

'England [he wrote—and he might without much loss of truth have said Britain] is the type of deferential countries, [countries] in which the numerous unwiser part wishes to be ruled by the less numerous wiser part. The numerical majority ... is ready, is eager to delegate its power of choosing its ruler to a certain select minority. It abdicates in favour of its *élite*, and consents to obey whoever that *élite* may confide in.'

Reverting then to his famous distinction between 'efficient' and 'dignified' parts of a constitution, he maintained (somewhat disputably) that while political power really rested in the hands of the middle classes (themselves, of course, rather deferential too), the masses were deferring not to them but to 'what we may call the *theatrical show* of society ... a certain pomp of great men; a certain spectacle of beautiful women; a wonderful scene of wealth and enjoyment ... a certain charmed spectacle which imposes on the many, and guides their fancies as it will.' Bagehot thought the political consequences of this star-struck deference very happy indeed. He knew about the poverty in which so many of his countrymen lived. 'There are whole classes', he conceded, 'who have not a conception of what the higher orders call comfort; who have not the pre-requisites of moral existence; who cannot lead the life that becomes a man.' But (remember that he was writing nearly twenty years after Chartism's last splutter, and just before the outcome of the political crisis of 1866-7 occurred to shake his complacency) the lower classes did not look to politics to change things, and the result, a result he applauded, was Britain's demonstration that 'A country of respectful poor though far less happy than where there are no poor to be respectful, is nevertheless far more fitted for the best government. You can use the best classes of the respectful country ...'. Britain, as if to prove it, made a lot of use of Bagehot.

Now all this Burkean stuff could have been comfortable make-believe. Some of it certainly was. Bagehot's second edition (1868) had a preface that went some way towards admitting that he had been inhabiting a fool's paradise. But he was far too shrewd an observer to be mistaken for much of the time, and his observations tally with so many other people's that his theory of 'deference'—i.e. willing acceptance of hierarchy—can be taken seriously. 'The essentially hierarchical plan of English society', remarked for example that sensitive observer Henry James, just ten years later, 'is the great and ever-present fact to the mind of a stranger; there is hardly a detail of life that does not in some degree betray it.'[10] Bagehot's generation was deferential, through and through, and what it was (in the strictest sense) deferential to, was rank and title: rank in the upper strata of that almost universally acknowledged hierarchy, and the title of 'Gentleman'. We must study what those ranks and titles meant, before examining the other sentiment that so much promoted social order, the common cult of respectability and independence.

Nobility and Gentry

Unchallenged on the topmost strata of the British hierarchy were the hereditary nobility and the county gentry. They had of course been there, under whatever titles, for many centuries. They looked as natural as the (carefully cultivated) landscape and as ancient as their (historically-attired) mansions. They certainly seemed to take their continued ascendancy in politics as in society as the most natural thing in the world. Perhaps indeed it was so. Perhaps Macaulay (who, goodness knows, had his head screwed on the right way) had seized the essential point when he argued that Britain had been spared a revolution in the nineteenth because she had had one in the seventeenth century. Deference may have been even deeper-rooted than even Bagehot dared to believe. One is driven to believe that it must have been extraordinarily strong during our period, when one considers the dangers and counter-attractions which that aristocratic ascendancy had so successfully and recently survived. The democrats' assault from the time of the French Revolution onward was not the whole, nor even perhaps the major part, of the danger. More serious really, because potentially capable of so much more organisation and persistence, was the righteous indignation of those 'numerous wealthy and respectable' men of the middle classes who had so many reasons for resenting their practical stigmatisation as second class citizens. Feargus O'Connor's analysis of the landlord's venison as dyed with orphans' blood and claret sweetened with widows' tears was not as menacing to the landlords as Cobden's statistics, Dickens's caricatures and Bright's lay sermons. During the forties these tribunes of the middle classes believed they were winning. During the fifties they were driven to admit that they had lost. Cobden was forced to say in 1857: 'During my experience the higher classes never stood so high in relative social and political rank, as compared with the other classes, as at present.'[11] That seems indeed to have been the case. The great 'middle class' movement—mainly urban, commercial and Nonconformist— which was channelled for a while by the Anti-Corn Law League could, in theory, have stayed in being after 1846 and gone on to other landlord-lowering objects. The league's leaders tried to do that. They failed, even though fate threw old aristocracy's monumental mismanagement of the Crimean War into their laps. Thus materialised another side of that mid-Victorian calm. The middle classes became either deferential or noticeably more deferential than they had recently been. For all their bluster they were, like the archetypal Meagles, toadies at heart (see below pp. 263–4). From Cobden's point of view, they had sold out to the aristocracy, just as had (from the point of view of an unrepentant democratic Chartist like, say, Harney) the working classes.

The aristocratic social élite of mid-Victorian Britain, while no more of a closed and caste-like body than the British aristocracy had always been, had nevertheless enough of an exclusive and caste-like air about it to keep it relatively select, small and homogeneous. The impregnable citadel of its prestige was its unquestioned leadership of 'society', metropolitan and/or county. London 'society' was much the more expensive to move in and it included more dubious elements of mere wealth and pretension. Only the richer members of county society could afford the London season, and not all of them liked it. It did however offer possible entrées for the really rich or unusually talented 'outsiders' (e.g. millionaires, beauties or novelists); London 'society' was more impressionable and unpredictable than county. 'Outsiders'—men like Sir Roger Scatcherd and Squire Muleygrubs (see below, p. 275) could break in by the county route too, if they really set their minds and purses to it. 'Society's' edge was permanently blurred by the jostling of the thousands who were trying to get in with the hundreds who were trying not to be pushed out. But its central parts were unmistakable: the hereditary nobility, the landed gentry and the professional gentlemen of the West End and the countryside; and, unless you were case-hardened to resist its appeal—as were the rich and talented members of some Nonconformist 'urban aristocracies' in great cities like Birmingham, Leeds, Norwich, Liverpool, etc.—that was the charmed circle you revered and envied.

The hereditary nobility was not, in our period, the very numerous body it had become by the 1920s; and its tone was hardly as yet affected by the industrial and commercial creations which only began to flood into it after 1886. These men of title and their relations formed the *corps d'élite* of the upper class. Peers had to be very bad or very peculiar indeed not to be accorded the conventional respectful treatment: as bad and peculiar as high-mettled military and sporting fanatics like the seventh Earl of Cardigan, for example, or profligate rakes like the third Marquess of Hastings. So high was peers' social value that even most distant relations could, if they wished, cash in on it; and relations were in fact plentiful, among the healthiest stratum of a population given to large families. Some hint of how these aristocratic families ramified is given in Bernard Cracroft's well-known calculation— made to demonstrate the control they kept of the parliamentary representation—that in the 1865 House of Commons there were at least 326 more or less aristocratic members, including 116 peers or sons or grandsons of peers and 110 ditto of baronets, and a hundred others 'connected with the peerage by marriage or descent'. Over a hundred more, said Cracroft, 'substantially belong to the same class'; making a good three-quarters of the Commons all connected to each other, and to the Lords, by blood as well as by interest.[12] From this same cohesive class were filled the bulk of the higher executive as well as the bulk of the higher legislative positions. One might suppose this *ancien régime*-like engrossment of political positions to have been intolerable to the men outside the charmed circle who, after all, paid for most of its official enjoyments. Indeed there were plenty of mid-Victorians who did think it intolerable. Dickens, who felt so strongly about it that he let it provoke one of his rare forays into politics (the Administrative Reform Association of 1855), characteristically digested the outsiders' point of view into his highly-coloured picture, in *Little Dorrit* (1858), of the Tite Barnacle 'clan, or clique, or family, or connection' (as one of its more cynical members called it); a member of which you could find 'wherever there was a square yard of ground in British occupation under the sun or moon, with a public post upon it . . .'. A shoal of the Barnacles condescendingly attended their relation Henry Gowan's marriage to middle-class Mr Meagles's daughter. Some were established, famous and great; some :

'. . . who had not as yet got anything, . . . were going through their probation to prove their worthiness. . . . And there was not a list, in all the Circumlocution Office, of places that might fall vacant anywhere within half a century, from a Lord of the Treasury to a Chinese Consul, and up again to a Governor-general of India, but, as applicants for such places, the names of some or every one of these hungry and adhesive Barnacles were down.'

All this was intolerable, normally, to Mr Meagles, and he certainly did not enjoy the snubbing and condescension to which these sponges and leeches subjected him; yet—so well did his creator know the bourgeois heart!—after the grisly ceremony was over, and his daughter had gone off with the well-connected wastrel whom the Meagleses (quite correctly) seriously distrusted, Mr Meagles got some consolation from reflecting on the rank of those who thus humiliated him. 'It's very gratifying', he said, often repeating the remark in the course of the evening, 'Such high company!'[13] One recalls Cobden's allegation, about the same year 1857, that 'The more contempt a man like Palmerston ... heaped upon them the more they [the middle class] cheered him.'[14] Dickens and Cobden were increasingly on the losing side in this debate about the merits of the aristocracy as a political and administrative ruling class. By the time Matthew Arnold presented his highly-coloured picture of them (a picture at least as much of a caricature as Dickens's), his was a cultured voice crying in a cultivated wilderness. 'One of the greatest industrialists in England, a radical and a supporter of Mr Bright', told Hippolyte Taine sometime during the sixties:

'It is not our aim to overthrow the aristocracy: we are ready to leave the government and high offices in their hands. For we believe, we men of the middle class, that the conduct of national business calls for special men, men born and bred to the work for generations, and who enjoy an independent and commanding situation. Besides, their titles and pedigrees give them a quality of dash and style, and troops will more readily follow officers who have that.... Let them govern, but let them be fit to govern.'[15]

Bagehot put much the same case in much the same way. It looks as if this easy and complacent acquiescence in the aristocracy's political as well as social ascendancy was dominant among the middle classes in the sixties and seventies, and was not seriously shaken until a new variety of rude noises began to make themselves heard in Birmingham.

This ascendancy could not, of course, have been so secure had the aristocracy neither lived satisfactorily up to its myth nor availed itself of the opportunities of usefulness thus confidingly offered to it. As Taine's friend said, the aristocracy had to govern efficiently; it had to give value for money. This demand was not difficult to satisfy, for an aristocracy with so many decades' experience of successfully absorbing the leaders and accommodating the demands of powerful 'rising' groups outside its own preserves. No hereditary aristocracy in Europe ever showed—ever has shown!—anything like the same sense for survival; a political sense, at bottom. But there was more to the aristocracy's ability to make itself not merely acceptable but also positively valuable than either its ultimate political wisdom or (a closely related thing) its ultimate accessibility to the well-qualified climber. It was, to a great extent, a working aristocracy. As politicians and administrators, peers and relations of peers were by our period working as hard as anyone else. That they took a leading part in the local government of the countryside, goes without saying; I doubt if any English peer who was not absolutely and embarrassingly mentally deranged was not a magistrate. Some were successful businessmen, active directors of big solid concerns like banks, railway and canal companies and docks; let alone their close and expert interest in the profitable use of their estates, urban and rural alike. Many lesser aristocratic fry were glad to realise the cash value of their social prestige as directors of sometimes less solid concerns; this commercial exploitation of title, which seems to have begun in the forties, had become standard practice and malpractice by the time Trollope wrote *The Way We Live Now* (1875). Aristocratic names were still more sought after by the promoters of philanthropic and charitable organisations. A new one could hardly hope to get off the ground without at least a spiritual peer's name on its notepaper. His name once given and his subscriptions paid, a prestigious aristocrat could sit back for 364 days of the year and let human nature and the secretary do the rest:

'Large fat private double letter, sealed with ducal coronet. [Contents lithographed, signature rubber-stamped, envelope addressed in a different hand.] 'Nicodemus Boffin, Esquire. My dear Sir,—Having consented to preside at the forthcoming Annual Dinner of the Family Party Fund, and feeling deeply impressed with the immense usefulness of that noble Institution and the great importance of its being supported by a List of Stewards that shall prove to the public the interest taken in it by popular and distinguished men, I have undertaken to ask you to become a Steward on that occasion. Soliciting your favourable reply before the fourteenth instant, I am, My Dear Sir, Your faithful servant, LINSEED.'[16]

Apart from these and other such socially useful activities in public service, business and philanthropy, the aristocracy made the very different claim on public respect and affection of being charmingly useless. Bagehot made much of this, and Bagehot may surely be presumed to have been right to do so:

'The office of an order of nobility [he wrote], is to impose on the common people.... The fancy of the mass of men is incredibly weak; it can see nothing without a visible symbol, and there is much that it can scarcely make out without a symbol. Nobility is the symbol of mind.'

Moreover it stood for something other than mere wealth, and performed the morally valuable service of counteracting the Englishman's too-ready reverence for riches (see below, p. 267). Granting that there might be an idolatry of rank as well as an idolatry of riches, Bagehot, surveying the doubly idolatrous society of his own day, concluded that the former was by far the less base:

'As the world has gone, manner has been half-hereditary in certain castes, and manner is one of the fine arts. It is the *style* of society.... The unconscious grace of life *may* be in the middle classes: finely-mannered persons are born everywhere; but it *ought* to be in the aristocracy...'

Thus, with a significant echo of Burke's purple passage about Marie Antoinette, Bagehot disclosed the emotional heart of the matter. The aristocracy was irresistibly fascinating to a historically- and hierarchically-minded, socially ambitious and envious society, because its members seemed to be *heroic*. They were supposed to look handsomer, love more passionately and behave more impressively than lower-bred mortals. Breeding was all. Aristocrats who did not look the part were something of a disappointment:

'Dined at the Mansion House [recorded an unusually critical Norfolk clergyman on 11 July 1855] "to meet", as the invitation ran, "the most noble the Marquis of Salisbury and the

Middlesex Magistrates". Certainly nothing could be fairer than the scene, or worse than the speaking. How is it that the aristocracy do not cut a better figure than they do? Here was one looking like a cadaverous Methodist, another like a German pipe-seller, a third so lost in a huge shirt-collar that it is hard to say what he *was* like.'

One gathers that the Reverend B. J. Armstrong thought their seediness almost culpable.[17]

Around this inner ring of the hereditary and titled blood group was gathered the 'county families' (often related to the inner circle, of course), boasting no titles higher than, at most, 'Sir' before and 'MFH' after, but capable of equal concern for lineage and racial purity and sometimes possessing more of them than the men of title themselves; the Thornes of Ullathorne were encouraged by the immemorial antiquity of their line to look down upon earls of recent vintage. The common characteristic of county families was landownership. That mattered not just because farmland usually, during our period, brought in a good income—even the most rustic-looking landowners might be getting more from urban ground-rents, mineral royalties, consols, etc., than from agriculture—but more because ownership of land and nothing else made possible the playing of the roles that country gentry conventionally played: the landlordly role in respect of tenants, employees and economic dependants; the sportsmanly role by due deployment of horses and hounds, coverts and streams; the society role by diligent attention to the rites of visiting, house and garden parties, church-going, charitable work, etc. If you owned land broad enough to be called a park or an estate, you had to be pretty unbearable (personally or politically) not to gain some degree of social acceptance among the established hierarchy of the county: enough acceptance, at any rate, to maintain a solid landowning class front in face of urban radicals, who menaced the whole lovely-looking system from without, and the rural lower orders—from farmers and tradesmen downwards—upon whose subordination and labour it actually rested. You could of course live safely among the elect without any land at all, provided you had a satisfactory connection to some satisfactory landowner; that was one of the several open elements of the hierarchical system, which significantly mitigated its exclusiveness and rigidity. So long as you were 'a gentleman' or the female equivalent, you would get in. But were you a 'gentleman'?

The Gentleman

It is necessary to investigate this 'gentleman' concept rather closely because, although it had been important and problematical since at least the middle of the eighteenth century, to mid-Victorians it became peculiarly so. So many men were not within striking distance of the title that it became as never before vital for the collective consciousness of the social heights to clarify its meaning. The questions, were you or were you not a gentleman, and if so, were you the right sort of gentleman (for the word meant different things at different social levels), were of rather agonising importance because, if you were, you could get into 'society' (in *any* of its manifestations: county, 'London' or provincial city) and if you were not, you couldn't. The late-Victorian Alfred Salteena's 'I am not quite a gentleman but you would hardly notice it...'[18] is only funny because of the way it's put; intrinsically his difficulty was no different from that of mid-Victorian Johnny Eames: 'Bless you, when you come to talk of a gentleman, who is to define the word? How do I know whether or no I'm a gentleman myself?'[19]

The short answer seems to be, that you could not be sure until judgment was delivered in your favour by the appropriate social authority—the particular élite group by whom you were anxious to be recognised. Because the unquestioned national élite was the aristocracy and county families, the socially ambitious or anxious principally sought recognition in their circles; which intersected with the unique and mixed phenomenon of 'London society'. To be accepted as a gentleman by the county or by 'London society' was virtually to guarantee acceptance by all other (cognate or interior) élite circles: by the sometimes quite old-established 'urban aristocracies' of the great cities which seem to have been capable of such local pride and self-sufficiency as to be able to exist independently; and, *a fortiori*, by the accepted élites which inevitably established themselves wherever two or three thousand Englishmen were gathered together and which might have little or even no connection with 'the county'. The term 'gentleman' was, as W. L. Burn noted in the course of his somewhat inconclusive section on it, elastic and relative:

'If a small town contained no gentleman as the word was understood in the county club, then the solicitor, the brewer, the doctor stepped into the breach; elsewhere the prosperous farmer or shopkeeper might have to serve; or someone who exhibited just a little more decorum, possessed a little more money than his neighbours, would have the role thrust upon him.'[20]

Such a man might pass as a gentleman in, say, Merthyr Tydfil, but he certainly could not rely on being accepted as such by the Nonconformist millionaires of Birmingham or Liverpool, let alone 'the county'. Least 'transferable' of all were the 'gentlemen' sometimes known as 'nature's gentlemen': persons of no social position and probably no property either, whose manners, bearing or achievements nevertheless marked them out as uncommon, admirable and civilised. Samuel Smiles insisted in the closing chapter of *Self-Help* (1859) that true gentlemanliness was within reach of any virtuous Briton. (Burn would have understood this; Burke wouldn't.) As an ideal, its appeal was unmistakable, and its moral content was clearly understood: morality, selflessness, courage, self-control, independence, responsibility. Its apparently very wide acceptance during our period compels us to regard it as an effectively civilising force. But we must take care not to confuse the moral ideal with the social reality. A true gentleman could be relied on not to push in where he wasn't wanted. A Highland gillie or a contented self-educated village schoolmaster were considered the finest sort. The idea of the gentleman was therefore much more influential than precise; and it was loaded to support the social hierarchy. It was not strong enough to topple the mighty from their seats, no matter how ungentlemanly a sort of gentleman they were. A gillie who showed himself to be no gentleman would remain a gillie. But so would a peer who showed himself no gentleman remain a peer.

The mid-Victorian's varied and continuous use of the gentleman concept thus had something but not very much to do with social mobility. It had more to do with social acceptance. The only sure way of knowing you were a gentleman was to be treated as such. But you were likelier to be so treated in some walks of life than others. If you were an officer in the army or navy, a lawyer, a civil servant, a doctor or a clergyman, and provided you were neither too obviously 'self-made' nor socially unadaptable, you were presumably eligible for acceptance. Clergymen of the established church started off with much in their favour. Advising her cousin against marrying an attorney, Lady Amelia de Courcy—a stickler for the proprieties—conceded that 'Clergymen—particularly the rectors and vicars of country parishes—do become privileged above other professional men.'[21] But not even the most prosperous parish, had Obadiah Slope contrived to get hold of it, could have made *him* privileged! When the courtly Dr Stanhope first met him, he was astonished and silent; 'in spite of his long absence, he knew an English gentleman when he saw him'. One sight of Slope sufficed for the born insider. Relative poverty in itself was no bar. Consider two more of those shrewdly observed Barsetshire clergy: Mr Quiverful, poor, harassed by an absurd superfluity of children, attached to an utterly unpresentable wife, and evidently without Oxbridge reputation and connection; and Mr Crawley, even poorer but with only three surviving children, a lady-like wife, and both academic distinction and 'good connections' dating from his Oxford days. Josiah Crawley was emphatically a gentleman, despite his 'dirty broken boots' and shabby garments. Even while under suspicion of having stolen a cheque, even though the most cussed and eccentric of his cloth, no one ever doubted his rank. And at the end of Trollope's last Barsetshire novel, it was memorably affirmed, when Crawley told his wife how he had expressed to Archdeacon Grantley (whose son his daughter was about to marry) his regret at being too poor to dower her:

' "My dear Crawley," the archdeacon said..., "I have enough for both." "I would we stood on more equal grounds," I said. Then, as he answered me, he rose from his chair. "We stand," said he, "on the only perfect level on which such men can meet each other. We are both gentlemen." "Sir," I said, rising also, "from the bottom of my heart I agree with you. I could not have spoken such words; but coming from you who are rich to me who am poor, they are honourable to the one and comfortable to the other." '[22]

What was true of the clergy was true, *mutatis mutandis*, of the other professional men of the period. The mid-Victorians recognised far fewer professions than we do in the 1970s but more than their predecessors had done. The demands of an industrial economy and a materially rich society, were by their time powerfully stimulating that gathering of educated men of particular valuable skills into organised and self-disciplined groups, for mixed purposes of material enrichment and social advancement which signalises the growth of the professions. The mid-Hanoverians had known only five professions: church, law, medicine, army and navy. By the 1860s it was possible to argue that there were also engineers (civil and mechanical), architects, administrative civil servants, accountants, actuaries and surveyors, artists (all kinds), teachers (perhaps), Nonconformist ministers (possibly), dentists. But there were no rules to determine the social status either of these *soi-disant* professions as professions, or of any individual members of them in any particular social situation. They were internally riven just like 'the old professions'. The status battle absorbed and bemused them all. Civil engineers thought themselves mighty superior to mechanical engineers, but had a hard enough job getting into high society; really rich ones like Cubitt, Peto and Brassey could buy their way into 'London society' like any other socially ambitious millionaires, but the unctuous moralising and ill-concealed glee which greeted Peto's downfall in 1866 showed clearly enough which way the social wind blew. Barristers carried much more social weight than solicitors; doctors, than dentists. A Nonconformist minister like R. W. Dale could hold as high a rank in Birmingham as an Anglican dean in a cathedral city—a higher rank, perhaps, than any Anglican clergyman in Birmingham; but he meant nothing to the county families of Warwickshire. The ambitious minister of Salem Chapel quickly discovered that neither did he mean anything in the country town of Carlingford.

My review of the social problems and hierarchical placings of those who thought they were or ought to be 'gentlemen' must close with a look at the most numerous group of all: the men whose commercial and industrial activities made Britain 'the workshop of the world' and kept the wealth-making wheels turning. I have left them till last because they were, socially, least. In élite circles dominated by aristocratic 'county' ideas, men connected with factories, banks and warehouses —let alone shops!—were generically suspect, clouded by the imputation of vulgarity. So were farmers, unless they could stake a credible claim to be counted as 'gentleman farmers'. The men of the factories, banks, etc., bodied forth the same endemic class-consciousness by establishing sub-hierarchies among themselves; sub-hierarchies which no doubt varied from place to place. An acute and astonished foreigner— French master at a first-class London school during the later seventies—noticed the fathers' multi-layered snobbery rebounding among the sons:

'In England boys begin swaggering about their social position as soon as they leave the nursery, and if you would have some fun, you should follow groups of public school boys in the playground or on their way home. . . . Here are the sons of professional men, of officers, clergymen, barristers. See them pointing out other boys passing: "Sons of merchants, don't you know!" These are not without their revenge, as they look at a group close by: "Sons of clerks, you know!" But you should see the contemptuous glance of the latter as they pass the sons of shopkeepers: "Tradespeople's sons, I believe!"' [23]

The 'tradespeople's sons' could however console themselves by looking down on the sons of artisans; who could themselves. . . . 'Are any of your clerks the sons of shop-keepers?' demanded the Civil Service Inquiry Commissioners of the Secretary of the London and Westminster Bank, in 1875. 'I should say none,' he judicially replied. 'We may have had one or two when we were not so rigid as we are now, but I should say that now, as a rule, we should not introduce the son of a shopkeeper.'[24] So that was that. Connection with shops had the same fatal stigma in the mind of Richard Jefferies's representative farmer's daughter, fashionably educated at boarding school to notions above her parents' station. Back home for the agonising annual visit, she reviewed the talent of the local town:

'A banker's clerk at least—nothing could be thought of under a clerk in the local banks; of course, his salary was not high, but then his "position". The retail grocers and bakers and such people were quite beneath one's notice—low, common persons. The "professional" tradesmen (whatever that may be) were decidedly better, and could be tolerated. The solicitors, bank managers, one or two brewers (wholesale—nothing retail), large corn factors or coal merchants, who kept a carriage of some kind—these formed the select society next under . . . the clergy and gentry.'[25]

Jefferies could not understand, or pretended not to be able to understand, what a 'professional tradesman' might be. A clue is offered by the prospectus for The Diocesan Mortual (*sic*) Insurance and Funeral Establishment, of 12 Edgware Road, about 1850. It announced:

'An important feature in this establishment will be to reduce the enormous charges . . . made by a class of tradesmen (under-takers) and raising the so-called trade to the dignity of a pro-fession, conducted by gentlemen of education and feeling, and under the control of the clergy. . . .'[26]

Whether his social situation seemed satisfactory or not to an industrialist, merchant or whatever, would depend on many factors. All mid-Victorian men of property, we can safely affirm, accepted that society should be ordered on the hier-archical principle. They were conscientiously inegalitarian, on the understanding that inequalities were and ought to be removable in the case of meritorious individuals. The degree of their satisfaction therefore would depend on whether they thought their merits adequately recognised by the arbiters of their hierarchy's élite, and their status adequately respected by equals and inferiors.

There was not much difficulty about getting respect from inferiors. Most of the inferiors with whom they ever came in contact were equally concerned to be respected by *their* inferiors; and those who would not willingly defer could easily be subordinated. Among more or less equals there could of course be much jostling for precedence and scoring of points in the great hierarchical game; Farmer Greenacre's wife, who at Ullathorne sports had gone according to custom into the enclosure for the non-gentry, would never forget or forgive Farmer Lookaloft's wife's tremendous triumph in breaking unbidden into the gentry's marquee.[27] Relations with unquestioned superiors however were much more difficult because of that indefiniteness about gentlemanly status which I have insisted upon, and because that indefiniteness in effect gave the arbiters of high society an unpredictable discretionary power to bind and to loose.

Bagehot was nearly correct in claiming that British theory and practice of aristocracy humbled the pride of Midas; that 'money alone ... will not buy "London society"'. I say he was only partly correct because it seems to me that he was as usual exaggerating the virtues of the aristocracy. That aristocracy knew the value of money *pur et simple* as well as its ancestors and descendants; it married money if it badly needed it, and the 'London society' which it effortlessly dominated was notoriously mixed and was certainly in some of its parts accessible not only to the Midas who really desired it and who had a wife and children capable of going through with it (e.g. the Potter girls), but also to every kind of attractive or plausible 'outsider' (e.g. Disraeli, Millais, Taine and Bagehot). 'Oh, caste's all right', said one of the aristocrats in T. W. Robertson's 1867 play of that name, 'caste is a good thing if it's not carried too far. It shuts the door on the pretentious and the vulgar; but it should open the door very wide for exceptional merit.'[28] Lady Amberley a year later affirmed that 'the highest London society' was potentially open to 'plebeians who were personally attractive'. Young girls, for example, she said, who were staying as guests in great houses, and who had strong points in the way of beauty or music or conversation, might have an immensely successful social career ... while whole families of magnates [she evidently meant the feudal sense] would come from the more distant counties for the London season and entirely fail of social success. 'I know lots of Duke's daughters', she said casually, 'who get no attention whatever.'[29] Professionally radical in thought and manner, she was of course laying it on thick for the benefit of her Yankee interlocutor; but it was true that talent, brain and beauty could, with the right patronage, rise quite high, and perhaps sleep better o'nights than the merely very rich, whose acceptance was implicitly conditional on their remaining so.

Happy, therefore, the mercantile man who, if he ventured on to the national élite's own ground, did so with the self-knowing assurance of a Jorrocks. Jorrocks's way certainly was the only way for a self-respecting 'city man' to approach county society without unconditional surrender to its terms. As a symbol, he is certainly not incredible; but there cannot have been many like him. Nor was there during our period, I believe, a growing army of men like that equally symbolic Marmaduke Muleygrubs, who 'had been a great stay-maker on Ludgate Hill, and, in addition to his own earnings ... had inherited a large fortune from a great drysalting uncle in Bermondsey. On getting this he cut the shop, bought Cockolorum Hall,' and set up as a country gentleman. Surtees drew his portrait in the forties, and it was in the classic tradition.[30] Very rich and socially ambitious city men had for centuries been buying country estates and relying on social acceptance coming sooner or later, for themselves or their posterity. That had for long been the approved, virtually the only, admissions procedure for financially qualified outsiders. By the early Victorian period that procedure was at last being superseded by another. During our mid-Victorian period that supersession was decisively accomplished. The instrument of supersession was the so-called 'public school' (for more about which, see above, pp. 182-5).

The number of such 'outsiders' had become too great, the supply of estates too small, and the desirability of the land-lordly way of life itself was coming to seem relatively less supreme as cities and manufactures asserted an ever more un-answerable claim to social respect and national appreciation. An *impasse* threatened, as the men of the new cities—secure on the topmost strata of their urban hierarchies indeed, and probably not at all anxious to set up as country landlords, but less than perfectly content while urban hierarchies were stig-matised as inferior to county ones—confronted the established immemorial élite of the countryside. For some years, from the early thirties to the middle fifties, this *impasse* soured the internal politics of the propertied classes and intermittently threatened to rupture their anti-revolutionary front. Then, in the fifties and sixties, it became clear that a way could be found round the difficulty, that the *impasse* had been tem-porary. County gentlemen and urban 'gentlemen' need not after all assimilate to one another, or even undergo the em-barrassment of meeting. Their sons could do it for them. The urban 'gentleman' would retain undisturbed ascendancy in his own social sphere and would seek no more of the reality of county life than the make-believe landownership of the sub-urban villa; his sons however would mix with the sons of the county on the common ground of a 'public school', and come out stamped as gentlemen together. Thus did the so-called public schools (the name is a classic instance of protective coloration!) begin during our period to perform the socio-political function they have performed ever since: preserving the quasi-hereditary social élite and satisfying the status ambi-tions of variously talented or wealthy professional and 'busi-ness' families, by endowing their children with a sense of shared superiority to everyone else. By the eighties, the un-certainty which had hung over the use of the word gentleman during our period had given way to this certainty at least, that anyone was a gentleman who had been to a public school or who successfully concealed that he hadn't.

This significant extension and clarification of the 'gentleman' idea was of immense importance in the history of British society, and not only because it represented the striking of a kind of bargain and *modus vivendi* between the traditional ruling class and their potential rivals. (It cannot be considered the utter sell-out that Cobden alleged, since one result of it was that the sons of men like Cobden would live free from the worry whether they were gentlemen or not. They could know that they were.) Its importance was more general because, developing within the secure scheme of deference, it added weight and (in our sense of the word) respectability to the social strata to which the middle middling and all lower orders deferred. Such had always been expected to defer to the broad-acred peers and gentry of the big house in the country and the big house in town, and it seems to have been deeply engrained in them to defer, in all but abnormal times, to the display of wealth and power. Most of them were still apparently willing to do so. These were still times when tradesmen were expected to extend credit to men of quality, the less limited in proportion of the quality, as if it was an honour to be bankrupted by a duke; and we know that, although the standards of respectability set for professional and business men expressly precluded the contraction of debts they might not be able to pay, some of the new suburban villa and metropolitan terrace folk (of whom the Dobbs Broughtons may stand as representatives) behaved as if large credit was no less their due than a marquis's, and were likely to get it. The tradesman was in no position to resist. As for peers, they had lost not a jot of their traditional standing and there is evidence that it remained viable in our rapidly industrialising society: e.g. this 'loyal and obedient colliers'' Address (who, one wonders, got it up?) to 'Our Great and Worthy Master, the Rt Hon Lord Francis Egerton; his virtuous and most gracious Lady; Mr Fereday Smith; and all in legal authority over us', proclaiming as recently as 1842 their 'Gratitude and Love' and readiness to lay down their lives (a readiness which, in view of their occupation, had some ironic literalness) on his behalf;[31]

or, in 1857, the second great entertainment for the three thousand men and boys employed in her collieries by the Marchioness of Londonderry, with Lord Adolphus Vane Tempest in the chair, the Bishop of Durham on the platform, sixty barrels of beer on the side-tables, a gracious motherly speech by the hostess, a reply by 'Thomas Nicholson, a working pitman [who] spoke at some length' on themes of duty, gratitude, education, and religion; and, two weeks later, a full report and picture in the *Illustrated London News*.[32] (see plate 7). That the proud and wealthy continued to command respect was unremarkable. But that this thickening accretion of gentlemen, not always wealthy and ideally not at all proud (for the Christian gentleman should not be so), should come to share that respect, demands the express notice I have given it, because, though not a novelty in our period (Jane Austen's urban gentlemen were respectable enough!), it was during our period that it became settled and decisive. The significance of this extension and modernisation of the gentleman idea is that it filled out and internally strengthened those upper social strata from which was drawn the bulk of the parliamentary, Whitehall, and county governing class, together with some proportion of the provincial governing class too. Without at all lessening the power and prestige of the aristocracy and the county gentry, it bracketed with them men more obviously of the new industrial and scientific age, and therefore more deserving of respect. The old ruling class of peers and squires had been expected to exercise authority, and themselves expected to do so in order to maintain subordination. The new ruling class of gentlemen had to work more tactfully in a quasi-democratic age and used gentler sounding words like 'responsibility' and 'leadership'. Nobility and gentry had commanded you to defer to their rank. Gentlemen persuaded you to defer to their quality. It is no surprise to read that, at a rather sensational police court trial in London in 1863, 'Viscount Raynham, MP, and other gentlemen present were accommodated with seats on the bench.'[33]

Respectability and Independence

The practice of deference, the 'removable inequalities' theory of society, and the concept of the gentleman occupy so much of our attention because they worked to maintain the 'vertical' ties of society, so far as those ties were voluntary ones; they explained and justified inequalities which might otherwise have driven men to conflict; and although there is some evidence that feelings of deference were weakening from the later sixties onwards (e.g. farmers began to show more independence vis-à-vis landlords, farm labourers began to show interest in trade unionism, the best organised unions began to get their leaders into Parliament), the weakening does not seem to have got far by the mid-seventies compared to its progress during the fifteen years thereafter. Now we must turn to the concepts of respectability and independence which enjoyed an undisturbed vogue throughout our period and had the same socially-soothing tendency, by assimilating even the most widely separated groups (separated socially or geographically) through a common cult. They need not keep us long because they were neither new nor complicated. Deference was not new either, but the removable inequalities idea was, and so was the importance of the gentleman idea as it became clarified in its new meaning; the student of mid-Victorian social history has to mark those applications and extensions of deference as peculiar characteristics of his period. But the ideas of respectability and independence were taken over lock, stock and barrel from earlier times; and since their content and their vogue remained stable until the eighties, one needs only to describe them to indicate their significance.

Respectability and independence ran together, because, for the mid and for the early Victorians, divinity and economics ran together: equal presciptions of the divine/natural order of conduct. Respectability was a style of living understood to show a proper respect for morals and morality; usually it meant some degree of formal Christianity, but you could be respectable and value your respectability without being Christian. Independence came to nearly the same thing in practice;

it meant such an accommodation of expenditure to income as would make possible the respectable style of life; it proceeded from the premise that it was immoral (viz., for Christians, unchristian) to depend on any but your own resources unless you absolutely had to; it presumed that the voluntarily dependent were disreputable, and it expected the involuntarily dependent to forego, for at any rate the term of their dependence, the respect due to the properly respectable man. Respectability was the outcome of a vulgarisation and perhaps secularisation of established Christianity. Independence was the main social consequence of the vulgarisation of the creed of classical economics in a Protestant country.

It goes almost without saying, that everyone except the very poor tried to be independent. (Everyone, that is, who had self-respect of a conventional modern kind. 'Aristocrats' at one end of society, and 'peasants', craftsmen etc. at the other, if their minds were still set in old ways, might not worry about it so much.) You were expected to pay your own way, to look after yourself, to keep out of troubles if you could and to bear them manfully, i.e. uncomplainingly, if you couldn't. That troubles would come to most mortals who survived long enough to identify them, the mid-Victorian generation had no doubt. Fortunate indeed the man who retained good health, knew not pain, lost no children, was never unemployed, and never had less than enough to maintain family life at the level he felt appropriate. Such painless security of life is not nowadays uncommon. It was then extremely so; and the mid-Victorians' common philosophy of independence, sensibly accepting the fact that life was on the whole a painful and arduous affair, justified its rigours as a proving-ground for character. Experience of adversities and temptations sifted out the tough characters from the feeble. No adversities could be so severe that a strong character could not retain at least his self-respecting sense of independence; examples of good men brought low through no fault of their own, but uncomplaining and still captains of their souls, were held up for admiration. Temptations (to idleness, waste, extravagance, self-indulgence, 'vice' etc.) likewise sorted out the sensible from the silly, the strong and prudent from the weak and wilful. It was part of W. L. Burn's seminal contribution to our understanding of the mid-Victorians to identify the heart of their thinking about it as 'the doctrine of the free choice'.[34] Men must be free to make mistakes, even irremediable ones. The processes of choice taught practical morality, and kept the morally defective (whether from choice or nature) where they belonged. The necessity of choice, the having to choose, was morally invigorating; the more so, when the fate of wife and children depended on the right choice being made. The ideally responsible man was therefore expected not to involve a wife and children in his fate unless and until he had a good chance (under providence) of making that fate a good one.

Nothing was new about 'the doctrine of the free choice' in the fifties and sixties except the extent of its vogue. It was proclaimed on high and on low. It became the common cant of popular moralists. Herbert Spencer, one of its strictest apostles, expressed it at its most rigorous in *Social Statics* (1850), the first full statement of his 'social Darwinism': e.g. 'Inconvenience, suffering and death are the penalties attached by nature to ignorance, as well as to incompetence. . . . If to be ignorant were as safe as to be wise, no one would become wise.' Self-appointed spokesmen of the working classes, admittedly superior workmen like William Lovett and J. D. Burn and Thomas Cooper, made confession of their faith in social progress by means of—why not use their own word for it?—self-help : especially in education. They certainly did not speak for the whole of their class but I share a general impression that more of their class thought like this than during any earlier or later periods of the century.

From the mid-Victorians' cult and sanctification of independence and self-help (epitomised of course in Samuel Smiles's best-selling book of that title in 1859) flowed these two consequences which especially strike the observer of their Britain. First, the necessity of at least seeming independent put an enormous pressure upon all poor people who valued the reputation of respectability. Second, the exaction from those who could not stay independent of a heavy price in humiliation and admission of failure. The helping hand of charity, when it reached *de haut en bas*, almost always had a disciplinary and/or a condescending glove on: disciplinary, in that the recipient had been adjudged 'deserving' (i.e. potentially if not actually respectable) and was expected to remain so (big, business-like charities often incorporated a system of surveillance); condescending, in so far as the recipient was pressed to make ample acknowledgment of his gratitude and dependence. The back-stop behind the team of voluntary philanthropists was of course the Poor Law, where the humiliation of failure to be independent was institutionalised in the forms and ceremonies of the workhouse, the relinquishing of personal possessions, the submission to what could, in a 'well-regulated' workhouse, be a somewhat prison-like discipline, the separation from spouse and children. Dependence on public relief did not have to mean 'the house'. As often it meant out-relief, doled out in weekly doses by the relieving officer, who might or might not use his position to bully the applicants. Merely to be a pauper—and so to lose whatever political rights one may have possessed—was however humiliation enough for any self-respecting person, and was avoided until it became, through sickness or hunger, unavoidable. There were of course plenty of poor people who did not seek to avoid the stigma of pauperism and who might even, considering their lowly standpoint, make quite a good thing out of it; but only those did so who set no store on the reputation of respectability.

So we come to the great Victorian shibboleth and criterion, respectability. Here was the sharpest of all lines of social division, between those who were and those who were not respectable: a sharper line by far than that between rich and poor, employer and employee, or capitalist and proletarian. To be respectable in mid-Victorian Britain had the same cachet as being a good party man in a communist state. It signified at one and the same time intrinsic virtue and social value. The respectable man was a good man, and also a pillar of society. He might be poor, he might be rich; it really made no matter which. A rich man who was evidently not respectable—who made no secret about his mistress, or who openly ran a disreputable business, or who was known to poke fun at contemporary religious practices—would need some extra-special recommendation to guarantee acceptability in respectable houses: the highest sort of title, the hugest fortune or repute of fortune, the most fascinating and ingratiating of manners. Without some such 'open sesame' to transcend conventional morality, he would have a difficult time in his social and business relations unless indeed they were themselves confined to the sphere of the similarly disreputable; as in London at any rate they might well be.

All gentlemen could be called respectable (although the most superior ones, up in the strata where gentlemen shaded into gentry, might not be flattered at being so called). The converse was however by no means the case. All respectable men wanted to be called gentlemen, but few were chosen. There was room for any number of respectable people; the idea of respectability allowed for the possibility—indeed, desiderated the possibility—of whole classes, whole nations even, being respectable; but the gentleman idea was an élitist one, and once the élite of any given section of society was made up, it was not easy to make room for more. Most would-be gentlemen, therefore, had to rest content with respectability, and make the most of that; priding themselves, perhaps, on respectability of a superior, solider style.

Respectability certainly came in a variety of styles; some on the lighter, some on the heavier side. They were differentiated from one another by the same means that respectability itself was differentiated from its opposite: by the strictness of their observances. It was respectable in some homes, for instance, to dance (decorously), to play cards, to drink in moderation, to go to the better sort of theatrical entertainments. In others it was not respectable so to do. Conventions of respectability varied from place to place, from denomination to denomination, from group to group, from level to level. You could, in respect of the stricter sort, easily make mistakes. But some hall-marks of respectability were absolutely standard. Respectable people did not get drunk (a test which of itself ruled out great numbers of men and women, most but not all of the lower classes) or behave wildly; they maintained a certain propriety of speech and decorum of bearing; they dressed tidily and kept their houses clean and tidy, inside and out; the men's dress and everyone's demeanour were especially sober and decorous on Sundays. They never did or said anything in the presence of persons of lower classes which might offer encouragement or excuse for ill conduct. That they were 'independent' and law-abiding goes without saying.

Being respectable essentially meant the maintaining a respectable front, and of course encouraged all the duplicities and hypocrisies fastened on by contemporary social commentators, in fiction or out of it. Historians will never conclusively settle the argument about 'Victorian hypocrisy'. Only purblind idolators of some imagined Victorian ideal can blink the facts of its existence. But such idolators are no more ignorant, wilfully or invincibly, than muck-raking critics of Victorian society who neglect to note that what may be called a kind of hypocrisy—the emulation of superior styles, the adoption of better manners, etc.—could, probably must, have had a refining and civilising influence in a hierarchical but mobile society, and that the motives for it need not always have been base. It is after all no sure sign of immorality, even in the much less hierarchical and and hidebound society of the nineteen-seventies, to wish 'to improve oneself'. That said, it remains true that conventional mid-Victorian respectability could be paltry and threadbare enough; as perhaps any compulsive or compulsory conventional code can be. How for instance can we withhold contempt for the code which prompted these travellers' tales? The French teacher Paul Blouet (already cited above, p. 272), staying with an English family, proposed a walk on a Sunday morning. 'A son of the family offered to accompany me. As we were leaving the house, he noticed that I had taken my walking-stick. "Take an umbrella", said he; "it looks more respectable".'[35] Remember the Lord's Day experiences of J. C. Fischer, cited above, p. 195. The mid-Victorians' fetish of Lord's Day Observance (it reached its Victorian climax in the mid-fifties and seems to have begun to subside by the early seventies) of course made hypocrites of them willy-nilly; it is the most perverse and unmanageable of Protestant rituals. But it was only the most impressive of a wide range of religious observances which could be sincere and no doubt often were, but which nevertheless offered the merely conformist and the positively hypocritical a royal road to seeming as respectable as the rest. I know of no more striking illustration of this than Mrs Catherick's outburst in Wilkie Collins's *Woman in White* (1860). She had run away from a disreputable past and was not best pleased when the mystery-unravelling Walter Hartright caught up with her at the country town where she had established a new existence:

' "I came here a wronged woman. I came here robbed of my character and determined to claim it back. I've been years and years about it—and I *have* claimed it back. I've matched the respectable people fairly and openly, on their own ground. If they say anything against me, now, they must say it in secret; they can't say it, they daren't say it, openly. I stand high enough in this town to be out of your reach. *The clergyman bows to me.* Aha! You didn't bargain for that, when you came here. Go to the church and inquire about me—you will find Mrs Catherick has her sitting, like the rest of them, and pays the rent on the day its due. Go to the town hall. There's a petition lying there; a petition of the respectable inhabitants against allowing a circus to come and perform here and corrupt our morals—yes! OUR morals. I signed that petition this morning. Go to the bookseller's shop. The clergyman's Wednesday evening lectures on Justification by Faith are publishing there by subscription—I'm down on the list. The doctor's wife only put a shilling in our plate at our last charity sermon—I put half-a-crown. Mr Churchwarden Soward held the plate, and bowed to me. Ten years ago he told Pigrum the chemist, I ought to be whipped out of the town, at the cart's tail. Is your mother alive? Has she got a better Bible on her table than I have got on mine? Does she stand better with her tradespeople than I do with mine? Has she always lived within her income? I have always lived within mine.— Ah! there is the clergyman coming along the square. Look.

Mr What's-your-name—look, if you please!"

'She started up with the activity of a young woman; went to the window, waited till the clergyman passed, and bowed to him solemnly. The clergyman ceremoniously raised his hat and passed on. Mrs Catherick returned to her chair, and looked at me with a grimmer sarcasm than ever.

'"There!" she said. "What do you think of that for a woman with a lost character?" '[36]

Respectability, then, was in the main an embracing of the established social order, within the reach of all who wanted it and could at the same time afford it. In the lower social strata it did not cost much: a whitened doorstep, a tidy house, a family cleanly clothed, an air of social aspiration and—what was almost a *sine qua non* for the would-be respectable working-class family—a dwelling in a respectable street, where the prevalent conformities made it safe and pleasant to be sober, thrifty, clean-spoken and private. But still it cost something to keep up the respectable front. The poor could not do it without considerable self-control (especially in respect of drink) and self-sacrifice. The destitute could not do it at all. Large numbers of mid-Victorians were thus shut out from the possibility of practising respectability. But, we must now ask, did they wish to practise it? And how many of all those who could afford it practised it or wished to do so? To put the questions a different way: how much dissent was there from the respectable and independent idea? And did that dissent *ipso facto* mean hostility to the hierarchical system?

Social Dissidence

My chief concern in this chapter being to examine the strength or otherwise of the social order, I need spend little time on the socially nonconforming elements of the middle and upper strata. Whatever dissent there showed from the conventional norms of respectability could not endanger the social order. In fact there does not seem to have been much conspicuous departure from those norms, and what did not dare to be conspicuous was even less likely to be socially disturbing. There was a colourful segment of aristocratic and county society which positively flaunted its disreputable (my word for it) tastes in the plurality of 'sporting' worlds: cards, drink, women, horses, prize-fighters, foxes, dogs etc. (See above, p. 221.) Some historians have pointed to this as a survival of 'the eighteenth century' or 'the regency' but that is surely to take too local a view of the matter. Such tastes are endemic among landowning aristocracies, and it is not the least important of their characteristics that, being shared with the 'fast' and the brutal of lower social orders, they actually bind 'the nobs' and their inferiors more closely together. The zeal that some of them showed for every kind of horse-racing, for blood-sports and for 'manly' pursuits like boxing and athletics was one aspect of the class-preservative 'common touch' for which the British and Irish aristocracies had long been famous. How much their free indulgence in these carnal tastes reduced the social acceptability of the well-born, I have no firm idea: not much, I suspect, provided they knew how to keep the more raw side of their lives out of sight of those who were bound to censure it. Those who did not know how to keep it quiet and/or those who had no indisputable blood-title to social distinction, might be ostracised and restricted to the company of their own kind, but they could certainly exist. Dickens heard of some such who existed somewhere in North Kent in the early fifties: a squire worth £7,000 a year:

'... drunken and utterly depraved and wicked; but an excellent scholar, an admirable linguist, and a great theologian [with] a mistress, aged five-and-twenty, and very beautiful, drinking her life away.... Tea or coffee never seen in the house, and very seldom water. Beer, champagne, and brandy were the three drinkables.... The Squire had married a woman of the town from whom he was now separated, but by whom he had a daughter. The mother, to spite the father, had bred the daughter in every conceivable vice. Daughter, then thirteen, came from school once a month. Intensely coarse in talk, and always drunk ... [etc.]'[37]

It sounds like the wildest fantasy, but Dickens had no doubt it was true. Nor have I.

Less flaunting but perhaps more interesting were the departures made by 'middle class' people from the norms of respectability that I have sketched. Mid-Victorian London certainly had its 'bohemian' circle of artists and writers. (Did Glasgow, Liverpool and Manchester have them too?' That circle was one of the several, the intersections of which made up Dickens's life. He took immense care, when he guiltily established a mistress in a cottage at Slough, that his non-bohemian circles should not know about her. His friend Wilkie Collins seems not to have taken the same trouble to conceal the existence of his mistress; but Wilkie Collins moved in no other circle than the bohemian one. Outside that, and 'the fast set', and whatever self-contained coteries might have established themselves in the larger towns (I suspect that the conventions were less strict in the foreign communities of London, Bradford, Manchester etc.)—outside those social citadels, discretion was of the essence. The eleventh commandment was the one which in respectable circles it was unforgiveable to break.

The practice of religion being a cardinal point of 'middle-class' respectability, partly because of the value as an example to the lower classes, it is of some interest that lower-class Britons were not the only ones to absent themselves from places of worship. Middle-class pews could be empty as well as working-class ones. That this cutting of church parade did not signify any real detachment from the prevalent system is however clear enough. Some of the most respectable eminent Victorians (e.g. Leslie Stephen, Edwin Chadwick, John Simon) kept as carefully away from church and chapel as some of the less respectable were careful to attend, but few respectable sceptics joined the small, struggling and noisy band of militant, proselytising secularism. Being of agnostic mind, they were exceedingly refined; and militant secularism on the whole was painfully ungentlemanlike. It is difficult to avoid the impression that the educated and the better-off sceptics of the nineteenth century were no less anxious than their eighteenth-century precursors had been, that the masses at any rate should be religious, for the sake of social and political order.

Matthew Arnold was one of the most penetrating and insatiable critics of the conventional middle-class respectabilities of our period, but what came instantly into his mind when he heard the sounds of the London mob breaking down the railings of Hyde Park was his father's classical injunction to 'flog the rank and file, and fling the ringleaders from the Tarpeian rock!'[38] Such respectable critics of their own kind and of the prevailing social order presented no serious danger to it. Most of them, like Arnold himself and George Eliot and Charles Kingsley, were really terrified of democracy and unpolished proletarians, and Disraeli's 1867 Reform Act gave them no less nasty a shock than it did oligarchs like Robert Lowe and aristocrats like Salisbury who had never even pretended to be friends of the people. Middle- and upper-class Liberal politicians who had actively befriended and helped to lead popular radicalism (Gladstone, Forster, Mundella, Bright *et haec genera omnia*), had one and all done so on the understanding that their working-class radical friends and supporters cared as much for independence and respectability and removeable inequalities as they did; the lusty 'Lib-Labism' that emerged from their efforts eventually lost hold of working-class voters because it valued them too much. The only non-working-class social critics who seriously and deliberately wished to overturn the existing social order and make a better one, were either applauded and ignored, or deplored and ignored: applauded, if like Ruskin they stood for fine things like art and unworldliness; deplored, if like J. R. Beesley they harped on empty stomachs and excused trade union militancy.

Let Ruskin's father speak for mid-Victorian property in general: 'My son',

'[he told a newspaper editor, that son having attained the modest age of forty] has fancies and is a thinker but ... he is too confident and positive and has got some strange notions from strange people the best and highest of whom are Carlyle, Browning, Tennyson and Maurice—but after them some atrocious Radicals and Louis Blanc people and scampish writers and working men who flatter and borrow money....'[39]

Ruskin *père* was alarmed lest his son's proclivities to

'thought' might encourage potentially disaffected working men to make trouble. The question is, how much serious disaffection or material for disaffection was there? The answer given by most reputable historians who have looked into the matter is, not much. That was of course what the propertied public wanted to believe, and one sees its mind mirrored in Tenniel's *Punch* cartoons through the Second Reform Bill time, contrasting the respectable and worthy working man with the disreputable and ruffianly, and—this was the significant point—taking it for granted that the good working man could be relied on to dissociate himself from, and to help the rest of the respectable community put down, the bad one. Governing classes (I use the term loosely, for *this* effectively governing class was very far from enjoyment of discretionary power) can often misunderstand underlying social situations and perhaps may as often err by trusting their social inferiors too little as by trusting them too much. But it looks as if the trust reposed by our middle- and upper-class respectable community in the basic law-abidingness and shared ideals of at any rate the influential upper levels of the labouring community was justified. Theirs was the perhaps unusual case of an effectively governing class which was not mistaken in believing what so many governing classes cannot safely believe: that their values were shared and emulated (and hence protected from revolutionary menace) by the lower classes whom they (with whatever degree of prudence) on the whole controlled. These were years when the mood of labour was unrevolutionary, with labouring men displaying a considerable willingness to accept the values and ideals obtaining among their economic and social superiors; and herein the mood of our period contrasted quite sharply with the mood developing from the later seventies onwards. (Whether it contrasted also with the mood of labour during the thirties and forties is for the present uncertain, pending the outcome of a current controversy about the dominant characteristics of Chartism.)

The economic values and ideals mid-Victorian workmen inclined to accept were largely those of economic individualism; the social ones, those of independence and respectability.

The alternative economic values of socialism were not during these years much voiced or followed. The language of trade unionism was indeed somewhat ambiguous; elements of socialist idealism, class solidarity and pragmatic collectivism being confusingly liable to turn up in statements and arguments otherwise as individualist and competitive as Henry Fawcett or The People's William could have wished. The general drift of British trade unionism—which is as if to say, the ruling notions of better-off working men (mainly miners, textile operatives, and skilled craftsmen)—was nevertheless unmistakably towards an acceptance, more or less willing, of a *modus vivendi* with capitalism; a drift which employers for their part increasingly recognised and encouraged by accepting unions as legitimate representative bodies of probably respectable character with whom it was possible (and probably profitable) to do deals. As for the social values of independence and respectability, the only alternatives to them lay in the proletarian culture of comradeship, improvidence and good cheer, etc., which made bearable the hardships and hazards of an unavoidably hard existence.

Labouring men's attitudes in respect of these social values were, as in respect of the economic ones, not as unambiguous as the high-priests of independence and respectability would have wished; the two value systems mingled and conflicted in, for example, friendly society or benefit club meetings where the prevalence of beer and tobacco tended to undo the organisation's avowed and ostensible purposes of thrift and prudence. At village and urban back-street level, the benefit or savings club often amounted to no more than a sociably cheerful means of diverting savings to the benefit of the publican. The 'better' sort of friendly societies were, however, fairly free from this dubious taint of improvidence, and their spectacular growth, together with that of allied institutions like savings banks, throughout our period, testifies to the spread of the independent ideal from the lower middle down into the lower classes; from which social strata such institutions' membership was mixedly made up. The number of contributors was by the end of our period immense; the reigning expert on the subject concludes that there probably were 'over four million members of various sorts of friendly societies, including burial societies, by 1872';[40] and perhaps more than any other statistical evidence it proves that for many upper working and lower middle class people, times were improving enough for savings to become a regular possibility. In the context of social order, its significance is as proof of the extent to which social value systems tied men of different classes together, in common pursuit of shared ideals. Along with other 'vertical' ties, like shared religious or educational interests (not to mention political ones like patriotism and xenophobia) it operated powerfully to hold mid-Victorian society together and to counteract the several forces of political and economic theory, and of social and economic hardship, which could otherwise have riven it.

The cohesion of mid-Victorian society and the maintenance of its chains of command did not, however, rest on such ties alone, unusually effective though they were. There were also other means by which the actually or potentially disaffected and troublesome were kept in fairly safe subordination.

Who were these actually or potentially discontented? We cannot simply say 'the poor' and leave it at that, because (as I hope I have shown) many poor people were respectable enough to wish not to appear as trouble-makers, and many who were not strictly speaking poor at all could nevertheless seem troublesome. Skilled workmen, for example, in their just mentioned ambiguous role as sporadically militant trade unionists, could prove more vexatious (because more unexpected) than striking miners (who were not, until at least the end of our period, considered respectable); and the sometimes quite prosperous denizens of the sporting and criminal worlds could not fairly be called 'poor' either. But it is certainly with the masses of 'the poor' that we must now be concerned, because, whether would-be respectable or not, they lived nearest to those privations and injustices which could make even the mildest men into rebels or murderers—and did make many Irishmen so.

Crime and Coercion

Whatever were the effective agents of social subordination, the army was not prominent among them. Here was a big change from the earlier nineteenth century. Cannon and cavalry had been public order's only defence against radicals and rebels before the thirties. Peel's new model police began to supplement them during the thirties; the first five years of Chartism kept the army busy in the old way, but the forties marked the shape of things to come. Truncheons were more conspicuous than sabres in 1848, and although the army remained available as a last resort, it was kept discreetly out of sight on the rare occasions when it was called upon. On a few notable occasions during our period, the military performed this back-street vigil; in 1855, during the Sunday trading riots; and in 1866 and 1867 during the massive metropolitan agitation for parliamentary reform. They were usually kept in reserve on during the Murphy riots of 1867/8; but they were regularly relied on for help in big emergencies by the Liverpool police. Liverpool was half-way to Ireland, which could not be governed as Westminster wished without coercion, and coercion of the Irish in Ireland meant the military, or the para-military Royal Irish Constabulary. But most of what overt coercion there was in Britain during our period was done by the police.

Serious investigation of the mid-Victorian police has only just begun, but I cannot rid myself of the impression that its main function was the protection of the property, the amenities and the institutions of the propertied: their homes and business premises, their parks and promenades, their religion and their politics. These good things badly neded protection. They reticulated like an arterial system (West Ends, commercial centres and stately homes as the vital organs; small shopkeepers, respectable artisans, clerks and farmers at the capillaries' vanishing points) through a turbulent land of often desperate need, customary roughness and endemic violence—a land teeming with tramps and vagrants, gipsies, nomadic and seasonal labourers, beggars and spongers, housebreakers, sneak-thieves, pickpockets, horse-thieves and 'loafers' (their expressive word for those who lived sometimes quite prosperously on the fringe of the underworld by menace of muscle and excellence of information). 'Why do I keep loaded firearms in my home: why do most people do the like?' rhetorically demanded 'S.G.O.' in an 1853 letter to *The Times*.[41] Why, one might further ask, were the ground-floor windows of all smart houses equipped with inside shutters or outside bars? Mid-Victorian Britain (and *a fortiori*, Ireland) was *not* an idyllically peaceful, secure, virtuous land. It does indeed seem to have been more peaceful and secure than early Victorian Britain, and K. Macnab's work[42] strongly suggests that it became more so as its years went by; but only a few days among local newspapers of the time suffice to convince one that there was still much lawlessness, violence and beastliness. Every country town and all but the best-regulated villages had their 'underworld' outlets, from the single suspect beer-shop where poaching, betting, bloodsports and sex interests could be safely discussed, to the street of pubs, low lodging-houses and makeshift brothels where down-and-outs and fugitives mingled with locals residing on the shady side of the law. The bigger the town, the larger this twilight area would be and the less determinate its boundaries: until in mid-Victorian London you found whole blocks of narrow streets and alleys in Westminster, Holborn, Lambeth, Southwark, Bermondsey, Whitechapel, Stepney and Bethnal Green, made over to this more or less lawless underworld which could not or would not 'respectably' earn its own living; an underworld largely though not wholly coextensive with the social 'residuum' considered in its other aspects on pp. 150–2.

'It has been stated on reliable police statistics [reported that eminently respectable periodical *The Builder* on 3 August 1867] that there is in London the enormous number of 100,000 persons who live by plunder, who do not know where their day's food is to come from when they get up in the morning. At every fire the police have a great deal to do to prevent these gentry breaking into adjoining houses and ransacking them, on the pretence of rendering assistance. The present instance [a terrible conflagration in Lambeth] formed no exception to the rule; the police had hard fighting with them, and, even then, were not always successful.'

On that occasion the police were fighting the 'plunder mob' outside their home territory. With them in their home territory the police only gingerly, during our period, began to interfere. They received some help from the public health and city improvements movements. 'Improvement schemes' deliberately drove broad new streets through bad old slums (Victoria Street, Chancery Lane, Farringdon Road in London, St Mary's Street in Edinburgh, and through the whole medieval heart of Glasgow). The public health movement armed policemen and sanitary inspectors with (optional) powers to control lodging houses and some sorts of overcrowded or otherwise noisome slum dwellings (see above, pp. 46–8). Protestant 'city missioners' and Roman Catholic priests, Ragged Schools and 'model lodging house' philanthropists established bridgeheads of sorts, or fought to extend the bridgeheads they had begun to establish before the fifties (see pp. 43–7, 179, 206–10). But this civilising and regulating offensive achieved little before the seventies, nor did the police during our period do much more than keep these twilight zones under a menacing sort of surveillance, punctuated by forays to seek out notorious malefactors against whom unusual good fortune had provided evidence for prosecution, or perhaps to put down a riot.

This 'underworld' being a ubiquitous and irreducible constant, beyond effective reach of the agencies that maintained a good showing of orderliness and morality in the 'civilised' parts of society, it was the main duty of the police to preserve the latter from the danger and nuisance of the former. It was not an easy assignment. It would have been much easier if all people of property had lived in remoter suburbs, or the unpropertied in 'ghettoes', as they are sometimes called. The term is misleading, inasmuch as it is a characteristic of a ghetto proper that its inhabitants stay within it. The inhabitants of our twilight areas moved freely out of them, in search of pleasure, profit or means of mere survival. Unable to keep these awkwardly poor and embarrassingly dirty or rough people within their own areas, the propertied classes could do no better than limit the occasions which justified their emergence (e.g. by abolishing public hangings in 1868), and the police had to concentrate on making sure they didn't linger. Just as gentlemanly clothes deflected, so ragged clothes attracted the mid-Victorian policeman's attention. 'Move on, there!' now became the policeman's characteristic expression. The police had to keep the better shopping areas clear; not only beggars, pilferers-presumptive, costermongers etc. but even workmen in their working-clothes were liable to be 'moved on'. The police had to keep the more respectable streets and pavements clear of that fantastic host of street-traders and entertainers described by Mayhew. They had to back the gatekeepers and watchmen controlling access to the private parks, estates and streets of the West Ends and richest suburbs. In short, they had to mitigate for the well-off the effects of a variously pathetic or threatening daily inundation of poverty, against which the men of property can plausibly be seen as standing on the defensive.

The other (and, it may be, lesser) task of the mid-Victorian police was to bring an ultimate element of coercion to support the social and economic agencies which were normally adequate to the task of social control. Fundamental to their operation was the fact that, irregular employment and barely adequate wages when employed being the norm for so many labouring folk, it was terribly important for most of them, first, not to lose their jobs and second, not to be cut off from the many forms of public or charitable relief which made all the difference, in bad times, between life and death. Over all but the most irreplaceable labour hung a whip of many thongs. Most workmen could usually be replaced without much difficulty. If the job they were quitting had any kind of 'benefits' attached to it (savings' fund, widows' and children's grants, burial fund; or tied cottage) they would have to sacrifice them. If they left with a bad name, several consequences followed: they would be unlikely to get another job as good in the district, and might be unable, if it was e.g. a domestic servant's or governess's job, for which references were regularly required, to get another job anwhere; they might become classified as 'undeserving' and get struck off the lists of the local distributors of charity; they might moreover be noted as troublesome by the Poor Law authorities and so have the terms of public relief made even more exacting. It is impossible to underestimate the extent to which the labouring and wouldbe labouring classes depended on 'relief' of some fairly regular sort; for a fuller examination whereof, see pp. 153 ff. above.

Behind the charitable agency which sought to persuade the necessitous of the wisdom of not breaking the law, and behind the policeman who could be so prompt to notice even the smallest nominal infringement of the law, lay the citadel of the law itself, with several batteries aiming straight at the working classes.

Principal among the legal means by which working people were subordinated, were the laws restricting trade union activity, and the laws enabling 'masters' to coerce 'servants'. I shall deal with the latter first and more fully, because, trade unions being throughout our period a minority activity, the Law of Master and Servant affected the lives of a greater number of workfolk, non-unionists even more than unionists; because it was made much use of; and because its abolition in 1875 after more than ten years' agitation made a landmark in the history of working-class emancipation. Daphne Simon, whom I here follow, tells us that between 1858 and 1875 there was an annual average of 10,000 prosecutions and nearly 6,000 convictions of workmen in England and Wales alone.[43] The great attraction to employers of the Master and Servant Law was its disciplinary convenience. Under the heading of an action for breach of contract, masters could prosecute men (by summons or arrest; in Scotland, always by arrest, perhaps at dead of night) for many kinds of unacceptable behaviour, ranging from the real culpable thing to disobeying even the most outrageous orders. The vindictiveness of many of the prosecutions recorded in the working-class press shows clearly enough that this law was as much valued by employers as a means of punishing disobedience and a handy device for strike-breaking as for its protection against defaulting employees. Assize judges set magistrates the example of construing the law largely to the employers' advantage. In theory this law worked both ways (with the notable proviso that whereas servants who broke contracts were until 1867 guilty of criminal offences, masters who did the same were guilty of civil ones only), and cases were not lacking in which servants brought actions against masters for non-payment of wages due, etc.; they were hampered however by the difficulties of persuading the court that they had not themselves provoked trouble, and of proving that the alleged contract existed. For less than yearly hirings there was not bound to be a written contract; and the so-called yearly hirings which still obtained in some farming areas and which had only gone from the Durham and Northumberland coal-fields in 1844 were actually for just under a twelvemonth. Employers therefore could be safe from the embarrassment of a written commitment without losing the particular power a long hiring gave them over strikers. Small strikes could be broken by arresting all the strikers for offending against the Master and Servant Law and then tactfully offering withdrawal of the prosecution on condition of return to work. Bigger strikes could be broken by arresting merely their leaders, and the miners' unions especially were thus punished until the sixties. The minor reform in 1867 of this branch of the law had no more than a minor effect; according to Mrs Simon, 'the number of prison sentences fell by two-thirds, but the total number of proceedings and convictions hardly declined at all'. Not until 1875 did the working classes, after more than a decade of agitation and lobbying, free themselves from this remarkable incubus. Its repeal by the Employers and Workmen Act of that year, was a notable point in the history of the freeing of labour from employer oppressions; just as the Criminal Law Amendment Act of the same year marked a similar phase in trade union law, by freeing strikers from the terrors of actions for criminal conspiracy, and making the withdrawal of labour and the picketing of premises at last lawful activities for a working man to engage in.

A peculiarity of the legal apparatus by which the lower orders of the countryside were disciplined was the game laws. Those ancient classics of class legislation had been modernised about 1830 and were formidably strengthened between 1860 and 1862 by a triplet of statutes, the last of which, the Prevention of Poaching Act, carried them to their furthest-ever pitch by empowering policemen to stop persons or vehicles in 'streets highways and public places' and to search them for game (anything from deer to rabbits) or the instruments of poaching. During the nine years 1863–71, an average of 908 actions were brought annually under that act alone, and 739 convictions made.[44] For obvious reasons it caused peculiar offence, and I see little reason to doubt the veracity of radicals like Joseph Arch who alleged that the county police sometimes used their power under this act vexatiously, and that labouring folk would not normally dream of bringing an action for false arrest or whatever, either because they would not know that they could or because they felt sure that the magistrates or county court judge before whom they brought it would side with the policeman. This act in fact served more than merely game-preserving purposes, for a labourer ordered to turn out his pockets might be discovered to have them filled with illicit firewood or filched turnips. The gentry's view of the labourer's rights is implied in one of the questions put to Arch by the chairman of the Commons' Select Committee on the Game Laws on 2 May 1873: 'Supposing that a policeman sees a man walking with a bulging-out pocket, it is not unreasonable, is it, for him to think that the man has something in it that he wants to conceal?'[45] One would certainly think it must have been risky for a labourer to have big pockets, or not to walk through the lanes at a smart pace with his arms swinging, had the size of the rural police force not been rather small (in 1872 only 119 in Hertfordshire, only 232 in Norfolk),[46] and had the policemen not presumably found it prudent to keep on reasonable terms with the people they lived among. Even less is yet known about the rural than the urban police of the nineteenth century, but it seems likely that poor people were as ready to dislike and, given a chance, to beat up policemen in the country as in the town. British magistrates however, unlike their Irish counterparts, never needed to fear the nocturnal blunderbuss, and could administer the game laws without fear or favour. Farmers (who of course suffered financially from them as well as in dignity) and radicals freely alleged that magistrates, being for the most part landlords themselves, enforced these laws with inhumane severity. The landlords' spokesmen in reply pleaded their character as British gentlemen, and pointed to the convention according to which a magistrate normally avoided hearing a case concerning his own property by handing it over to one of his fellows. They also remarked that poaching—which within reach of main railway lines could be big business—was the natural occupation of layabouts and criminals, and that men who found no ready supply of private pheasants and hares would probably go after private chickens and piglets. It is difficult not to feel that they had a point there. But it is no less difficult to emerge from some study of the evidence without concluding that the bulk of convictions under the game acts were for petty offences committed by poor people not habitually dishonest or lazy. Such convictions were numerous, hovering through the sixties at around 9,000 a year (which was between four-fifths and five-sixths of the number of prosecutions).[47]

It is fitting to conclude this survey of the social order and its sustaining sanctions in the place which the mid-Victorians themselves liked to think of as its strong, still centre: the home. Every schoolboy knows that the Victorians cultivated a high ideal of the home and proclaimed the British Christian home as at once the finest source of human virtue and the firmest foundation-stone of social order. Their theory was that morality and piety were best inculcated 'at the mother's knee', before any spots of the extra-domestic world's slow stain had touched the growing child; that good habits of obedience, honesty, diligence, loyalty etc., learnt in the home, stayed with the citizens for life; and—following their principle enunciated on p. 251 above, that the best society was the one that governed itself—that the home was one with the other institu-

tions of social self-discipline. It needs hardly a moment's reflection to suggest flaws in these arguments; flaws which have
been particularly well detected, without removal from their
context, by W. L. Burn.[48] The home envisaged by the high
priests and publicists of the cult can have been a practical
possibility only above the manual labouring line, and a reality
only where father and mother were morally and intellectually
capable of fulfilling so exalted a role and willing moreover to
spend time enough with the children to accomplish it. The
demands of fashion, towards one end of society, could be as
domestically disruptive as the exigencies of poverty at the
other, though the formal deficiencies might in the former case
be made up by servants, governesses etc.; some of whom are
convincingly recorded as having had intensely moralising
effects on their charges (of others, quite the opposite is known
to have been the case!) or, *more Anglice*, by schoolmasters.
There can be no doubt that this moral and moralising ideal
home was likelier to occur below the highest and above the
lowest social strata; likeliest to occur, where vital religion
fertilised the pursuit of respectability. Many 'poor' homes of
actively and pleasantly Christian families must have provided
a 'better' upbringing than many more prosperous ones. But
beyond such safe and simple reckoning we reach an impassable morass of ignorance and variety. We actually know so
much less about the interior conduct of ordinary respectable
families than we do about, on the one hand, rich and stately
ones (whose inhabitants tended to write copiously about them)
and on the other hand the really poor ones which were subjected from the forties onwards to such a clinical glare of
publicity. Contemporary novelists' domestic middle class
scenes, the most seemingly fruitful body of evidence, must
indeed often be photographically life-like but they present
such a variety of scenes, such an infinitude of possibilities, that
most generalisations about the quality of middle class family
life crumble at the critic's touch.

Three fundamentals of the mid-Victorian home's social
structure may however be singled out: first, it was normally
a patriarchate, woman's place within it being subordinate and,

to a modern eye, in some respects unenviable; second, religion powerfully helped to hold it together and to mitigate its apparent hardships (perhaps to the point where they were not felt as hardships at all); third, woman's position was beginning to become a little less unenviable, and the dominant male's powers were beginning to suffer erosion, as our period unrolled.

Law backed the social tradition that, within the family, father's will was supreme. With actual historical exceptions we are not concerned. Of course they were legion. Formidable or fortunate women could in our period as in any earlier period of known history manage their men and make their way in the world. But they were bound to be exceptions, and except among the higher propertied classes (where lawyers had centuries of experience in so 'settling' property on wives and heiresses as to secure it from misuse by the men to whom they were otherwise legally subject), the law awarded to husbands nearly absolute powers over wives, and even more tremendous powers over children. What greater power can a father have over his child than the power to keep it uneducated? Yet this was general in Britain until after 1870, broken only where parents had forfeited their natural rights by becoming paupers or convicts or (interesting exception!) where their child worked as a half-timer in a textile factory. Parental powers to knock children about were legally limited only by the common law on assault, subject to the readiness of someone to bring a case; the overwhelming consensus of adult opinion in any case favoured corporal punishment, for which biblical command was commonly cited (as it still may be by fundamentalist bigots).

A mother living apart from a demonstrably intolerable husband had under the 1839 Custody of Infants Act a right to apply to Chancery for custody of her children so long as they were under seven years old, and for access to them if they were older. This made a significant crack in the defences of male prerogative, but only a small one, and the matter was taken no further until 1873 when the age was upped to sixteen. A wife's right to leave an intolerable husband (if she could afford and dare to) only received the backing of the common law in 1852. Thitherto husbands, no matter how detestable, were supported by the courts in endeavours to recover possession of runaway wives. It was Lord Campbell who cracked the defences in this quarter, declining in the case of Regina v. Leggatt (Mrs Sandilands' brother) to issue a writ of *habeas corpus* to enable Mr Sandilands to recover her. Other judges presumably (I have been unable to find evidence one way or the other) followed his lead. But here again it was the mere fact of the change, not the extent of the change that signified; the slightness of the extent can be judged from the fact that it seems not to have been until after our period that a husband's right to keep an unescaped or a recaptured wife in custody was similarly terminated.

The state of the law on divorce was more decisively changed. From 1857 there were available, for all in England who could afford the still considerable expenses, facilities for divorce that had since the reign of William III been open only to the well-connected and very wealthy. The heat and fury of the opposition—mainly, of course, ecclesiastical in inspiration—was extreme. So far as it was not mainly ecclesiastical, it rested on the argument that the basis of social order was in the home, and that the ruin of civil society would ensue. To a modern mind the act itself seems no masterpiece of humanity and morality, since it carefully made it much more difficult for a woman to divorce a man than vice versa. 'In a husband's petition', writes the historian of *Divorce in England*, 'simple adultery sufficed; a wife was required to prove not only adultery but the additional aggravation of desertion, cruelty, incest, rape, sodomy or bestiality.'[49] The only part of the British Isles where a fairer (and incidentally a cheaper) law of divorce obtained was in Scotland, where it constituted one of that country's legal system's many superiorities. The English (and also, I suppose, the Irish) law remained unpleasantly peculiar in the distinctions it enforced: distinctions between male and female, and between rich and poor. The act of 1857 had cheapened divorce, but it was still far too expensive for the lower classes. No facilities in any way comparable were placed within the lower classes' reach until 1878, when magistrates' courts were empowered to grant separation and maintenance orders to wife victims of persistent husband assaults. Much legislation on that painful topic followed quickly thereafter, but it is all too late to be relevant to our purposes. Throughout our period the absolute rule for all sub-affluent marriages was—like it or lump it; and for even affluent marriages the same crude rule might hold, for beyond getting legally free of an obnoxious partner lay the terrible economic problem: how could a woman—let alone a woman with dependent children—make an independent livelihood? The 1857 Divorce Act made a notable departure from all precedent by allowing a judicially separated woman control over whatever property she might acquire *after the divorce*; but thirteen more years had to pass before Parliament extended this equitable principle, in the half-baked Married Woman's Property Act of 1870, to protect property earned or acquired by a woman *while married*.

Beneath the legal bonds which were so slowly loosening during our period lay economic compulsions which, as yet, were hardly beginning to relax. 'Jobs for women' matter much more in the history of female emancipation than 'votes for women'; and all but the least eligible jobs were, as I have more fully said on pp. 121 ff., few and far to come by. It was this desperate shortage of opportunity to survive socially outside the respectable home that compelled its wives, if they were wretched, to put up with their wretchedness, and (not less important in our context) its daughters either to accept whatever offer of marriage they could get or to put up with lifelong dependent subservience to father and mother at home. For most middle and upper class girls who could not get married, *no other course was open*. The ways they could earn an independent livelihood were few in the forties and not much more numerous by the seventies. It was the churches' joy and their parents' interest to rub in the fifth commandment; unmarried sisters were indispensable in so many domestic contexts. That many such women successfully embraced their faith's instruction to accept their lot with resignation or even cheerfulness need not blind us to the essential truth, clearly stated by Burn (than whom no great historian of this period was less prone to either smart Stracheyism or unhistorical sentimentalism): 'The dependent daughter was one of the fundamentals on which the mid-Victorian home was based.'[50]

Epilogue

At many stages of writing this book I have felt like a lonely mid-Victorian traveller in Spain: often benighted, even in daylight likely to be unsure of direction, a prey to potholes, pitfalls, and the possibility of bandits. I have had to generalise, so far as I have dared, but even more than at the outset am I conscious of the hazards of those generalisations on which a social history of this sort depends, on the relative paucity still of those fresh and solid researchers' conclusions on which alone better generalisations may be based, and of my own failure to master more than a fraction of all the existing literature that could be relevant. My most comprehensive critic to date has justly remarked upon my neglect of, for example, the armed forces, farm labourers, family life, the places and circumstances in which work was actually done. . . .

I find myself at the end of my labours anxious to make three points.

First, there is so much about this period that we don't understand. Some people have an extraordinary idea that historical understanding must become more perfect in proportion as the twentieth century is neared, and that we therefore understand the nineteenth century better than the seventeenth, the seventeenth better than the thirteenth, and so on. One might plausibly argue the opposite. This is not the place for such an argument, but it is worth repeating what has often been admitted *en route*, that some important matters of mid-Victorian social history remain dark, among them, for example:– social mobility, business and professional incomes, the interior design of houses and offices, patterns of middle-class domestic life, the extent to which houses were owned or leased, types and quantities of crime, the workings of the police, the persistence or otherwise of regional and local pecularities, the extent of Scottish differences, and almost everything about Ireland.

Second, I feel obliged to emphasise something that may have got lost in the multitude of separate allusions to it, i.e. the character of the changes that begin to come over British society during the closing third of my period. In economic terms, 1873 is the obvious turning point but in social and political terms it looks as if the big shift sets in from a few years earlier, from the middle sixties. That is where Burn judicially called down the curtain on his *Age of Equipoise*. The change of mood and tempo is most obvious in politics, with the determined and effective reappearance upon the political stage of distinctively working-class organisations, and the onset within the two major political parties of certain polarising tendencies which were to have dramatic consequences within the next thirty years: the strengthenings of the radical and popular elements within the Liberal party, and of the non-rural, non-landlordly, simply property-owning elements of the Conservative. The Liberal party, whose leadership Gladstone inherited in the mid-sixties, quickly became a very different thing from what Palmerston had presided over; and by the time Disraeli laid down the leadership of the Conservative party, its tone and its electoral appeal (though not so much the social composition of its leadership) were becoming very different from what they had been for Lord Derby. The Age of Equipoise gave way to an age of oscillation, while cabinet ministers who had known the *douceur de vivre* before 1865, when the pressures upon them had been mainly administrative or (if it is not too grand a word for it) philosophical, pressures that could be comfortably handled by juggling and speechifying within the parliamentary arena, found themselves having to cope with importunate and disagreeably election-conscious political organisations and economic interest-groups, which needed to be handled in much more realistic ways.

In administrative and educational history, the same years mark an epoch. Urban local government, the piecemeal extension and improvement of which had never ceased, was in the seventies recast into a simpler and stronger mould; and the continuing sanitary or public health movement, which had been mainly an urban thing before about 1870, at last hit the countryside. Soon thereafter, town and country alike became straddled with those radically new local authorities, the school boards. The nationalisation of the ancient universities was completed. The Civil Service, the armed services, the judiciary, from all of which reformers had been snipping gnarled remnants of nepotism and patronage for many years, were severely shaken into new and more business-like shapes. A new age of reform opened, dedicated to the principles of entry and promotion by examinations, and the ideal of *la carrière ouverte aux talents*. The extreme traditionality of the criteria by which those talents were to be assessed, however, and the resourceful gearing of the best parts of the school and university system to helping the sons of the better-off to show such talents, remind us that the degree of social revolution accompanying these new principles was less than Napoleonic; while the approaching shadows of Lord Salisbury and Lansdowne remind us that their splendid set remained secure in powers as well as privileges for many years yet. Something of an aristocratic comeback was indeed to follow the liberal-radical upsurge of 1866–86. Thereafter were hastily drafted to the aid of our old nobility plentiful reinforcements of new wealth and new men, in newer and rougher shapes than men had known for centuries. Already by Lady Bracknell's time (1895) there was ironic point in her question, were you born into the purple of commerce or have you risen from the ranks of the aristocracy? But this apparent recovery of the aristocratic principle, however astonishing one might think it, had little profound significance. Its gay lights of leisure and privilege, which seemed so stable in the early twentieth century, were not extinguished only by the force of the cataclysm which actually marked its overthrow: the First World War. Its foundations were by then thoroughly eroded by the semi-subterranean forces of economic and social change, some of which we have seen welling up (or re-surfacing) during the later sixties and early seventies. Of the major forces of this ultimately irresistible complex, only Marxist socialism and militant feminism were not yet conspicuous by 1875.

Third and last, I am irresistibly drawn to attempt a balance sheet: a felicific calculus of mid-Victorian happiness. The difficulties of doing so are, strictly speaking, insuperable; yet something of an impressionistic sort may be attempted. Writers of the sixties and seventies were not loath to attempt it, anyway; and their tendency was to confirm Clapham's opinion which I cited on p. 250, that the mid-Victorian world was one 'which was demonstrably getting more comfortable'. Their attempts at demonstrating with wage and price statistics a rising standard of working class living do not convince us that a great deal was happening in that line before the late sixties (see above, pp. 111–14), but they had no difficulty in producing lists of inventions which had, they thought, dramatically changed the texture of common life, and changed it, surely, for the better. The pioneer feminist and philanthropist Frances Cobbe, for example, looking back from 1867 only as far as the forties, thought she saw

'. . . the whole cycle of changes represented by the words— the steam-engine locomotive by land and sea, steam applied to printing and manufacture, the electric telegraph, photography, cheap newspapers, penny postage, chloroform, gas, the magnesian and electric lights, iron ships, revolvers and breach-loaders of all sorts, sewing-machines, omnibuses and cabs, parcel deliveries, post-office savings banks, working-men's clubs, people's baths and wash-houses, turkish baths, drinking fountains and a thousand minutiae of daily life, such as matches, Wenham ice, and all the applications of india-rubber and gutta-percha. . . .'

One might wish to dispute a few points of dating in that list, but its tenor is unmistakable and, after all, the important thing is that this is how it seemed to someone who lived at the time; it was her direct sense of the period, and we should think twice before saying she was wrong. Of those wonderfully miscellaneous items, only 'revolvers and breach-loaders' seem to be less than clearly in the category of inventions tending (one dare not say more than 'tending') to the increase of human happiness.

For whom, for what groups, was life likely to be becoming more comfortable? My book has suggested many: e.g. everyone above the poverty line whose generally increasing income enabled them to afford more of the good things that a world-wide trade, an increasingly sophisticated economy and a dramatically rising national income put within their grasp; everyone whose hours of work were a little shortened and whose chances of holidays improved; everyone who lived in a town where the basic amenities of urban culture were beginning to be systematically provided; everyone who could have chloroform for a surgical operation and carbolic acid for a wound; poor people and members of the forces who had to go into hospital. For such people and groups of people, the prospects of a more comfortable life must be judged to have improved.

For whom did our period probably make little improvement? One may hazard the judgment that it must have been thus for everyone below the poverty line: for domestic and workshop workers in decaying and sweated trades; for agricultural labourers in 'backward' counties, for miners in disorganised or failing areas; for convicts in HM Prisons, where the regimen got distinctly tougher; for many children perhaps, if the school or reformatory they were made to go to had (as one fears was often the case) a prison-like and punitive air. But such generalisations don't carry us far. The incalculables are all too numerous and, in this sort of argument, all too important. Would relief from the treadmill of childbearing or the necessity of daily factory employment make wives into better mothers? Would the Divorce Act of 1857 bring (as its opponents in effect argued) unhappiness into the home, by suggesting to unhappy wives that there might be some point in their admitting to feeling so? Did the decay of religious faith, if there was indeed much of that, increase unhappiness by robbing people of the consolations of hope, or increase happiness by freeing people from terrors and inhibitions? What penalties of social isolation were paid by those who 'rose' from the earthy comradeship of the sub-respectable back-street to the prim privacies of the genteel suburb? And so on.... On these mysteries, the historian of the nineteenth century is at one with his friends of the seventeenth and thirteenth. We are all in the dark.

Guide to Further Reading

General

As was remarked in the Introduction, the early-to-mid-Victorian years have been made the object of special study by several fine historians, to whose writings all later comers, whether they agree with them or not, must owe much. First in time was G. M. Young whose collection of informative long essays on *Early Victorian England, 1830–1865* (2 vols, 1934) begins with the brilliant essay of his own which he later expanded into the famous *Portrait of an Age* (1936). So valuable did that book prove, and so tantalising its profusion of unannotated references and quotations, that George Kitson Clark published a fully annotated edition of it in 1977. Of the more manageable recent books, Kitson Clark's *Making of Victorian England* (1962) is often held to be the best starting point. On its own peculiar social and psychological grounds unmatched is W. L. Burn, *The Age of Equipoise* (1964). Asa Briggs has made at least three different approaches to our period: *Victorian People: A Reassessment of Person and Themes* (1954); *Victorian Cities* (1963) (it includes essays on aspects of Manchester, Leeds, Birmingham, Middlesbrough, Melbourne and London); and the last section of his big text book on England between 1783 and 1867, *The Age of Improvement* (1959) which has more social history in it than most such; as also does R. K. Webb's excellent big history of *Modern England from the Eighteenth Century to the Present* (1980). Harold Perkin, *The Origins of Modern English Society, 1780–1880* (1969) is an original, stimulating and controversial book which covers some of my ground, in a style all its own. F. Bédarida, *The Social History of England, 1851–1975* (1979) is uniquely valuable for its social-scientific approach. My Sussex colleague J. F. C. Harrison's *Early Victorian Britain* (Fontana, 1979, originally published as *The Early Victorians*, 1971) is a natural companion volume, much to be recommended.

As to Bibliographies, H. J. Hanham (ed.), *Bibliography of British History 1815–1914* (1976) has knocked out all others.

J. H. Clapham's classic *Economic History of Modern Britain*, vol. 2 (1932) runs from 1850 to 1886; it is economic history of the most liberal and spacious interpretation, and I have not concealed the extent of my debts to it. No other economic history book comes as close to our period, but there is necessarily much to our purpose, in S. G. Checkland, *The Rise of Industrial Society in England, 1815–1885* (1964) (he really means 'Britain'); W. Ashworth, *Economic History of England, 1870–1939* (1960); Peter Mathias, *The First Industrial Nation* (1969); J. D. Chambers, *The Workshop of the World* (1961); and E. J. Hobsbawm, *Industry and Empire: an economic history of Britain since 1750* (1968). Fruitfully mixing economic with other historical interests, and partly concerned with our period, are three collections of essays: E. J. Hobsbawm, *Labouring Men* (1964); Henry Pelling, *Popular Politics and Society in late Victorian Britain* (1968); and Royden Harrison, *Before the Socialists* (1965). Culturally interested readers should not miss H. House, *All Due Time* (1955), which like much of the same great scholar's study of *The Dickens World* (1942) touches on many mid-Victorian themes. Walter Houghton's *The Victorian Frame of Mind* (1957) is a valuably suggestive anthology of (by my chronological definitions) early and mid-Victorian points of view; *1859: Entering an Age of Crisis* (ed. Appleman, Madden and Wolff, 1959) contains an engaging scatter of relevant essays.

Our two most obvious public 'turning-points' – the Great Exhibition and the Second Reform Bill – have each by now a literature of their own. For the former see especially C. R. Fay, *Palace of Industry, 1851* (1951); C. H. Gibbs-Smith (ed.), *The Great Exhibition of 1851: a commemorative album of the Victoria and Albert Museum*, (1950); C. Hobhouse, *1851 and the Crystal Palace* (1950);

and N. B. L. Pevsner, *High Victorian Design* (1951). For the Second Reform Bill crisis, see particularly F. B. Smith, *The Making of the Second Reform Bill* (1966) and Maurice Cowling, *1867: Disraeli, Gladstone and Revolution* (1967), and Harrison, *op. cit.*

Readers who want more political history than is available in these rather specialised books and the general books of Briggs and Webb may consult D. Read, *Cobden and Bright* (1967); H. J. Hanham, *Elections and Party Management: politics in the time of Disraeli and Gladstone* (1959); John Vincent, *The Formation of the Liberal Party 1857–1868* (1966) and (ed.) *Disraeli, Derby and the Conservative Party; the political journals of Lord Stanley* (1978); Olive Anderson, *A Liberal State at War* (1967); H. C. G. Matthew (ed.), *The Gladstone Diaries*, vols. 5 and 6, covering 1855–68 (1978); E. J. Feuchtwanger, *Disraeli, Democracy and the Tory party* (1968) and his *Gladstone* (1975); J. B. Conacher, *The Aberdeen Coalition 1852–5* (1968); Paul Smith, *Disraelian Conservatism and Social Reform* (1967); Robert Blake, *Disraeli* (1969); Lucy Iremonger, *Lord Aberdeen* (1978); John Prest, *Lord John Russell* (1972); and James Winter, *Robert Lowe* (1976). David Cresap Moore's *Politics of Deference* (1976) has excited much argument; a different sense of politics in particular communities is given by Richard W. Davis, *Political Continuity and Change, 1780–1885; a Buckinghamshire study* (1972) and R. J. Olney, *Lincolnshire Politics, 1832–1885* (1973).

By now there is a sufficiency of good books on Ireland. To the relevant passages in J. C. Beckett, *The Making of Modern Ireland* (1966) add F. S. L. Lyons, *Ireland since the Famine* (1971), Leon ó Broin, *Fenian Fever: an Anglo-Irish Dilemma* (1971), Desmond Bowen, *The Protestant Crusade in Ireland, 1800–1870* (1978), L. P. Curtis, Jr, *Anglo-Saxons and Celts: a study of anti-Irish prejudice in Victorian England* (1968), and his *Apes and Angels: The Irishman in Victorian caricature* (1979) and E. R. Norman, *The Catholic Church and Ireland in the Age of Rebellion* (1965). For all Scottish matters, the first call must be to W.

Ferguson, *Scotland, 1689 to the Present* (1968) with its exemplary bibliography. H. J. Hanham, *Scottish Nationalism* (1969) is largely about the nineteenth century, when most of it was invented.

Chapter 1

The process of urbanisation is now scientifically studied. Pioneer with respect to the Victorian period was W. Ashworth, *The Origins of Modern British Town Planning* (1954), which is less specialised than it sounds. Briggs's *Victorian Cities* on the other hand is more selective than you might think. Leader in this great field was H. J. Dyos, whose *Victorian Suburb* (1961) has much in it about that swelling metropolis of which Camberwell was a sizeable part. He brought together a useful collection of essays: Dyos (ed.), *The Study of Urban History* (1968) and his articles 'Agenda for Urban Historians' in that collection and on 'The Speculative Builders and Developers of Victorian London' and 'The Slums of Victorian London' in *Victorian Studies* xi (1968, Supplement) 641 ff. and xi (1967) 5 ff. respectively are important, not least for their copious bibliographies. With Michael Wolff he edited the splendid two-volume *Victorian City: images and realities* (1973) which now towers over the whole great topic and deals well with almost all imaginable, and some unimaginable, aspects of it.

On London, start with Francis Sheppard, *London, 1808–1870: the infernal Wen* (1971), Donald J. Olsen, *The Growth of Victorian London* (1976), Anthony S. Wohl, *The Eternal slum: housing and social policy in Victorian London* (1977) and Gareth Stedman Jones, *Outcast London: a study in the relationship between classes in Victorian Society* (1971). F. M. L. Thompson, *Hampstead* (1974) is mostly about the nineteenth century; his *Victorian England: the horse-drawn society* (1970), an inaugural lecture, is on too important a subject not to be mentioned somewhere. Geoffrey Crossick, *An Artisan Elite in Victorian Society* (1978) deals with Kentish London, 1840–1880. There is something to our purpose in *London: aspects of change* (1964), published by London University's Centre for Urban Studies as its Report no. 3. London's transportation history is adequately dealt with by T. C. Barker and M. Robbins, *History of London Transport* vol. 1 (1963). The sanitary matters which are fundamental to Victorian urban history can best be got at via R. J. Lambert, *Sir John Simon and English Social Administration* (1963) and M. W. Flinn's edition of A. P. Stewart and E. Jenkins, *Medical and Legal Aspects of Sanitary Reform, 1867* (1969). N. Longmate, *King Cholera* (1966) includes the epidemics of our period, D. Hodgkinson, *Origins of the National Health Service* (1966) throws new light on the Poor Law too, and F. B. Smith is brilliantly hair-raising about *The People's Health, 1830–1910* (1979). Other worthwhile books on (mainly urban) health history are J. Woodward and D. Richards (eds), *Health Care and Popular Medicine in 19th century England* (1977), J. Woodward, *To Do the Sick No Harm: a study of the British voluntary hospital system to 1874* (1974), Jean Peterson, *The Victorian Doctor in London* (1978), and Angus McLaren, *Birth Control in 19th Century England* (1978). *A Social History of Housing, 1815–1870* has been written by John Burnett (1978) and *Victorian Homes* have been nicely surveyed by David Rubinstein (ed. 1979).

Hermione Hobhouse, *Thomas Cubitt: master-builder* (1971) is a fine book about the man who more than any one other made Victorian London look the way it did and, where permitted, still does. On the other cities see, for instance, A. Redford, *History of Local Government in Manchester*, 3 vols. (1939–40), B. D. White, *History of the Corporation of Liverpool* (1951), C. Gill and A. Briggs, *History of Birmingham*, 2 vols. (1952), Roy Church, *Nottingham in the Nineteenth Century* (1964), the *Victoria County History*, Warwickshire vol. vii (for Birmingham), Leicestershire vol. iv (for Leicester) and Essex vol. v (for London eastwards), M. J. Daunton, *Coal Metropolis: Cardiff, 1870–1914* (1977), A. Temple Patterson, *History of Southampton, vol. 2, 1836–67* (1977) and (just its beginning) S. G. Checkland, *Upas Tree: Glasgow, 1875–1975* (1975). Much may be learnt about Auld Reekie from R. Q. Gray, *The Labour Aristocracy in Victorian Edinburgh* (1976). For city politics and administration see above all E. P. Hennock, *Fit and Proper Persons* (1977) and Derek Fraser, *Urban Politics in Victorian England* (1976). J. R. Kellett, *The Impact of Railways on Victorian Cities* (1969) is the basic book on that side of things.

There is no lack of evidence as to what London life was like; perhaps we should say, what the varieties of London life were like. The novels of Dickens were accepted by his contemporaries as extraordinarily faithful, in one mode or another, to the middle and lower class realities they represented. Trollope delighted to paint scenes of smarter London but knew little of the rest. Dyos's works refer *passim* to the many lesser contemporary novelists who handled themes of city and suburban life. Low and shady mid-Victorian London is vividly sketched in Michael Sadleir's documentary novels mentioned on p. 237; they rest in part on Henry Mayhew's *London Labour and the London Poor* (which has been reprinted in paperback, 1968) and on the anonymous demi-monde autobiography *My Secret Life* (1880s), which has been recently republished in various abridged and/or expurgated versions. A much less vicious but still extraordinary secret life is revealed in Derek Hudson, *Munby: man of two worlds . . . 1828–1910* (1972). P. McHugh, *Prostitution and Victorian Social Reform* (1980) is about the Contagious Diseases Acts. The richness and drama of London life attracted hosts of contemporary journalists and commentators, many of whom wrote well; e.g. G. A. Sala, *Gaslight and Daylight, with some London scenes they shine upon* (1860); James Greenwood, *The Seven Curses of London* (1869) and *The Wilds of London* (1874); John Hollingshed, *Ragged London in 1861* (1861); etc. etc. Various of these have been reprinted.

Provincial city and small town life is not so well served by the novelists, much less well by the journalists. Trollope's Barchester cannot be considered representative of much! Mrs Oliphant's 'Chronicles of Carlingford' (1863–6), regrettably inaccessible nowadays, were probably more so: the volume called *Salem Chapel* (1863) is particularly effective. Cotton towns of the fifties are powerfully suggested in characteristically different ways by Dickens in *Hard Times* (1854) and by Mrs Gaskell in *North and South* (1854–5). None of what journalists' writings there were about provincial cities have been reprinted, so far as I know; not even those of Mayhew's collaborators, whose provincial reports alternated with his in the *Morning Chronicle* from October 1849 through 1850. The mid-Victorian countryside is best approached through Clapham's *Economic History* vol. 2; F. M. L. Thompson, *English Landed Society in the 19th Century* (1963), J. D. Chambers and G. Mingay, *The Agricultural Revolution 1750–1880* (1966), and Mingay (ed.) *The Victorian Countryside* (2 vols., 1981). Eric Richards, *The Leviathan of Wealth: the Sutherland Fortune in the Industrial Revolution* (1973) is a powerful reminder of how close landbased wealth often ran to industrialisation; J. P. D. Dunbabin, *Rural Discontent in Victorian England* (1977), of how uneasy the foundations of landed wealth often were. James Obelkevich, *Religion and Rural Society: South Lindsey 1825–1875* (1976) takes the lid off many strange things. David Spring (ed.), *European Landed Elites in the 19th Century* (1978) has an introduction by the editor and a chapter by Thompson of great value. The life-styles and domestic economies of the rulers of the countryside may be viewed close-up in Mark Girouard, *The Victorian Country House* (1971) and *Life in the English Country House* (1978).

For Wales, see D. W. Howell, *Land and People in 19th century Wales* (1977); for Ireland, J. S. Donnelly, Jr., *The Land and the People of 19th-century Cork* (1975) and B. L. Solow, *The Land Question and the Irish Economy, 1870–1930* (1972).

Of the many accounts of British attitudes and British social life left by foreign visitors, the best known to me are those of Hippolyte Taine, translated by Edward Hyams (1957) as *Taine's Notes on England*; and Henry James's slightly later essays, collected in *English Hours* (1960).

Chapter 2

Of the economic history books already mentioned, Clapham's will be found the most informative on the topics of chapter 2. For *Professional Men*, see W. J. Reader's little history of that title (1966) and relevant parts of Perkin, *op. cit.*, and their references. On all matters to do with the standard and style of living of the middle classes, J. A. Banks, *Prosperity and Parenthood: a study of family planning among the Victorian middle classes* (1954) is pre-eminently valuable; how they actually might have done it may be read about in Angus McLaren, *Birth control in 19th Century England* (1978). There is no exact equivalent in respect of the working classes but Hobsbawm's *Labouring Men* contains much to the point. Most of the literature on working women and children is sloppy or sensational, but M. Hewitt, *Wives and Mothers in Victorian Industry* (1958) is good and their story is of course an integral part of the theme of B. L. Hutchins and A. Harrison, *A History of Factory Legislation* (1903). The serious study of Victorian diet, a matter of equal importance to men, women and children of all classes, has been got off the ground by J. Burnett, *Plenty and Want: a social history of diet in England from 1815* (1966) and in *Our Changing Fare* (ed. T. C. Barker, J. V. McKenzie and J. Yudkin, 1966). What life as a whole was for working men is more difficult to judge at this than at any subsequent period; there is, alas! no mid-Victorian equivalent to Alfred Williams, *Life in a Railway Factory* (1915) and Lady Hugh Bell's wonderful little book, *At the Works* (1907). Some illustrative extracts, mostly of the gloomier kind, are printed by E. Royston Pike in *Human Documents of the Victorian Golden Age* (1967). The life-and-work-styles of several notable groups of toilers are examined by Pamela Horn, *The Rise and Fall of the Victorian Servant* (1975), Gregory Anderson, *Victorian Clerks* (1976), Lee Holcombe, *Victorian Ladies at work: middle-class working women . . . 1850–1914* (1973), and

Robert Colls, *The Colliers' Rant* (1977). Alan Skelley, *The Victorian Army at Home* (1977) and E. M. Spiers, *The Army and Society 1815–1914* (1980) have let new light into the world of the barracks. Rather superior as a working man was Thomas Wright, alias 'The Journeyman Engineer', whose non-fiction works richly deserve to be reprinted: *Some Habits and Customs of the Working classes* (1867), *The Great Unwashed* (1868), and *Our New Masters* (1873).

Mayhew's great series contains much direct evidence about working class life and work; he specialised in interviews and historians have accepted his reports of them as generally trustworthy. E. P. Thompson and Eileen Yeo rightly make much of him in *The Unknown Mayhew* (1971).

The nation-wide field of philanthropy and its applications is best approached through Kathleen Heasman's small-scale *Evangelicals in Action* (1963) and David Owen's big *English Philanthropy 1660–1960* (1964), to which it is worth appending Brian Harrison's article in *Victorian Studies*, ix (1966) 353–74. Of local philanthropic apparatuses, I know only the excellent little book about Liverpool by Margaret Simey (1951). The Webbs' great *History of the Poor Laws in England* remains basic, but must now be used in the light of a new wave of learning, summarised (as much of it has been led) by Oliver MacDonagh, *Early Victorian Government 1830–1870* (1977). For the Poor Law in particular, see Derek Fraser (ed.), *The New Poor Law in the 19th Century* (1976). For the 'civil service', Henry Parris, *Constitutional Bureaucracy . . .* (1969). Many branches of Scottish philanthropy and poor relief can be glimpsed in Thomas Ferguson, *The Dawn of Scottish Social Welfare* (1948) and *Scottish Social Welfare, 1864–1914* (1958).

Chapter 3

For Education, begin with John Hurt, *Education in Evolution: Church, State, Society, and Popular Education,*

1800–1870 (1971). Stimulating and enjoyable are W. F. Connell, *The Educational Thought and Influence of Matthew Arnold* (1950) and Brian Simon, *Studies in the History of Education, 1780–1870* (1960). *The Schoolteachers* have been written about by A. Tropp (1957). The Revised Code episode must now be studied via D. W. Sylvester, *Robert Lowe and Education* (1973) and see Winter's biography of him. For the so-called public schools, see T. W. Bamford, *Thomas Arnold* (1960) and *Rise of the Public Schools* (1967), E.C. Mack's studies of *Public Schools and British Opinion* (1938, 1941), David Newsome, *Godliness and Good Learning* (1961) and *History of Wellington College* (1959), Brian Heeney, *Mission to the Middle Classes: the Woodard Schools* (1969), and, perhaps above all, J. R. Honey, *Tom Brown's Universe* (1977). J. F. C. Harrison, *Learning and Living* (1961) is more than the history of adult education it is primarily meant to be. Parts of the Scottish educational scene are brilliantly (and controversially) illuminated by G. E. Davie, *The Democratic Intellect* (1961) and the whole is lightly sketched by H. M. Knox, *250 Years of Scottish Education* (1953), heavily by James Scotland, *History of Scottish Education* (1969). On Universities and (by no means coterminous!) Intelligentsia, read Michael Sanderson, *The Universities in the 19th Century* (1975), Sheldon Rothblatt, *The Revolution of the Dons* (1968), W. R. Ward, *Victorian Oxford* (1965), the appropriate Victoria County History volume for the other place, Christopher Kent, *Brains and Numbers* . . . (1978), Christopher Harvie, *Lights of Liberalism* (1976) and, still unmatched, Noël Annan's famous essay on 'The Intellectual Aristocracy' in Plumb (ed.), *Studies in Social History* (1955). Davie (1961) is the key book for Scotland.

On Religion, Owen Chadwick's big *Victorian Church* (1966, 1970) must be the usual starting point, backed up by Alan D. Gilbert, *Religion and Society in Industrial England* (1977) and the relevant parts of R. Currie, A. Gilbert and L. Horsley, *Churches and Churchgoers: Patterns of Church Growth in the British Isles since 1700*

(1977). E. R. Norman, *Church and Society in England, 1770–1970* (1976) and G. Kitson Clark, *Churchmen and the Condition of England, 1832–85* (1973) cover much ground; not much of it resembling the South Lindsey of Obelkevich (1976). Brian Heeney, *A Different Kind of Gentleman: parish clergy as professional men in early and mid-Victorian England* (1976), and Peter Hammond, *The Parson and the Victorian Parish* (1977) go well together. P. T. Phillips (ed.), *The View from the Pulpit* (1978) is a valuable collection: so is Anthony Symondson (ed.), *The Victorian Crisis of Faith* (1970). Landmarks of recent non-Anglican history are Robert Currie, *Methodism Divided* (1968), Elizabeth Isichei, *Victorian Quakers* (1970), Edward Royle, *Victorian Infidels* (1974), and John Kent, *Holding the Fort* (1978). We still badly need R. K. Webb on the Unitarians. From K. S. Inglis, *Churches and the Working Classes in Victorian England* (1965) something about the rechristianisation campaign of our period may be learnt, and from the first volume of R. Sandall, *History of the Salvation Army* (1947) a great deal about that particular side of it. J. E. Orr, *The Second Evangelical Awakening in Britain* (1949) is enthusiastic. No one has yet done for any other city what E. R. Wickham did for Sheffield in his *Church and People in an Industrial City* (1957). I find no reason to distrust Trollope's picture of the better-off sector of rural clerical society, so far as it goes; but it doesn't go far. For Nonconformity, which Trollope never touched and Dickens only glimpsed, we are well served by Mrs Oliphant (1863) and by Mark Rutherford's *Autobiography* (1881), *Deliverance* (1885) and *Revolution in Tanner's Lane* (1887) chapter 16 onwards, which although set in the forties reflects the author's later experience. Edmund Gosse, *Father and Son* (1907) remains a key document. For Scotland, get what is relevant to our period from A. A. Maclaren, *Religion and Social Class: disruption years in Aberdeen* (1974). Dim outlines of the mid-Victorian kirk (in several of its branches) may be described in S. Mechie, *The Church and Scottish Social Development, 1780–1870* (1960). Strong sidelights on Irish Roman Catholicism are provided by K. H. Connell in his essays on *Irish Peasant Society* (1968), and in the books by E. R. Norman and Desmond Bowen already mentioned.

The serious study of Recreation has begun. The pub is a fundamental starting-point; begin there with Brian Harrison, *Drink and the Victorians* (1971), then go on to H. Cunningham, *Leisure in the Industrial Revolution* (1980), John Lowerson and John Myerscough, *Time to Spare in Victorian Britain* (1977) and James Walvin, *Leisure and Society 1830–1950* (1978). Of many jolly books about the music hall, the most scholarly (though it is not easy to follow) is Harold Scott, *The Early Doors* (1946). R. Mander and J. Mitchenson, *British Music Hall* (1965) is a good simplified introduction and has fine illustrations. M. R. Booth, *English Melodrama* (1965) includes a readable account of popular mid-Victorian theatres. What was the finest sport of all for some may be studied in David Itzkowitz, *Peculiar Privilege: a social history of fox hunting 1753–1885* (1977) and Raymond Carr, *English Fox Hunting* (1976). Percy Scholes, *A Mirror of Music* (1947) is a fathomless mine of fascinating information, E. Mackerness, *A Social History of Music* (1964) is helpful, and William Weber, *Music and the Middle Class . . .* (1975) has a lot about England in it. *Popular Fiction a Hundred Years Ago* (1957) is the title of a good survey of that important subject by Margaret Dalziel; R. D. Altick, *The English Common Reader* (1957) is a more solemn and comprehensive coverage and Amy Cruse, *The Victorians and their Books* (1935) a more popular one that ranges wider. Altick has also thoroughly covered *The Shows of London* (1978). The development of the newspaper press is lightly sketched in course of E. Francis-Williams, *Dangerous Estate* (1957), but there seems to be nothing thicker, except H. R. Fox Bourne's good old *English Newspapers: chapters in the history of journalism* (2 vols. 1887), the admirably broad-gauged *History of the Times*, vol. 2 (1939) which goes from 1841 to 1884, vol. 1 of S. E. Koss, *The Rise and Fall of the Political Press in Britain* (1981), and the last chapters of Stanley Morison, *The*

English Newspaper: some account of the physical development of journals printed in London . . . (1932) – the unique value of which is, that it presents a multitude of facsimiles.

Chapter 4

So many of the books already mentioned are relevant to the matter of this chapter, there is not much more to be said about it. The later chapters of Perkin, *op. cit.*, cover much of the same ground and make some of the same points in the course of a more sophisticated and ambitious argument. Cast in an older-fashioned mould but full of good things are O. F. Christie, *The Transition from Aristocracy* (1927) and *The Transition to Democracy* (1934). Cast in an older-fashioned mould still, but refreshing and amusing in a sub-G. M. Young style, are E. Wingfield-Stratford's *Victorian Tragedy* (1930) and *Victorian Sunset* (1932). The meaning of the 'self-help' concept has been examined by K. Fielden in *Victorian Studies* xii (1968) 155 ff. and by P. H. Gosden (1974).

Working-class attitudes to social order are best approached through the already mentioned works of Hobsbawm, Pelling and Royden Harrison, T. Tholfsen, *Working-Class Radicalism in Mid–Victorian England* (1977), F. M. Leventhal, *Respectable Radical George Howell and Mid-Victorian Working-Class Politics* (1971) and F. B. Smith, *Radical Artisan: William James Linton* (1973). See also Gray (1976) and Crossick (1978). Respectability and constitutionalism dominate these studies. For more violent vistas, see (besides R. Harrison) H. Collins and C. Abramsky, *Karl Marx and the British Labour Movement* (1965), Colls's *Colliers' Rant* (1977), and J. Foster, *Class Struggle and the Industrial Revolution* . . . *in three English towns* (1974). For trade unionism through our period, the Webbs' famous big book, *The History of Trade Unionism* (third edn 1920), has become outdated. Pelling's short *History of British Trade Unionism* (1963) gives a succinct outline and includes a good bibliography. E. Allen (ed.), *The North-East Engineers' Strikes of 1871* (1971) gets to some grass roots. P. H. Gosden's is the standard scholarly account of *The Friendly Societies in England, 1815–1875* (1961).

The mid-Victorian underworld is best approached through Mayhew's vol. 4; Philip Collins, *Dickens and Crime* (1962), J. J. Tobias, *Crime and Industrial Society in the Nineteenth Century* (1967) and L. Radzinowicz, *History of English Criminal Law* vol 4. (1968). On the operation of the Victorian police, I have to make do with parts of T. A. Critchley, *History of Police in England and Wales, 900–1966* (1967) and good articles by Henry Parris in *Public Law* (1961) pp. 230–55, and by Jennifer Hart in *English Historical Review* lxx (1955) 411–27, and *Public Administration* xxxiv (1956) 405–17, and E. C. Midwinter's Borthwick Institute Paper No. 34, *Law and Order in Early Victorian Lancashire* (1968).

The history of women has boomed since this book was first published. To J. A. and O. Banks, *Feminism and Family Planning in Victorian England* (1964), O. R. McGregor, *Divorce in England* (1957 and his pioneer bibliographical article 'The Social Position of Women in England, 1850–1914' in the *British Journal of Sociology* vi (1955) 48–60, and some ideas thrown out by Brian Harrison in his suggestive article 'Underneath the Victorians' in *Victorian Studies*, x (1967) 239–62, add Martha Vicinus (ed.), *Suffer and Be Still: women in the Victorian age* (1972), Pamela Branca, *Silent Sisterhood: middle-class women in the Victorian home* (1975), A. John, *By the Sweat of their Brow* (1980), Eric Trudgill, *Madonnas and Magdalenes: the origins and development of Victorian social attitudes* (1976), and Sara Delamont and Lorna Duffin, *The Nineteenth–Century Woman* (1978). My summary of the state of the law on females comes mainly from Erna Reiss, *The Rights and Duties of Englishwomen* (1934). It seems that the Scottish law was significantly different.

NOTES

Chapter 1

1 David S. Landes in the *Cambridge Economic History of Europe*, vol. vi (1965), p. 353 n.
2 B. R. Mitchell and P. Deane, *Abstract of British Historical Statistics* (1962), p. 366.
3 J. H. Clapham, *Concise Economic History of Modern Britain to 1750* (1949), Introduction.
4 Landes, *op. cit.*, p. 433.
5 H. J. Habakkuk, 'Free Trade and Commercial Expansion', in the *Cambridge History of the British Empire*, vol. ii (1940), p. 803.
6 Mitchell and Deane, *op. cit.*, p. 64.
7 Clapham, *Economic History of Modern Britain*, vol. ii, p. 451.
8 C. M. Law in *Transaction of the British Institute of Geographers*, xli (1967), 125 ff.
9 J. T. Coppock, in Coppock and Prince, *Greater London* (1964), p. 34.
10 Henry Mayhew, *London Labour and the London Poor*, vol. iv, Introduction.
11 Henry James, 'London', written in 1888, in *English Hours* (1960), pp. 1–6.
12 Figures taken from Mitchell and Deane, *op. cit.*, pp. 24–7.
13 In his article 'Population Change and the Victorian City', in *Victorian Studies*, xi (1968), 277 ff.
14 John Saville, *Rural Depopulation in England and Wales, 1851–1951* (1957), pp. 54–5.
15 Ravenstein, as cited by A. Redford, *Labour Migration in England, 1800–1850* (ed. W. H. Chaloner, 1964), p. 190.
16 H. J. Dyos, *Victorian Suburb*, p. 59.
17 H. A. Shannon in *Economic History Review*, v (1934–5), 79 ff.
18 Dyos, *Victorian Suburb*, p. 58.

19 T. C. Barker and M. Robbins, *History of London Transport* (1963), i, 57–8.

20 *Georgian London* (1945), p. 159

21 M. W. Flinn (ed.), *Edwin Chadwick's Report on the Sanitary Condition of the Labouring Population of Great Britain, 1842* (1965), p. 6.

22 C. Gill, *History of Birmingham* (1952), i, 368.

23 Sanitary ('Adderley') Commission, in *Parlty Papers 1868–9*, xxxii. *First Report*, pp. 345 ff; Qs. 6329 and 6350–1.

24 John May, 'Sanitary Measures in a Provincial Town', in *Transactions of the National Society for Promoting Social Science*, i (1857), 403 ff.

25 Newsholme, *Fifty Years in Public Health* (1935), p. 203.

26 Ravetz, in *Victorian Studies*, xi (1968), 435 ff.

27 In *The British Workman*, 3 March 1866, pp. 137–8.

28 Mayhew, *London Labour and the London Poor* (1851 edn), i, pp. 253–4, 408–9.

29 *Ibid.*

30 Rawlinson, *Lectures, Reports, Letters and Papers on Sanitary Questions* (1876), pp. 103–4.

31 Beames, *The Rookeries of London* (1850).

32 J. P. Marquand, *The Late George Apley*, chapter 3.

33 Sadleir, *Forlorn Sunset*, chapter 2. See p. 237.

34 Adderley Commission, as in n. 23 above: Q. 6304.

35 Dr John Simon to the same, Q. 1810.

36 Dr Ramsey to the same, Q. 4295.

37 Adderley Commission, *Report*, p. 16; in *Parlty Papers 1871*, xxxv, 22.

38 A. P. Stewart, in Stewart and Jenkins, *Medical and Legal Aspects of Sanitary Reform* (1867), p. 9.

39 *Ibid.*

40 See Manchester's Town Clerk's evidence to the Adderley Commission, Q. 2319 ff.

41 Stewart, *op. cit.*, p. 20.

42 In respect of Merthyr Tydfil I must acknowledge help from Tydfil D. Jones's admirable University of Wales M.A. thesis.

43 R. W. C. Richardson, *Thirty-two Years of Local Self-Government* (1888).

44 Select Committee on Local Taxation, *Parlty Papers 1870*, viii, 68.

45 London and Liverpool figures from Local Government Board's Statistical Memoranda etc. on Public Health and Social Conditions, *Parlty Papers* 1909, ciii 699.
Birmingham's, from Gill and Briggs, *op. cit.*, i, 369 and ii, 76.
Glasgow's, from A. K. Chalmers, *The Health of Glasgow 1818–1925* (1930) p. 190.

46 Chalmers, *op. cit.*, p. 282.

47 Originally delivered to the Park Parish Literary Institute, on 27 February 1888, it is printed in A. K. Chalmers (ed.), *Public Health Administration in Glasgow: a Memorial Volume of the Writings of James Burn Russell* (1905), pp. 189 ff.

48 Simon, *Public Health Reports* (1887), i, 49.

49 Dyos, 'Railways and Housing in Victorian London', in *Journal of Transport History*, (1955), ii, 14.

50 Nicholas Taylor, *Monuments of Commerce* (1968), p. 39.

51 Briggs, *Victorian Cities*, chapter 4.

52 See its *Transactions* for that year, the chairman's speech.

53 Surtees, *Mr Sponge's Sporting Tour* (1853), chapter 28.

54 Jack Simmons, *The Railways of Britain* (1961), p. 18.

55 Clapham, *op. cit.*, ii, 489.

Chapter 2

1 W. O. Henderson, *Johan Conrad Fischer and his Diary* (1966), 21 June 1851.

2 1854, pp. 82–3.

3 'Max O'Rell', *John Bull and his Island* (English 1884 edition), p. 26. I owe to the late Edward Welbourne the identification of O'Rell as Paul Blouët.

4 These extracts are taken from a 'Notice to Employees' reproduced—as a joke—in the magazine *Autoworld*, January or February 1968. I presume it is genuine.

5　*Morning Chronicle*, 21 March 1850.

6　R. D. Baxter, *National Income* (1868), p. 41.

7　Extracted from *Journal of the Royal Statistical Society*, xlix (1886), pp. 314–435.

8　From P. Deane and W. A. Cole, *British Economic Growth, 1688–1959* (1967), Table 37, p. 166.

9　A. L. Bowley, *Wages and Income Since 1860* (1937), p. 99.

10　Since writing that I have noticed in chapter 10, part one, of Perkin's *Origins of Modern English Society* his independent conclusion that, whatever contemporaries may have thought, 'the rich were getting richer at a faster rate than the poor'; and moreover that 'inequalities were increasing within as well as between classes, from top to bottom of society'.

11　From J. Verveka, 'The Growth of Government Expenditure in the UK since 1790', in *Scottish Journal of Political Economy*, x (1963), pp. 111–27.

12　*Hemel Hempstead Gazette*, 21 February 1874.

13　*Op. cit.*, chapter 7.

14　The idea and most of the figures come from Banks's table, *Prosperity and Parenthood*, J. A. Banks, pp. 104–5

15　I have redefined this schedule, following Goschen in *Journal of Royal Statistical Society*, l (1887), 594.

16　*British Incomes and Property* (1916), pp. 264–5.

17　Banks's table in *op. cit.*, p. 110.

18　*Ibid.*, p. 111.

19　Booth in *op. cit.* (note 7 above), pp. 414–15. I confess I cannot reconcile them with the figures offered by W. J. Reader in his useful *Professional Men* (1966), Appendix I.

20　Booth in *op. cit.*, pp. 418–19.

21　*Ibid.*, pp. 422–3.

22　The parish was St Clement's.

23　Banks, *op. cit.*, pp. 83–4.

24　Adapted from Banks, pp. 83 and 86–7. His 'females' tally quite well with Booth's but his 'males' are so different, I cannot imagine how Booth got them. I have been unable to extract detailed comparable figures for 1881.

25　Since 'the Civil Service' was still, until the seventies, a congeries of dissimilar departments, generalisations on my scale are extraordinarily difficult. These figures are my deductions from B. U. Humphreys, *Clerical Unions in the Civil Service* (1958); M. Wright, *Treasury Control of the Civil Service, 1854–1874* (1969); and Marios Raphel, *Pensions and Public Servants* (1964).

26 *Parlty Papers 1875*, xxiii, 446 ff; Appendix G.

27 Cited by Banks, *op. cit.*, p. 105.

28 R. D. Baxter, *The Taxation of the UK* (1869), pp. 105–6.

29 Cited by Banks, *op. cit.*, pp. 76, 49.

30 Jack Simmons, *St Pancras Station* (1968), p. 78.

31 *Contemporary Review*, xi (1869), 321 ff.

32 Briggs, somewhere.

33 See Perkin, *op. cit.*, pp. 413–14.

34 Checkland, *Rise of Industrial Society in England* (1964), pp. 228, 351.

35 *Ibid*, p. 229.

36 Hobsbawm, *Labouring Men*, pp. 134–5.

37 Baxter, *National Income*, Appendix IV, pp. 88–93.

38 Extended from Booth, *op. cit.*, p. 321.

39 *Ibid*.

40 Figure from D. C. Marsh, *The Changing Social Structure of England and Wales* (1965), p. 54.

41 Deane and Cole, *Growth of the British Economy*, Table 30, p. 142.

42 Gervas Huxley, *Victorian Duke* (1967), p. 137.

43 See Booth, *op. cit.*, pp. 366–7 nn.

44 Banks, *op. cit.*

45 Booth, *op. cit.*, pp. 366–7.

46 *Ibid.*, as in notes 19–21, above.

47 *Parlty Papers 1883*, xxx, General Report on the Census, p. 33.

48 Banks, *op. cit.*, p. 81.

49 From Mitchell and Deane, *op. cit.*, Tables in ch. VII, and from the decennial censuses.

50 Booth, *op. cit.*, Tables in Appendix A (1, 2 and 3) as appropriate.

51 *Ibid.*, in Appendix A (1 and 2) as appropriate.

52 Clapham, *Economic History of Modern Britain*, ii, pp. 414–5.

53 *The Working Man*, 21 July 1866.

54 Farr, *Vital Statistics* (1885).

55 W. Ashworth, *Economic History of England 1870–1939* (1960), p. 203.

56 Clapham, *Economic History of Modern Britain*, ii, p. 447.

57 Railways figures from P. S. Bagwell, *The Railwaymen* (1963). Mines estimate from C. Walford, *The Insurance Cyclopedia* (1871–80) i, 'Collieries'.

58 Dickens, 'A Small Star in the East', in *The Uncommercial Traveller* (1861), no. 32.

59 Ashworth, *op. cit.*, pp. 251–2.

60 Booth, cited by John Gross in *New York Review of Books*, 30 January 1969, p. 14.

61 Calculation in *Journal of Royal Statistical Society*, xliii (1882), 535.

62 Mitchell and Deane, *Abstract of British Historical Statistics*, p. 64.

63 Clapham, *Economic History of Modern Britain*, ii, 454.

64 Ashworth, *op. cit.*, p. 23, citing Baxter's *National Income* (1868).

65 The observation of a later observer, H. Dendy, in B. Bosanquet (ed.), *Aspects of the Social Problem* (1895).

66 Wright, *The Great Unwashed* (1868), pp. 137–49.

67 *Parlty Papers 1870*, liv, 357, Fitch's Report, p. 89.

68 *Parlty Papers 1884–5*, xxxi, 51; Q. 19141.

69 *Parlty Papers 1909*, xxxvii, part vii sec. 121.

70 Wright, *op. cit.*, pp. 287–8.

71 Owen, *English Philanthropy* (1964), p. 277.

72 *The Times*, 11 and 12 February 1869, citing the work of G. M. Hicks.

73 *Parlty Papers 1909*, xxxix. Appendix v (15).

74 *Ibid.*, Appendix v (16). I have taken the definitions from Appendix ii, Pitt's memorandum, secs. 92–5.

75 *Parlty Papers 1870*, xxxv. 22nd Annual Report, p. xv.

76 *Durham Chronicle*, 2 January, 1852.

77 For these Lancashire workhouses see Rhodes Boyson's

Manchester MA thesis on *The History of Poor Law Administration in North East Lancashire, 1834–70.*

78 *Household Words*, i, 361–4: 'A Day in a Pauper Palace'.

79 See Aschrott and Preston-Thomas, *The English Poor Law System* (1888), p. 282, n. 1.

80 S. and B. Webb, *English Local Government*, ix (1929), 1041–2. (i.e. the second part of their English Poor Law History: Part II, *The Last Hundred Years*).

81 *Ibid.*, p. 1043.

Chapter 3

1 As types of bad schools I cite Dickens's creations in *Nicholas Nickleby* and *Great Expectations*.

2 Characters in *Our Mutual Friend* (1864–5). Dickens was fascinated by schools and their inmates. Philip Collins, *Dickens and Education* (1963) constitutes a valuable commentary on many of the educational problems of our period.

3 *Parlty Papers, 1867–8*, xxix, 669–74.

4 For Arnold *père*, see T. W. Bamford's biography (1960); for Woodard, see Brian Heeney, *Mission to the Middle Classes* (1969).

5 The Argyll Commission, *Third Report* p. 155. Its admirable reports fill several Parliamentary Papers between 1865 and 1867. My figures of university attendance are from the report of the Scottish Universities Commission. There is always uncertainty about figures of this sort but I notice that the Commission's figures for Edinburgh tally with those of D. B. Horn, *Short History of the University of Edinburgh*, (1967), p. 180.

6 In *Learning and Living* (1961), chapters 2–5.

7 'Absolute and Abitofhell', in *Essays in Satire* (1928).

8 Rutherford [i.e. William Hale White], *Deliverance* (1885), chapter 1.

9 J. C. Fischer, in W. O. Henderson, *op. cit.*, 22 June 1851.

10 Taine, *Notes on England* (1957 edn), p. 283.

11 Letters to Mrs Lehmann, 6 December 1868.

12 K. S. Inglis in *Journal of Ecclesiastical History*, xi (1960), 74 ff. W. S. F. Pickering in *British Journal of Sociology*, xviii (1967), 382 ff. D. M. Thompson in *Victorian Studies*, xi (1967), 87 ff.

13 He has kindly allowed me to borrow from his Oxford B.Litt thesis, *Matthew Arnold and the Nonconformists*.

14 His Cambridge Ph.D. thesis, *The Role of Religious Dissent in the Reform of Municipal Government in Birmingham, 1865–1876*.

15 His Cambridge Ph.D. thesis, *Nonconformity in the Eastern Counties, 1840–1885*.

16 A. A. MacLaren, 'Presbyterianism and the Working Class in a mid-19th century city', in *Scottish Historical Review*, xlvi (1967), 115 ff.

17 In *Methodism Divided* (1968).

18 R. Howie, *The Churches and the Churchless in Scotland* (1893).

19 His Edinburgh Ph.D. thesis should be completed by the time this is published.

20 R. W. Dale, *Life and Letters of John Angell James* (1851 edn), pp. 495–6.

21 *Oldham Chronicle*, 25 April 1874. The same issue reports the flogging and tar-and-flouring of a man who tried to seduce a Heywood girl.

22 *Durham Chronicle*, 23 July 1869.

23 His thesis, mentioned above in chapter 2 note 77.

24 This was the Friday evening boat by which bourgeois fathers went down river to join their wives and children for the weekend.

25 G. and W. Grossmith, *Diary of a Nobody*, 30 July–20 August *passim*. That was 1890, but the Pooters had been going there for many years.

26 The publication of his prodigious researches is anxiously awaited by all who have heard him talk about Blackpool and its poorer relations.

27 Briggs was a sub-Jorrocks figure, anti-hero of many of Leech's *Punch* cartoons c. 1850.

Brown, Jones and Robinson were Richard Doyle's creations for *Punch* in the later forties.

28 I am indebted to Dr J. Kelly for this extract, which occurred in a lecture he gave to the Victorian Society's conference in Liverpool, 1967.

29 Cited in Charles Knight, *Passages of a Working Life* (1864–5), iii, 17.

30 John Timbs, *Curiosities of London* (1868 edn), p. 841.

31 Cited by R. Mander and J. Mitchenson, *British Music Hall*, p. 19.

32 Hugh Shimmin, *Liverpool Life: its Pleasures, Practices and Pastimes* (1856), Essays I and II. These essays had originally appeared in the *Liverpool Mercury*.

33 Robert King, *North Shields Theatres* (1948).

34 Compare them with, e.g., the 1963 figures for England and Wales: 0·31 gallons of spirits, and 13·1 of (generally weaker) beer. *United Kingdom Alliance, Annual Report for 1965/6*, p. 52.

35 These are no more than well-considered speculations.

36 Webb, *The British Working Class Reader* (1955), and, e.g., in *University Quarterly*, xii (1957), 32–3.

37 *Coventry Herald*, 5 January 1849.

38 This was in a lecture to the Anglo-American Historical Conference in July 1966.

39 *Publishers' Circular*, 16 May 1864.

Chapter 4

1 Clapham, *Economic History of Modern Britain*, ii, Preface.

2 Cited by Briggs, *Victorian People* (1954), chapter 2.

3 Barrington Moore jun., *Social Origins of Dictatorship and Democracy* (1967).

4 *Newcastle Commission Report* Part One, p. 199. *Parlty Paper 1861*, xxi, Part One, p. 216.

5 G. O. Trevelyan, *Life and Letters of Macaulay*, chapter xiii.

6 Cited by Fay, *Palace of Industry*, p. 131.

7 *Oldham Chronicle*, 29 July 1854 and Saturdays following.

8 In his classic work *The English Constitution,* from which all my Bagehot quotations are taken.

9 I take it from the *Illustrated London News,* 8 April 1865.

10 James, 'London at Midsummer', in *English Hours* (1960 edn), p. 99.

11 Cited by N. McCord in R. Robson (ed.), *Ideas and Institutions of Victorian Britain* (1967), p. 113.

12 B. Cracroft 'Analysis of the House of Commons . . .' in *Essays on Reform* (1867), pp. 155 ff.

13 *Little Dorrit,* chapter 34.

14 As in no. 11, above.

15 Taine, *op. cit.,* p. 155.

16 Dickens, *Our Mutual Friend* (1864–5), chapter 17.

17 H. B. J. Armstrong (ed.), *A Norfolk Diary* (1949), p. 36.

18 Daisy Ashford, *The Young Visitors,* (1919), chapter 1. The book refers to British society as it was before 'the flood destroyed them all'.

19 Trollope, cited by Burn, *op. cit.,* p. 255.

20 Burn, *Age of Equipoise,* p. 264.

21 Trollope, *Doctor Thorne* (1858), chapter 38.

22 Trollope, *Last Chronicle of Barset* (1867), chapter 83.

23 'Max O'Rell', *Drat The Boys!,* (English version, 1886).

24 Cited by David Lockwood, *The Blackcoated Worker* (1958), p. 24, n.1.

25 Jefferies, *Hodge and his Masters* (1880), chapter titled 'Mademoiselle the Governess'.

26 Cited by C. Walford, *Insurance Cyclopaedia* (1871–80), ii, 293–4.

27 Trollope, *Barchester Towers* (1857), chapter 39.

28 Cited by M. Savin, *Thomas William Robertson: his Plays and Playcraft* (1950), p. 110.

29 Bertrand Russell (ed.), *The Amberley Papers* (1937), ii, 112.

30 Surtees, *Handley Cross* (1843), chapter 39.

31 *Parlty Papers 1846,* xxiv, 432, p. 50. (Tremenheere's report on Glamorganshire p. 50).

32 *Illustrated London News,* 22 August 1857.

33 *The Times,* 20 July 1863. One must remark that the

presence of at any rate Lord Raynham had a philanthropic justification. This was a trial of a brothel-owner for maltreating a fourteen-year-old girl, and Raynham was President of the Society for the Protection of Women and Children.

34 After identifying it in earlier articles, he summarises it in *Age of Equipoise*, pp. 118 ff.

35 'Max O'Rell', *John Bull's Island* (English version, 1884), p. 231.

36 Collins, *Woman in White*, Third Epoch, chapter 8.

37 John Forster, *Life of Charles Dickens*, Book VII, chapter 5 (at the end).

38 Arnold, *Culture and Anarchy* (ed. J. Dover Wilson, 1935), p. 203.

39 A letter to the editor of *The Witness*, 24 June 1859, cited in *Bulletin of the John Rylands Library*, xliii (1960–1), 522.

40 Gosden, *The Friendly Societies in England, 1815–75* (1961).

41 Sidney Godolphin Osborn (The Revd Lord), *The Letters of S.G.O.* (1890), ii, 328.

42 His University of Sussex Ph.D. thesis, *Aspects of the History of Crime in England and Wales, 1805–60*.

43 Her essay in J. Saville (ed.), *Democracy and the Labour Movement* (1954).

44 *Parlty Papers 1872*, x, 450–1.

45 *Parlty Papers 1873*, xiii, 383. Q. 8338.

46 *Parlty Papers 1872*, x, 26.

47 As in n. 45, above.

48 *Age of Equipoise*, pp. 246 ff.

49 O. R. McGregor, *Divorce in England* (1957), p. 18.

50 Burn, *op. cit.*, p. 251.

Index

INTO UNKNOWN ENGLAND 1866-1913

SELECTIONS FROM THE SOCIAL EXPLORERS

Edited by Peter Keating

How did the poor live in late Victorian and Edwardian England?
In the slums of London and Birmingham? In the iron-town of
Middlesbrough? In a Devon fishing village? In rural Essex?

This is a fascinating sequence of extracts from the writings of
those individuals, journalists and wealthy businessmen, a
minister's wife, and a popular novelist, who temporarily left the
comfort of their middle-class homes to find out how the other
half lived. Peter Keating includes material from Charles Booth,
Jack London, B. S. Rowntree and C. F. G. Masterman as well as
by such lesser-known figures as George Sims, Andrew Mearns
and Stephen Reynolds.

'. . . a brilliant and compelling anthology . . . *Into Unknown
England* is not only an education in itself, throwing into three-
dimensional chiaroscuro the flat statistics of "scientific" history,
but a splendid example of prose which is always immediate and
alive.'
Alan Brien, *Spectator*

'The writers collected here used all the techniques they could to
solicit sympathy. Their descendants are a thousand television
documentaries.'
Paul Barker, *The Times*

'. . . a rich collection of passages, intelligently presented.'
The Guardian

Fontana Paperbacks: Non-fiction

Fontana is a leading paperback publisher of non-fiction, both popular and academic. Below are some recent titles.

You can buy Fontana paperbacks at your local bookshop or newsagent. Or you can order them from Fontana Paperbacks, Cash Sales Department, Box 29, Douglas, Isle of Man. Please send a cheque, postal or money order (not currency) worth the purchase price plus 10p per book (or plus 12p per book if outside the UK).

NAME (Block letters) _____

ADDRESS _____

_____

_____